Contents

Les corps cellulaires des neurones

Consciousness

Consciousness

J. Allan Hobson

SCIENTIFIC AMERICAN LIBRARY

A division of HPHLP
New York

Interior design: Blake Logan

Library of Congress Cataloging-in-Publication Data

Hobson, J. Allan, 1933–
      Consciousness / J. Allan Hobson.
       p. cm.
   Includes bibliographical references (p.   ) and index.
    ISBN 0-7167-5078-3 (hardcover)   0-7167-6040-1 (paperback)
    1. Consciousness.   I. Title.
BF311 .H57 1999
153—dc21

                                        98-42628
                                            CIP

ISSN 1040-3213
© 1999 by J. Allan Hobson. All rights reserved.

Printed in the United States of America

Scientific American Library
A division of HPHLP
New York

Distributed by W. H. Freeman and Company
41 Madison Avenue, New York, NY 10010
Houndmills, Basingstoke, RG21 6XS, England

First printing 2000

Prologue

Consciousness has always seemed to me the single most fascinating process in the natural world. I vividly recall sitting on the steps of the food storage shed behind the kitchen of Camp Waya-Awi in Rangeley, Maine, one spectacularly starry night in the summer of 1948. Responding to my teenage companions' awe at the vastness of the heavens, I, the budding neuroscientist, extolled the capacity of our minds both to construct an image of that cosmos and to generate our romantic reactions as we beheld the starry skies on a clear night.

For many of us, such adolescent "aha" experiences confirm early religious teachings. They can also prompt a nascent mysticism. For me, they served to deepen an already firm conviction that behind my stargazing eyes lay the physical instantiation of my vision, my perception, my emotion, my mental construct of the universe, and my already monistic model of consciousness.

I had by then been told by my mentor, the educational psychologist Page Sharp, that a deeper understanding of the dyslexia that hindered the reading comprehension of hundreds of Waya-Awi's student campers could come only from studying the brain. Sharp convinced me that anyone wishing to ground any part of psychology firmly in science needed a medical school education and training in neurobiology or psychiatry—that is, to become a neuroscientist.

The Cellular Bodies of Neurons *To begin to understand consciousness as a natural process, we must explore subjective experience as well as objective scientific data. (Courtesy of Paul Conpille.)*

Approaching Consciousness

One key concept that compels the model of brain-mind unity that lies at the heart of this book is the organization of mental life as an orderly sequence of conscious states. That all of us humans—mystics and scientists alike—wake, sleep, and dream in symphonic harmony with the cosmos that inspires our conscious awe denotes a set of biologically based brain mechanisms as reliable as the cycles of light and dark that make our conscious states by day so different from those of the night.

The goals of this book are to explicate this conscious state paradigm, to compare it with other intellectual approaches to consciousness, and to show how it can accommodate both classic research on sleep and the techniques that are emerging in cognitive neuroscience today. These techniques include behavioral measures of such conscious state features as memory, attention, and visualization as well as the various approaches to brain scanning and imaging. Last, but not least, I will attempt to introduce the reader to the ways in which the conscious state paradigm can be used to inform practical approaches to the management of normal and abnormal conscious states.

I will introduce those brain structures and functions that science now recognizes as fundamental to our conscious experience by recounting what I have learned about consciousness in the half-century since my camp counseling days. And I will explain how my youthful model of the brain-mind as a single, unified system has been strengthened by my scientific research on sleep and dreams as conscious states.

Can consciousness really be grounded? Brought down to earth? Rooted in the brain? I think it can, but if, and only if, our approach is both bold and modest in admitting the inability of science at present to go much beyond the preliminary set of formal rules that constitute the conscious state paradigm. To begin to understand consciousness as a natural process, we must be subjective as well as objective: we must welcome psychology's prodigal child, subjective experience, back into the family of science.

By employing objectivity, neuroscience now can redress the youthful excesses of subjectivism by taking all its claims with a physiological grain of salt. By

The expression "field of consciousness" has but recently come into vogue in the psychology books. Until quite lately the unit of mental life which figured most was the single "idea," supposed to be a definitely outlined thing. But at present psychologists are tending, first, to admit that the actual unit is more probably the total mental state, the entire wave of consciousness or field of objects present to the thought at any time; and, second, to see that it is impossible to outline this wave, this field, with any definiteness.

WILLIAM JAMES, 1908

employing subjectivity, neuroscience can investigate how the conscious experience of individuals illustrates general physical laws that reflect the universality of the brain mechanisms of conscious state control.

I have voiced these sentiments in *The Chemistry of Conscious States*, the book that first got me thinking in earnest about better ways to conceptualize and study consciousness itself. And it is the conscious state paradigm that clearly distinguishes this volume from its predecessor in the Scientific American Library series, *Sleep*. When *Sleep* was written ten years ago, the field of cognitive neuroscience was a barely visible dot in the scientific heavens. Now it is an explosively expanding nebula, needing many mappings to help us appreciate and evaluate its claims on that now more clearly visible galaxy called consciousness.

Toward a Science of Consciousness

What do we think a science of consciousness—when it is ultimately developed—will be like? We no longer believe that consciousness wafts like wind or water through the hollows of our cerebral ventricles. But are we satisfied to imagine that consciousness pops out of the cerebral cortex when it is electrically stimulated by the brainstem? And does it comfort us to think that consciousness may be a symphony of vibrations emanating from tiny microtubules inside our nerve cells?

In my view, consciousness is not now and will probably never be reducible to any one particular brain function, much less to any particular brain region, brain network, brain cell, cell part, molecule, ion, or wave function. As crucial as the traditional reductionistic approach of science is to our understanding of brain-mind unity, we are certain to be disappointed if we expect consciousness to reveal itself in an electron micrograph, an ion channel, a recording, or an electrophoretic plot of brain proteins.

In addition to reductionism, we need three other -isms not always appreciated by scientists. We need emergentism to keep us aware that complex phenomena such as consciousness emerge at higher levels of system organization and cannot be discerned or analyzed at the level of the system's elemental building blocks. We need holism to keep us aware that we must be conscious of something, and that something, be it the world, our bodies, or our selves, serves to structure consciousness every bit as much as the brain does. We need subjectivism because, since it is subjectivity that we wish to explain, we had better know—as precisely as possible—just what it is.

At the same time, we must not let our commitment to the evidence offered by emergentism, by holism, and by subjectivism become a screen for romantic mysticism, a dodge from quantitative rigor, or an evasion of experimental hypothesis testing. I will therefore endeavor, always, to be of two minds at once: bold and modest, subjective and objective, psychological and physiological, brainful and mindful.

A Caveat to the Reader

To many readers, this book may seem superficial. Rather than ascribing consciousness to some deep and invisible state of quantal energy, I present conscious experience as the natural integration of several higher brain functions, each of which entails subjectivity and all of which evince a brain state dependency that is robust, observable, measurable, and—to a first approximation, at least—explainable.

To other readers, the book may appear overly narrow. Instead of surveying the whole field and its parts with impartiality and balance, I commit myself to that particular set of brain-mind data emerging from the study of sleeping, dreaming, and waking, and to one particular model of the brain-mind based on those conscious states. I have elaborated that conscious state space model in the decade since its first introduction in *Sleep* and its verbal explanation five years ago in *The Chemistry of Conscious States*. Here it is extended to a visual presentation and to a wider range of normal and abnormal conscious states.

To still other readers—perhaps to most—this book will seem naive, wrong-headed, or even foolish. In the place of a sophisticated and cool professional reserve about such daunting issues as the mind-body question, free will, psychic energy, and mind-as-causal, it substitutes a set of radically innocent, commonsense claims. These claims are justifiable only by adopting a pragmatism that is as assertive of open-minded liberty as it is respectful of tough-minded scientific assessment. And only when enough empirical evidence has been gathered for consciousness to reveal its ultimate face will we know if these choices are wise or foolish.

I am no stranger to criticism. And while I sometimes wince at its lash, I have learned to welcome its recognizance—especially when my scolders are respectful! Indeed, I welcome the dialectic that I hope this book will inspire. Let it be healthy, creative, inclusive, and expansive. After all, consciousness belongs to everyone. Everyone has a stake in how consciousness is described, in how consciousness is conceptualized, and in how consciousness is used. On the eve of the third millennium, we are not only aware, and aware of our aware-ness, but we are now also aware of how and why we are aware and how and why we are aware of our own awareness. The assumption of brain-mind unity means that we are our brains and our brains are us. The more we learn about the brain-mind, the more we learn about the nature of our selves.

A Paradigm
for Consciousness

The sea this morning is calm, rippled only slightly by a gentle northerly wind. From my writing table, this view is framed by the large leaves of an ancient fig tree and the tendrils of an invasive wisteria that seems to want to grow everywhere, even at the expense of the figs. The thick white walls and porch pillars of the Mediterranean house where I write radiate coolness and support the bamboo awning shielding me from the sun. All around me the red-orange flowers of a trumpet vine proclaim the glory of a new day.

Girl Before a Mirror, Pablo Picasso, 1932 The mirroring function of consciousness is epitomized in this painting. Our conscious awareness of the world, our bodies, and ourselves is always a construct, as Picasso reveals through the selectiveness and distortion of the image in the mirror. (The Museum of Modern Art, New York. Gift of Mrs. Simon Guggenheim. Photograph © 1998 The Museum of Modern Art, New York. © 1998 Estate of Pablo Picasso/Artists Rights Society (ARS), New York.)

At the center of this idyllic scene is my conscious mind: awake, alert, and anxious; eager to begin this new experiment in scientific analysis and literary expression. My mind tingles with excitement and apprehension at the challenge of the task. I am convinced that what I am experiencing perceptually, emotionally, and conceptually at this and every other moment of my conscious life is a function of the activity of my brain. And I think I know enough about the science of perception, emotion, and thought to give a clear account of the dependence of each of these mental functions upon brain physiology.

But will I succeed in reducing consciousness to brain activity, as many scientists, myself included, believe may ultimately prove possible? Almost certainly not. Can I marshal enough evidence to prove that consciousness is brain activity and nothing else? I doubt it. And if I should fail, would such a failure encourage—even vindicate— those who believe that consciousness—with its attendant spirit and soul—is irreducible to brain structure and function? Encourage them, certainly. Vindicate them, just as certainly not. Why not? Because the scientific study of consciousness is today as incomplete as was knowledge of the earth when Columbus set out for India and encountered, instead, the Americas.

Columbus's discovery did not convince the skeptics of the time that the world was round any more than today's neuroscientific revolution will convince everyone that the brain and mind are one. But while our exploratory enterprise is incomplete and fraught with risk, it points clearly to the affirmation of its guiding hypotheses. Brain science promises unanticipated revelations, revelations that will change our view of the mental world at least as much as Columbus's discovery of America changed our view of the physical world. Our future evolution as philosophers, psychologists, physiologists, spiritualists, moralists, and theists will be shaped by brain science in ways that we cannot yet imagine.

Measuring Conscious States

A simple definition of consciousness is awareness: awareness of the world, the body, the self. At an elemental level, consciousness is nothing more than sensitivity to a stimulus, such as light. As consciousness emerges across species or within an individual over time, sensitivity deepens into varying levels of awareness, or primary consciousness, and eventually into self-awareness, or secondary consciousness. It is by linking objectively measurable brain mechanisms to subjective mental experience that we can begin to explore the concept of consciousness.

So consistent and so robust are certain formal features of mind and brain as both change conscious state together that I use the hyphenated term "brain-mind" to denote this integrated system. This term extends the assumptions of the dreaming brain to the waking brain. After all, it is the brain whose physical state determines the nature of waking, sleeping, dreaming, and all other conscious states. And now that the physical state of the human brain can be studied in detail as its conscious states evolve naturally, the day of deep brain-mind integration is at hand.

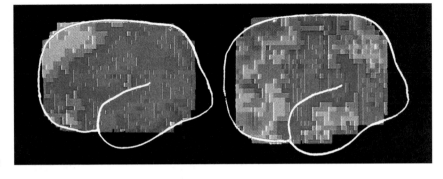

Early Brain Scan That the activity of the human brain could be quantified in relation to ongoing mental events was first demonstrated in 1985 by the Swedish neurologist Per Roland, who asked his subjects to imagine walking along a familiar street. Compared to the resting condition (left), imaginary walking (right) was associated with increases in parietal and temporal lobe blood flow.

It is as much the purpose of this book to make clear the reasons for excitement about the far-reaching implications of brain-mind research as to review the evidence in favor of the more specific hypothesis of brain-mind unity. By reporting on the scientific study of consciousness as work in progress, and therefore necessarily incomplete—even grossly inadequate—I will not give an inch to doubt about its ultimate success. To those who still harbor such doubt, I will appeal for openness of mind and for active collaboration in reconstructing our picture of our selves.

Five hundred years after Columbus, we are entering a New World of self-understanding. The dynamic maps being made today of the human brain in conscious action provide prophetic symbols of how we will see ourselves tomorrow. How long will it take for us to incorporate and internalize our discovery of ourselves as conscious brains? Give it a century. Give it a millennium if need be. It is well worth the time.

Consciousness as Subjective Experience

Why begin a book on brain science with a personal snapshot of a moment of conscious experience? Because it is subjective conscious experience that we seek to explain. If we assume that we already know enough about what conscious experience is without carefully examining its richness and its vicissitudes, we risk missing important opportunities to tie the details of subjectivity to the objective material that is the brain. As unappetizing as subjectivity may be to science, we miss the point of our efforts if we ignore it. I will take a strongly objective, scientific approach to describing the subjective differences in conscious state that characterize waking, sleeping, and dreaming.

In my 35 years as a scientist, I have encountered only two first-hand accounts of subjective conscious experience that were sufficiently extensive, detailed, systematic, and free of gratuitous interpretation to warrant quantitative analysis. One was a collection of normal dream reports made by an individual, the other a compendium of lucid dreams (dreaming with accurate self-awareness) made by three subjects who had trained themselves to regain the self-reflective awareness of waking while continuing to dream. Sadly, neither of these two remarkable data sets includes the essential control observations of waking—or waking fantasy—that basic scientific research demands in order to compare the features of one conscious state quantitatively with the features of another in the same individual.

By pointing out how incomplete these descriptions of conscious states still are, and how these inadequacies impinge critically upon brain-mind science, I hope to encourage—and even to vindicate—the efforts of those psychologists in all branches of the humanities who seek a more adequate depiction of conscious experience. We need to use psychology wisely and strategically, as I will attempt to make clear in discussing this new approach to all states of consciousness.

And we need art. Stimulated by the bold assertions of Freudian psychoanalysis at the beginning of the twentieth century, many writers and painters began to describe and to depict their conscious states as well as the unconscious processes that they imagined might shape them. To capture the essence of subjectivity, we need James Joyce and Marcel Proust every bit as much—and possibly more—than we need Sigmund Freud and Carl Jung. These writers are interested in the same thing as the brain-mind scientist: conscious experience. Because art attempts to capture and render consciousness in detail, artists have contributed more, in a way, to explaining consciousness than have many self-proclaimed scientists who overlook the details and too quickly jump to conclusions about the underlying mechanisms. But art is embellished verisimilitude, not mental description. Our quest to quantify subjectivity cannot be satisfied by Proust or Joyce.

How, then, should conscious experience be rendered? Should I, for example, further deconstruct the porch scene at my house on the Mediterranean island of Stromboli with a view to enriching its associative reverberations? Should I mention that I have been here twice before with Lia, the woman who is now my wife, and how these memories color my experience? Should I say how my experience of this scene has changed as my relationship with Lia has evolved? Should I mention the impact of bringing the children of our previous marriages together here in celebration, three months after the birth of our twin sons, Andrew and Matthew? At a personal level, these are certainly relevant details that might make for a psychoanalytic psychology of my own particular, subjective conscious and unconscious mental processes, especially if tied to my earlier experiences of love.

Or should I embed my experience of sea, wind, and vine in a mythological context—that of Odysseus, for example, who may have experienced some of these same impressions and feelings in his legendary odyssey 2500 years ago? I could, for example, describe my anxiety when the hydrofoil whizzing us here from Messina yesterday suddenly stopped with a thump. The hydrofoil had collided with an unseen underwater object, a material Cyclops, exactly midway between the real Scylla and the real Charybdis. I was suddenly aware that my anxiety had many points in common with Odysseus's mythological ambivalence about Penelope and Calypso as he navigated these alluringly dangerous and beguiling seas long ago.

Such allusions could be valid bridges between my particular current experience and my more general historical and cultural context: my membership in Western culture. All writers, scientists included, need an armature, a strong line, a metaphor, and a hypothesis if their work is to transcend the particular and touch the universal aspects of conscious experience. Whatever means are chosen are inevitably reductionistic. Art and science thus share the same fate: whatever path is taken excludes all others. Proust and Joyce, Freud and Jung all shared a fascination with the associative nature of consciousness. They focused on the content of the consciousness, especially as it relates to universals of desire, longing, and love. This is

Consciousness and Myth *Homer's Odyssey, stunningly visualized on the surface of this ancient Greek vase, is of enduring interest because it speaks to the restless inquisitiveness and experimentalism of human consciousness. In tying himself to the mast of his ship, the Argo, the better to resist the allure of the Sirens' song, Odysseus also foreshadows the perpetual conflict between the instinctual impulses and rational restraints that are parts of everyone's conscious experience.*

the reduction of modernism: Whatever we think or feel derives from our instincts and primordial emotions.

Freud's Theory

Anyone who trained in psychiatry a generation ago knows well that neuroscience was not a part of the curriculum. Even today, psychiatry can be monolithically psychodynamic. The goal of analytic psychotherapy is to make our feelings—often so painfully evident to others—known to ourselves. In this sense the Freudian mission remains entirely viable today, despite the problems with many of its mechanistic assumptions.

Because of our obsessive abstinence from the symbolic interpretation of dreams, slips of the tongue, and memory lapses, my friend Willard Quine called the seminar group of young psychiatrists that I convened at Harvard in the late 1980s "Freudians Anonymous." Freud's theory, as science, had long since gone stale and sterile. And, no doubt, many readers will wonder why anyone would still struggle with a theory that probably should have been rejected out of hand to begin with. One reason for its persistence is that so many psychiatrists fell for it. Subsequently, many other branches of scholarship have fallen for it, and are continuing to do so.

The history of Freudianism reveals clearly the folly of any psychology independent of neurology. And yet today there are still many vociferous advocates of this brainless approach. Some psychoanalysts speak of hermeneutics (theories of meaning), some behavior therapists speak of cognition (theories of mind), and some philosophers speak of qualia (theories of subjective experience) as if these phenomena could exist outside a biological context.

One may be justifiably disappointed in the contribution neurology has made to date, and even reasonably suspicious of its current claims. But to assume that the mind is in any sense brainless is a grave error. So far, neither neurology nor psychology has come up with a satisfactory model of the brain-mind. Such a model would specify how many compartments there are, describe each of them objectively, and formulate the dynamics of information interchange among them. Not an easy task.

Despite a hundred years of vigorous intellectual promotion, Freud's dynamically repressed unconscious is still difficult to define with anything approaching scientific rigor. For example, I take "repression" to mean the active exclusion from consciousness of sensory data (psychic blindness), bodily data (hysterical anesthesia), or personal historical data (neurotic amnesia). Now I know that I personally am quite capable of evincing all these symptoms. So are most of my patients, and I daresay many readers will also show these traits. Hence we may overlook the most obvious but painful visual cues, not feel losses, and not remember certain birthdays. But the assertion that these processes are either unconscious or irretrievable by means other than the free association techniques prescribed by Freud is still an unproved and highly dubious assumption.

Freud's diagram of inhibition as repressed nervous energy

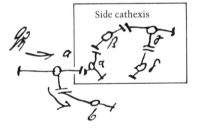

Nervous energy is diverted into a "side-cathexis," $\alpha \rightarrow \beta \rightarrow \gamma \rightarrow \delta$ instead of along the normal $a \rightarrow b$. This unproved physiologic diversion of energy is isomorphic with Freud's psychological concept of repression.

Sigmund Freud, with his two chows, in his house in London after he had fled his native Vienna and long after he had abandoned his Project for a Scientific Psychology in favor of psychoanalysis. (At right) Freud's concept of psychodynamic repression was nonetheless based upon his imaginative notion of the redirected flow of nervous energy from its normal path to a side cathexis, as depicted in his hand-drawn neural circuit diagram.

In fact, my own clinical experience has convinced me that in every case, alternative explanations *are* possible. Among those alternative explanations, the most satisfactory are those presented by neurology. This was the source that Freud himself first drew from, then abandoned, but always proclaimed as the ultimate ground for a science of the mind.

Nowhere is the need for such explanations more clear than in the neuroscientific study of conscious states. As I explained in greater detail in my first book, *The Dreaming Brain,* Freud was as preoccupied with the bizarre content of dreams as he was with the occurrence of peculiar utterances, acts, and lapses during waking. Freud assumed that we are all born with impulses—predominantly sexual—that are repressed when they come into conflict with prohibitive social conventions. These impulses emanate from the unconscious id in the depths of the psyche. But, like the pulsatile pressures driving Stromboli's volcano, these repressed impulses constantly threaten to erupt. The potential victim of such an upheaval is consciousness itself, a structure as highly socialized as the village of Fico Grande, where I sit writing, under the omnipresent volcano.

According to Freud, the repression that protects consciousness from the eruption of unconscious impulses is a counterforce exerted upon the id by the ego and superego. These controlling elements function most effectively when we are awake, and manage, even when challenged, to detoxify the id's impulses by transforming them into universal neurotic symptoms such as slips of the tongue or pen.

When we go to sleep, the ego relaxes its guard upon the id, and the pressure upon consciousness becomes so great as to overwhelm it, causing awakening. The bizarreness of dreams, in this view, is the result of successful bowdlerization of the id impulses during dreaming.

Domains of Consciousness

But what about the *form* of conscious experience, the difference among waking, sleeping, and dreaming states? Is consciousness to be reduced to transforms of desire: to permission and prohibition, to yes and no, to impulse and blockade? Freud and Jung thought so, but I have my doubts. How, in such terms, am I to explain that exactly four hours ago, when it was still dark and the glorious porch scene I now behold was invisible, I could see, with perfect clarity, the northern fence line of my house in Brookline, four thousand miles away? Then

I was asleep—and dreaming—but my conscious experience was no less rich and no less intense for all its independence of the now vivid particulars of my Mediterranean waking-state consciousness.

In my dream, from a vantage point that could only have been the little sleeping porch of my Brookline house, I looked down on a new line of fence post holes dug by my northerly neighbor, Bob Sands, and was surprised to see that he had moved them two feet in his direction. The net effect of this supremely generous neighborly act was a gift of about 200 square feet of valuable real estate.

Now, a theory of consciousness that emphasizes desire has little problem with the particular content of this particular conscious experience. I am territorial. My dream reveals it. But besides being disappointingly uninformative—since I am already quite conscious of my territoriality—the desire paradigm leaves unsolved—and even untouched—the completely *autocreative* aspect of my conscious experience while dreaming.

The lights are out. I am lying in a bed within 20 feet of this writing table, yet my consciousness is four thousand miles away, effortlessly annexing new territory. Talk about Columbus! Talk about Odysseus! Whatever its content, my mental voyage must have been in the vessel of my brain. My brain is transformed by some universal agency, a particular physical state called REM (for rapid eye movement) sleep, the same REM sleep state that affects my wife and twin babies, who are sleeping beside me, each in their own particular conscious world. It is this shared physical state that gives all our dreams their remarkably consistent formal properties.

While lying in my bed on the Mediterranean island of Stromboli as I dreamed of my fence in Brookline, Massachusetts, my brain was undergoing the same universal dream state process that changed the consciousness of James Joyce and Stephen Dedalus, of Sigmund Freud and the Wolf Man, of Marcel Proust and Swann, and of Homer and Odysseus himself when they went to bed at night. The most general—and universal—theory of consciousness would capture the subjective features that are common to all conscious states. In this way—and only in this way—can we hope to succeed in reducing consciousness to neurophysiology.

We cannot, today, expect to know how and why the particular contents of conscious experience are chosen by the brain-mind. As scientists, we must wait patiently for that golden opportunity to present itself in the form of some new but now unimaginable technology. At the same time, we must seize the chance to account for some of the most fascinating formal features of conscious experience that the currently available technology has given us—such as how I can "see" my Brookline house while lying, eyes closed and asleep, in the dark Strombolian night.

Visual Awareness

Vision is a universal biological process with some stable, formal properties that are independent of culture, personal history, and literary style. And vision—that is, sensitivity to light—is an aspect of all conscious states. It may be more or less vivid, more or less detailed, and more or less sharply focused, but you and I both see objects, people, and places whether we are awake (the fig tree that shades my writing table) or dreaming (the fence posts that my Brookline neighbor has moved). The subjective I—the one who sees—cannot tell the difference between these two radically different conscious states, precisely because, in some of their aspects, they are identical. If we could know how such a remarkable identity of formal conscious state features is achieved by the brain, we would be a step closer to understanding the brain basis of consciousness.

The genesis of visual representation is that fashioning by Nature of a picture of herself, in the mind of man, which we call the progress of science.

THOMAS HUXLEY, 1869

The same is true of the differences among conscious states. By understanding their universal brain basis, we might gain as much as, or more than, we would learn from their similarities. Memory is a good example. My recall of the waking consciousness that I experienced yesterday is far richer than my recall of the dreaming consciousness that I experienced last night. Why? Answering this question—in terms of brain physiology—would solve many of the problems that beset Sigmund Freud and fascinated Marcel Proust.

And if my memory is as deficient in dreaming as my vision is keen, that fact could help explain why the subjective I is so poor a judge of what conscious state it is in. Without memory, I cannot analyze the temporal and spatial continuity linking sequences of events. If I cannot remember that I am actually in Stromboli, I am easily fooled into believing that I am in Brookline. Two aspects of this comparative approach to the study of consciousness deserve notice at this early juncture. One is philosophical; the other is clinical.

Monism and Dualism

The philosophical aspect of the comparative approach to consciousness concerns the ancient debate between monism and dualism. The natural tendency to regard mind and body as radically distinct was clearly articulated by the French philosopher René Descartes (1596–1650). In his *Discourse on Method* (1637), Descartes's epigram *Cogito, ergo sum* ("I think, therefore I am") crystallized the belief that consciousness was a primary, indubitable entity divorced from the body. Only the body was explainable in mechanical terms. To account for the obvious parallelism between mind and body, Descartes was forced to resort to the highly improbable notion that the two entities behaved like perfectly synchronized watches wound up, timed, and set in motion by the mind of God.

This strongly top-down viewpoint accorded well with the dogmas of the Church, but it rankled the common sense of more scientifically oriented philosophers like Thomas Hobbes (1588–1679). Imbued with the laws of planetary motion enunciated by Galileo and Kepler, Hobbes developed a contrastingly bottom-up view, arguing that if material things and all their parts were always at rest, or in uniform motion, there could be no distinction and no perception. In his *De Homine* (On Man) (1658), Hobbes held that human cognition and motivation were explicable as differentiated movement. Although Hobbes was neither a physiologist nor even an experimentalist, his viewpoint set the stage for subsequent investigations of the brain— the search for its own laws of motion as the physical basis of cognition. Today, brain scanners are offering us the first clear vision of the planetary motions within our heads.

When I use a phrase like "the brain basis of consciousness," I am succumbing to linguistic dualism. The danger here is the assumption of deep philosophical dualism that a brain state is one thing and a conscious state another. But suppose that it is the brain itself, and not the mind, that is conscious. That means that many more or less conscious brain states, when better understood, will reveal their conscious or nonconscious aspects in terms of brain state difference *only*. Because subjectivity is so vital a tool in investigating itself, we may need linguistic dualism well into the indefinite future. But if our philosophical stance is to be monistic, we need to be on guard against the tendency of our linguistic dualism to pull us into the Cartesian separation of brain and mind.

How the Brain Goes Out of Its Mind

The clinical aspect of a comparative approach to studying consciousness concerns the severe disturbances of consciousness to which the human brain-mind is vulnerable. Consider visual hallucination, a grave symptom indicative of severe psychosis. Or consider amnesia

Thomas Hobbes *After he was summoned back to England from Paris in 1630 to teach the young Earl of Devonshire, Hobbes was surprised to realize that none of his learned conferees could answer the question, "What is sense?" Hobbes reasoned that perception depended upon the diversity of movement of material things and took up the study of geometry to learn the principles of motion. His deliberations were published as* A Short Tract on First Principles.

and disorientation to time and place, fearsome symptoms for anyone with a family history of Alzheimer's disease. Since my Brookline fence dream was a visual hallucination, why didn't I worry? And since I was hopelessly disoriented—in both space and time—why didn't I run to the hospital for a brain scan? The answer is simple: when I woke up, those "symptoms" were gone. I was cured of my dream psychosis simply by waking up.

> *Dreaming permits each and every one of us to be quietly and safely insane every night of our lives.* WILLIAM DEMENT, 1959

But wait a minute. If I asked, "It was I who had the symptoms, wasn't it?" would you tell me, "No, it was your brain that had them"? If you said *that,* you would already have grasped the main point of this book: It is the brain that is conscious; it is the brain that is "I"; it is the brain that is psychotic in one of its normal conscious states, dreaming. In other words, a study of consciousness that uses a comparative approach to its various states promises a payoff in that most practical of all domains, the medical, as well as taking a significant step toward solving the mind-body problem that Western philosophy has wrestled with unsuccessfully for two and a half millennia.

Defining a Conscious State Space

How can an object, a brain, become a subject, a self with self-consciousness? This question has been called by some philosophers the "hard problem" of consciousness. At the risk of seeming hopelessly naive, let me state my commonsense position. If the brain is capable of creating an abstract or representation of the visual world (and it is), and if that representation is an activated state of the brain (which it is), then I do not find it so hard to believe that the brain can create a representation of that representation (as it does when a visual image arises spontaneously or is voluntarily summoned in the absence of an external stimulus).

From the crucial point at which my brain has an entirely self-contained but externally referenced vision, it is but one small step for my brain to step back and contemplate its own activated state. In doing so, not only is my brain seeing things, it is seeing that it is seeing things. It is fully conscious. In this sense, I agree with Francis Crick and Christof Koch, who have concentrated on visual awareness in their study of consciousness. If vision can be thoroughly understood, a model for all the rest of consciousness will be at hand.

Consciousness, defined here as our awareness of our world, our bodies, and our selves, has a global, all-inclusive aspect, but at the same time is composed of easily identifiable components. And consciousness is graded in its intensity, ranging from absent through partial to full according to many factors, including species, age, and time of day.

To inventory the universal formal properties of consciousness systematically, we now turn to their specific enumeration, definition, and clarification. We will discuss three aspects of consciousness: the global (or unitary) aspect; the componential (or modular) aspect; and the graded (or dynamic) aspect.

The Unity of Conscious Experience

In the global sense, we recognize that all conscious states are surprisingly unitary and single-minded. Although our minds may jump from one subject to another, and while the several biochemical molecules of consciousness contribute components to our integrated awareness in parallel, consciousness can at any given instant concern itself with only a single idea, a single percept, or a single emotion.

As long ago as 1890, the pioneering psychologist William James understood that it is the brain, with its billions of neural elements, that mediates the conscious states that integrate for us an experiential world of infinite complexity. Given the complex nature of reality,

Henry and William James (ca. 1900) called themselves "asthetic twins" who had been sacrificed on the altar of their father's radical education program. Henry (on left, in bowtie) became famous as a novelist and William (on right, bearded) achieved his fame as a psychologist. Some claim, however, that Henry was the better psychologist and William the better writer. This photograph was taken at about the time that William gave the Gifford Lectures at the University of St. Andrews, Scotland, which were later published as The Varieties of Religious Experience.

James asked, why wasn't conscious experience a "great buzzing confusion"? The philosophical binding problem is the modern scientist's expression of this same conundrum: How can any aspect of perception be unified if the brain is simultaneously computing multiple maps of the world? Where in the brain are all these maps brought together, and how are they integrated so that I behold only one seascape as I look out from my writing table?

On the basis of our experience, most of us would accept the principle of conscious unity—that is, global binding—unquestioningly. Certainly consciousness is not utterly chaotic; indeed, it may be even less chaotic than the world it represents. When we later consider the mental faculty of attention, we will see that this function allows the mind to focus on one thing at a time. But the fact remains that the vaunted unity of consciousness has been little studied from a scientific point of view. Is it true that we think of one, and only one, thing at a time? Is it true that we are always one, and only one, person? Is it true that we always are in one, and only one, state of mind?

Several caveats should make us cautious about prejudging the answers to these questions. One concerns the fragmented quality of dreams. Although we experience our dreams as if they were as seamless as skillful movie plots, dreaming is notably disjunctive when analyzed objectively. At the formal level of times, places, and persons, dream consciousness displays a superabundance of both incongruity and discontinuity. These dream features are both microscopic, characterizing every second of dream experience, and macroscopic, suddenly interrupting one plot and replacing it with another. But what about waking? Is it really so different? Just how disjunctive the constantly flowing stream of consciousness can be is hinted at in Joyce's *Ulysses,* but made intolerably clear in *Finnegan's Wake.*

Inspired by the evident discontinuity of dreams, psychologists have recently begun to explore waking consciousness using the concepts and measuring tools of dream research. In the darkened rooms of John Antrobus's sleep laboratory in New York City and on the streets of Boston, where they carry Bob Stickgold's beepers, subjects' consciousness is interrupted and they are asked to report their thoughts, imaginings, and fantasies. The data show waking consciousness to be an exceedingly choppy stream, if it is a stream at all.

The modern psychologists and the modern artists who are interested in the connections among successive thoughts, feelings, and ideas have assumed that a connective tissue of desire links even grossly disjunctive mental associations in a deeply meaningful way. To make this reductionistic hypothesis even plausible, many psychoanalysts and their artist followers have relegated the supposed unity of conscious experience to the constant throbbing of an instinctual heart of desire in the unconscious. For them, the dissociations seen on the surface of the stream of consciousness—the ripples, the currents, the whirlpools, and even the whitecaps—are turbulence designed to protect the conscious self from the disgrace of recognizing the instinctual self.

But why need we assume that conscious or unconscious mental processes should always be either instantaneously unitary or sequentially seamless? It is obviously useful for the mind to have some built-in tendency to be continuous. But should it always be? Would such mental inertia prove occasionally or even often disadvantageously restrictive? Should consciousness not be subject to some internal turbulence whose adaptive function it is constantly to change our minds, the better to cope with the constantly changing demands and opportunities presented by constant change in the external and internal world?

In this view, the mind is intrinsically subject to both associative and dissociative forces. The apparent self-contradictions of this hypothesis are overcome by the enormous advantages it provides in explaining many otherwise inexplicable data. Remembering the prescient insights of Thomas Hobbes, might we not now propose that cerebral motion has its own mechanism of inertia and its own dynamic mechanisms for changing speed and direction? The laws of cerebral inertia guarantee mental continuity and enough constancy for us to present a semblance of a self, while the laws of cerebral dynamics allow us to shift our attention and to change our mode of analysis. In this way a wide range of subject matter can be tracked and processed over a wide range of mental levels.

Moreover, the discontinuity hypothesis mirrors the paradigm shift in the physical sciences from the Newtonian mechanics that prompted Freud to assume a more or less constant inertia of desire to the Lorentian chaos that views all complex systems as unpredictable in the face of deterministic but unanalyzable noise. Later on I will try to show how such chaotic noise may be useful to consciousness, since it confers the constancy of change, and with it, variety, originality, and creativity.

The Modularity of Consciousness

Another intrinsic opponent to the unity of consciousness is the modularity of the brain-mind. Even at its most impressively unified moments, consciousness is made up of different experiential components—its building blocks. We have already alluded to several of these modules and have emphasized, for example, perception (the scene I behold from my writing table) and memory (the personal history of my previous visits to Stromboli and the cultural and literary history of Homer's *Odyssey*). But the comprehensive list is much longer, with contributions from at least the thirteen components listed in the accompanying table.

For convenience, it is possible to subdivide these components in two ways. The first, represented by the groupings in the table, divides them according to the classic reflex paradigm that links sensory inputs (or information sources) to motor outputs (or behavioral acts) via neuronal transactions or internal processing. This was the model that informed the neurophysiological work of Charles Sherrington and led to the founding of learning theory, or behaviorism, via the conditioning studies of Ivan Pavlov. Along the way, the reflex paradigm became incorporated into the psychoanalytic model of Sigmund Freud, who saw all mental life in its very limited terms.

The second subdivision scheme, represented by the rightmost column of the table, recognizes differences between primary and secondary levels of consciousness. Primary components are those experi-

Building Blocks of Consciousness

Component	Definition	Level
	Input sources	
Sensation	Reception of input data	1
Perception	Representation of input data	1
Attention	Selection of input data	1
Emotion	Feelings about representations	1
Instinct	Innate propensities to act	1
	Elaborative processing	
Memory	Retrieval of stored representations	2
Thought	Reflection upon representations	2
Language	Symbolization of representations	2
Intention	Representations of goals	2
Orientation	Representations of time, place, and persons	2
Learning	Automatic recording of experience	1
	Output actions	
Volition	Decisions to act	2
Movement	Motor acts and behaviors	1

enced by all mammals and by human infants (for example, sensations, perceptions, attention, emotions, instincts, and movement); secondary components are those fully experienced only by adult humans (memory, thought, language, intention, orientation and volition). While the reflex model is focused upon temporal sequences, the primary-secondary model is based upon levels of complexity. But neither model accommodates the binding properties of spontaneous activity, parallelism, and integration that conscious states evince so clearly.

As our subsequent examination will reveal, both methods of subdivision are empirically and theoretically arbitrary and therefore highly risky. Whether emotion is a stimulus or a response, or both, is one critical question. Whether animals possess language is another. We will include both modular models, for now, as oversimplified working hypotheses. The variety and complexity of modular consciousness make one point clear: Consciousness is a many-splendored thing, a stupendous synthesis of diverse components.

This undoubted fact presents a major dilemma for science: In deciding how to study consciousness, should we take an analytic or a synthetic approach? Until recently, scientists have answered this question with resounding unanimity: analysis, yes; synthesis, no! As a result, we now know many details about each of the parts, but little about the whole. Holism, while intellectually justifiable, has tended, until now, to be a rather sterile protest against analysis.

The Graded Complexity of Consciousness

Is there a middle way—or, better yet, a comprehensive and truly integrative way—of proceeding? Can we call such an approach either analytic holism or holistic analysis? I believe that we can. The successful application of analytic holism depends upon our recognition of the third robust and general attribute of consciousness; namely, the way that consciousness is graded across species as they develop over evolutionary time (phylogenesis) and within species over each individual's lifetime (ontogenesis). Add to the mix the way consciousness is modulated (tempered or tuned) in every one of us over the course of each 24-hour day, and you will grasp my point more easily.

It is in this last strategy, the study of the diurnality of consciousness, that modern science makes common cause with Joyce (whose Ulysses-Leopold Bloom lives out one day) and with Proust (whose Swann-Marcel moves back and forth across the edges of sleeping and waking). In seeking the rules that govern these dynamic aspects of consciousness, we can hope to discover the rules of its constant alteration.

Many scientists, most prominently physicists, espouse analytic holism in another way. They suppose that consciousness is elemental—even particulate—in the sense of proteins, electrons, and quanta. In his book *The Dreaming Universe*, Fred Alan Wolf holds that consciousness is an elemental attribute of any correlational mechanism and, hence, a trait of even inanimate objects.

In making this claim, Wolf is going far beyond the already extreme claim that artificial intelligence—and hence consciousness—may plausibly reside in computers. He is claiming that all physical objects that change their informational state dynamically are capable of *some* degree of consciousness, however infinitesimally small. While I understand Wolf's point about correlation as an essential

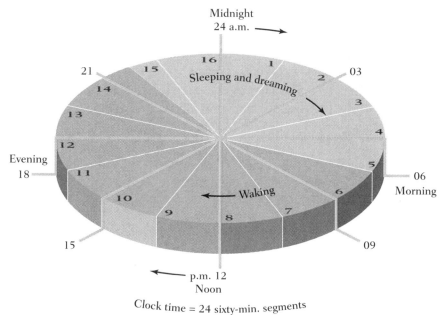

Brain Time and Clock Time *There are two important differences between brain time and clock time. One is that the brain's daily rest–activity cycle is usually longer than 24 hours (the circadian brain clock), and must be reset each day. The other, shown here, is that the brain's nightly NREM–REM 90-minute sleep cycle is much longer than one hour. Although, the 90-minute clock is suppressed in waking, it does express itself in cycles of attention, fatigue, and appetite so as to contribute an internal structure to external behaviors (mealtimes, exercise scheduling, film and class durations).*

aspect of consciousness, I would not expect to learn much about my conscious states from a close study of rocks and minerals, even if they could be shown to keep a record of their experience. Many other physicists see the study of consciousness as not only tied to quantum mechanics, but dependent upon its resolution. Those of us who have trouble even grasping what quantum mechanics is all about tremble at such a prophecy.

But let us grant that it may be so, and let us encourage the physicists to tell us what to look for at higher levels of self-organization, just as Roger Penrose has encouraged us to investigate such subcellular elements as microtubules, those tiny capillaries within nerve cells that serve as a sort of internal circulatory system for proteins. If the physicists are right, so much the better. If consciousness can be studied at many levels at once, the task of integrating across those levels will be all the more challenging—and positively rewarding.

David Kahn, the physicist who works with our group at Harvard, has convinced me that the spontaneous tendency of complex systems to change state from chaos to self-organization is relevant to our understanding of dream consciousness. One very attractive aspect of Kahn's self-organization model is that it closes the door on the leg of that annoying little person in our heads, the homunculus, who is supposed to be doing the thinking, the seeing, and the remembering for us.

Are Animals Conscious?

Pet owners will easily comprehend the assertion that so-called "lower" animals possess aspects of consciousness often erroneously denied them by those who suppose that only humans are conscious. It is true that pet owners are often guilty of the opposite fallacy, that of supposing that their animal protégés are every bit as conscious as their fellow humans. The cat that begs for scraps of fish at a restaurant table is clearly responding to an internal drive, hunger. It expresses that state with communicative clarity in its seductive postures and meows. Cats also learn, associatively to be sure, which guest is a feeder, and they remember that fact from meal to meal. But I very much doubt that they think about these vital matters in abstract terms. Otherwise they would write books about the brain basis of cat consciousness.

The componential view of consciousness relieves the animal mind of considerable strain by revealing this to be a false dilemma. Each side is partially correct. Yes, the scientific evidence favors the

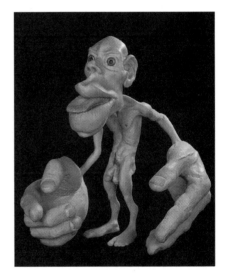

Homunculus *The notion of a little man living inside the head has been perpetuated by images such as this imaginary creature, the size of whose body parts is proportional to the amount of brain cortex devoted to the sensation arising from them. It is now known that there is not one, but a vast multiplicity of orderly maps of each sensory modality. At least 27 distinct visual worlds have so far been discovered within the brain. As with the stars and planets, we can expect more to be mapped as neuroscience develops further.*

view that only adult humans are fully conscious: only we are able to represent our own mental processes to ourselves via the abstractions of language and thought. Only we possess both primary and secondary levels of consciousness. And, yes, the scientific evidence favors the view that other animals sense, attend, feel, and learn in ways that are every bit as interesting—and worthy of respect and study—as those processes in humans. They too possess primary consciousness.

Two important consequences follow. The first is that animals are suitable models for the study of aspects of consciousness in humans. The second is that any such exploration must take the animal's consciousness into account by performing only such studies as are warranted by the promise of relief of human affliction, and only in such ways as are morally acceptable. In later chapters I will say more about these two important issues as I try to answer two questions: To which scientific inquiries about consciousness can animals provide definitive answers? By what techniques should such inquiry be pursued?

And what about babies? Because they cannot yet talk, our twin boys are no better than the biggest cats at telling us what they feel when they cry or smile. One thing is clear, however: they are much more likely to cry before being fed and much more likely to smile

The Animal Mind "Mirror, mirror on the wall, who is most conscious of them all?" This curious chimp appears to be scratching his head in wonderment. Or is he simply grooming? And, in any case, does he have the conscious awareness of self that even the simplest of such mirror gazing behaviors would seem to imply?

afterward. Presumably they experience—at some level—pain, or at least discomfort, in the hungry state and pleasure, or comfort, when they are sated. But are they conscious of these states? Do they say to themselves, as we could, I am feeling irritable because I am hungry? I am feeling content because I have had a good meal? Presumably not.

Like the ruminations that have preoccupied philosophers for millennia, such questions as these may seem hopelessly futile. But our reasons for asking them now are more practical. We want them to help us shape a strategy that could lead us to definitive answers. If every mind state, like feeling hungry (the cat and the baby) or knowing that one is hungry (like us adult humans), is associated with or identical to a brain state, and if each particular brain state is differentiable from all others, then we could, given world enough and time, create a reliable catalogue of correlated states that would enable us to say, with confidence, yes, the cat feels hungry, and yes, the baby feels discomfort, but no, the cat and our twins cannot tell themselves about their state, develop strategies to avoid the disgrace of crying, or do brain research and write books about it.

The Conscious State Paradigm

The conscious state concept opens the door to an analytic and holistic approach to consciousness by recognizing—and attempting to explain—the three major features of consciousness: its constant oscillation between unity and plurality, its extensive componential modularity, and its graded, modulated quality within and across species. It attempts to explain all three features by focusing upon the formal aspects of the three cardinal states of consciousness: waking, sleeping, and dreaming. By defining and measuring formal aspects of these three states at both the phenomenological (mental) and physiological (cerebral) levels, the conscious state approach permits comparison across levels within each state as well as comparison of one state with the others.

Such an exercise makes it possible to seek an integrative, neurocognitive explanation of each module of consciousness. Thus, if one conscious state (waking) is characterized by accurate recent memory and another (dreaming) is not, it should be possible to find a hypothetical explanation for that difference in their differential physiology. In fact, a brain chemical essential to memory is present in the brain during waking but is not secreted when dreaming occurs. Contrastingly, if one state (dreaming) is more intensely or more variably emotional than another (waking), it could be possible to explain the difference in terms of spontaneous and quasi-random neuroelectrical activation of known emotion centers in the brain during the sleep-with-dreaming state.

Both of these explanations and others have already been achieved. Thus the conscious state paradigm provides an effective set of working hypotheses about how the brain effects changes in consciousness. As satisfying as such an achievement may be, it will fail to satisfy those who seek an explanation of consciousness itself. To them we say, be patient. Take it one day at a time. Let us develop our theory bit by bit, little by little, but always standing on the firm ground of empirical science, whether that science be cognitive or neurobiological or even mathematical.

It may strike such critics as surprising that even that most essential attribute of human consciousness, reflective self-awareness, may yield to analysis by this state-based approach. That is possible because in one state, waking, self-awareness is present and in another, dreaming, it is not. When we dream, we erroneously suppose we are awake. At the level of the brain, what is lost, besides an accurate representation of the external world, that could explain this loss of self-reflective awareness? What has been subtracted from my dreaming brain in Stromboli that could account for my situating myself on my sleeping porch and thinking myself to be awake in Brookline? When I am lying in a bed on an island in the Mediterranean and experiencing such bizarre events, I should surely be able to accurately diagnose my conscious state as dreaming, but I cannot.

The answer to this fascinating question is not yet available. But it may come soon through the combination of two experimental techniques: lucid dream induction and brain imaging. Since human subjects can be trained to turn on—and turn off—self-reflective awareness during their dreams and to signal when they are lucid (accurately self-aware), it could be possible to identify critical brain correlates of self-awareness (for example, activation of the brain's frontal lobe during lucid dreaming, inactivation during nonlucid dreaming). This would be a dramatic experimental triumph of the conscious state paradigm.

Many formal features of conscious states were identified by scientists working in the field of sleep and dream research before the current upsurge of interest in consciousness began. The methodologies used have included the electroencephalogram (EEG),

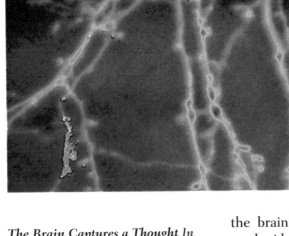

***The Brain Captures a Thought** In the span of a decade, building on the pioneering work of neuroscientists like Per Roland (see the photo on page 3), advances in cellular imaging techniques now allow us to view the activation of a single neural synapse.*

the analysis of subjective reports elicited in sleep laboratories, the development of reliable formal measures of such reports, and the analysis of differences in the report data in terms of the neurophysiology and neuropharmacology of the brain states with which they are associated.

Never has the brain-mind problem been so hotly pursued as today. I hope to describe the excitement of the chase and to evoke in the reader the scent of the prey. Scientists are poking into every nook and cranny of the brain in quest of the consciousness quark. And if I tell you that the brain-mind problem is in principle already solved, will you scoff and close the book with disgust, or hear me out and perhaps permit yourself to be convinced?

Compartments of the Mind

At first, the buzzing of a motorbike and the cry of its driver are consciously inaudible to me. I behold the Strombolian seascape as before, except that today the atmosphere is hazy and the air heavy with humidity. But because the cry is plaintively high-pitched and repetitive, I begin to tune it in and listen to it. After three or four passages through my conscious mind, the whining chant can be decoded as "Pes-che-fres-co." My still primitive Italian vocabulary, primed by the sea and seafood, translates the cry as "Fresh fish," which is less musical but more meaningful to me than "Pesche fresco."

Illumined Pleasures, Salvador Dali, 1929 *Dali appreciates the parallelism that characterizes the flow of even disparate mental processes simultaneously going on in the many compartments of the mind. His multiple light box collage represents sensation, perception, emotion, instinct, language, and motor action. And a voyeuristic observer peeps through the keyhole of consciousness. Or is it the unconscious that he is gazing into? (The Museum of Modern Art, New York. The Sidney and Harriet Janis Collection. Photograph © 1998 The Museum of Modern Art, New York.)*

I recount this scene to reveal a common truth: Only a very small portion of the universe of data available to us is represented in our consciousness at any one time. In the case of data from the outside world, it is obvious that we make a selection by directing our sense organs and tuning them to various inputs via the faculty of attention. This selection process determines what we are aware of perceiving. That we are already perceiving more than our awareness can acknowledge has been amply documented by studies of subliminal perception.

I recently had a vivid first-hand experience of this phenomenon when I participated in an experiment that my colleague Bob Stickgold designed to see whether the quality of sleep can affect our ability to retain a learned skill. Will I be better able tomorrow to detect and decode the fishmonger's cry that I learned today if I sleep well tonight? The answer appears to be yes.

The task that my colleague asked me to perform in the lab is less exotic than the fishmonger's challenge, but much more frustrating. The visual stimuli that I am asked to discriminate are flashed on the computer screen too fast for me to perceive consciously, and I therefore feel that I am failing miserably. Nonetheless, my nonconscious brain-mind does see the differences among the stimuli because I guess more and more of them correctly even as the exposure time diminishes. It is the learning of this unconscious perception that sleep helps me retain, or even improve, again without any conscious awareness.

The same limitations that gate data from the external world apply to internal data generated within our bodies. Most of the time we are not consciously aware of our posture, the beating of our hearts, our digestive processes, or even the movements of body parts that are the direct expression of our conscious experience. Indeed, it is only by contemplating what I am now writing that I can focus my awareness on the automatic but exquisitely complex movements of my left hand as it guides my pen across the page. Most of the data available to us from the external world and from our bodies never enter consciousness. We process many inputs automatically, and we have no conscious idea of the vast amounts of data that are saved or discarded.

*W*hy does the eye see a thing more clearly in dreams than the imagination when awake?   LEONARDO DA VINCI, CA. 1500

But consciousness is supraautomatic in that it is the mental attribute that allows us, occasionally at least, to transcend automaticity. And it is a surprisingly human attribute, giving us a mental freedom that most animals do not enjoy and that most of our own behaviors do not possess. This dichotomy between the unconscious reflexive and the conscious deliberate aspects of behavior lies at the heart of the philosophical problem of free will.

How we conceive of the brain's ability to support such an improbable property as freedom of choice has a practical bearing upon our concept of legal responsibility. The law assumes that the will is free, that consciousness directs decision making, and that we are therefore responsible for our acts. The conflict between the social exigency and the scientific uncertainty of these assumptions reverberates in courtrooms, in prisons, and in communities throughout the world. Until we can better negotiate between the large part of our behavior that is automatic and the rather small part that is deliberate, we will remain in a sad state of civil war with ourselves in matters relating to the notion of free will.

Yet we are naturally impatient when asked to wait for such vital information as cognitive neuroscience can provide. "So many neurons, so little time," laments the T-shirt worn by fledgling neuroscientists at a recent summer institute sponsored by the McDonnell-Pew Foundation. The mind boggles at the staggering array of possibilities. Some are stunned, stopped in their tracks by the classic discrepancy between the time courses of opportunity and obligation. Indeed,

Life is Short
And art long
Opportunity Fleeting
Experiment Treacherous
Judgment difficult.

These words were penned by the Greek philosopher Hippocrates almost 2,400 years ago in 377 B.C. When one looks at how far research on consciousness has advanced in just 50 years, we can only wish we might be alive 2,400 years hence to read and reflect on what brain-mind science accomplished in its short, artful life. Who knows, even the brain basis of free will may be clear by then.

Background and Foreground Compartments of Consciousness

Waking consciousness proceeds on at least two levels all the time. The surface, or foreground, level deals with our transactions—with the task at hand, if you will—and with our conscious intentions. The background level wells up in us from the fonts of emotion, memory, and experience. The discourse between these two levels may be coherent, such that the background level is in constant touch with the foreground level, informing and shaping it. But the two levels can also become split, or dissociated, in ways that can illustrate what neuroscience knows about processes as wide-ranging as chaos and creativity. James Thurber's comic sketch "The Secret Life of Walter Mitty" is an extreme case in point. Stuck in traffic, Mitty suddenly breaks with his foreground reality and becomes a fearless ship captain, heroically guiding his storm-threatened vessel to safe harbor.

For most of us, the traffic between the immediate perceptions in the foreground of our consciousness and the internal cognitive framework that forms its background is more mundane. As we make our daily rounds, our perceptions are oriented around those expectancies or goals that constitute our program, our plan of attack for the day. Stuck in traffic, we may simply reorganize our schedule and our priorities, revise our route, or cross less important items off our "to do" list. But we all approach Walter Mitty's state when we engage in the near-fantasy level of background processing that I call review and rehearsal.

Review and rehearsal is a cognitive self-monitoring of behavior in which we reiterate recent interactions, especially those that dissatisfy us, and imagine alternative scenarios, including ways to make amends, to clarify our aims, or to assert ourselves more vigorously. These imaginings are usually reality-bound, but often press on the borders of dramatic heroism and self-debasement. Because they are so furtive and so often embarrassing, this fantasy aspect of consciousness has proved very difficult to study. So surreptitious are our private reveries that some critics even relegate these fantasies to the unconscious and include them as a target for investigation via free association in the context of psychoanalytic therapy. On the fly, in the press of the routine of urban life, many of us are wholly unaware of the dialogues we are conducting with our background selves.

But we don't necessarily need to lie down on an analyst's couch to investigate this process. Each of us has our own bed in which to access our background consciousness. This is the lesson that eloquent stay-a-bed Marcel Proust taught us. We may not have the luxury of ruminating while awaiting our maid's arrival with our morning coffee, but we can lie or sit still (even in traffic) and let our fantasies carry us into the land of our schemata, our memories, and our emotions. When I do just that right now, I can easily summon a vision of meeting with my collaborative companions in our conference room for a reality-based discussion of the issues relevant to fantasy research.

For about three years, between 1984 and 1987, my colleague Steven Hoffman and I tried to collect fantasy data from ourselves and several other highly motivated co-workers. We hoped that these fantasy reports would have the same face validity as the dream reports from which we had derived robust measures of bizarreness and for which we needed suitable controls. Although we did overcome many obstacles to the recording of these evanescent wisps of conscious experience, we still lack a fantasy data set comparable in validity, extent, or length to our dream material. Why? What is so difficult about capturing fantasies?

One issue concerns attention. Basically, attention is the process of devoting more cerebral resources to an analytic task by narrowing the focus of a data channel. The ability to focus our attention involves changing channels or selecting a topic within a channel. But it seems that when the background fantasy channel is sharply tuned, the foreground perceptual channel is out of focus, or even lost.

So strongly do external and internal data compete for the limited resource that is attention that when fantasy is up and running, the capacity to chase and capture it is unavailable, and vice versa. This slippery, "now you see it, now you don't" aspect of fantasy consciousness led Freud to the concept of the preconscious, by which he

A One-Person Fantasyland *In the hilarious film version of "The Secret Life of Walter Mitty," Danny Kaye switches brain-mind modes from the processing of external reality (left) to internal fantasy (right).*

meant to emphasize the intermediate position of fantasy between the easily reportable aspects of foreground consciousness and the deeply buried unconscious that he saw as omnipotent.

Rather than speculating, as Freud did, about the deep forces that may drive fantasy, we prefer today to devote our scientific attention to the diverse phenomenology of these compartments of consciousness, the better to bring them under the microscope of experimental analysis. The tools are available for understanding their brain mechanisms and functions. What we now need most are trained subjects and the critical experimental paradigms in which to apply those tools.

Some promising avenues of research to be discussed in more detail in later chapters include brain-imaging studies of two groups of subjects. One group has become so expert at lucid dreaming that they can not only turn lucidity on and off in REM sleep, but also signal their conscious state to the experimenter. The second, a group of highly hypnotizable persons, can likewise turn on and off visual imagery of hallucinatory intensity during trance states.

Conscious and Unconscious Brain States

Does the brain shift its conscious state when subjects shift their attentional focus from foreground to background processing? Or is there a third brain state associated with "parallel processing" at both the foreground and background levels?

The classic tool of sleep research, the electroencephalograph (EEG), has proved unequal to the task of answering these important questions. And no wonder. It is a much more global and remote measuring device than we need to detect what may be the highly localized and deep neuronal processes that underlie such relatively subtle states as fantasy and other forms of background processing. The EEG has been used by scientists investigating consciousness ever since its discovery in 1928, by the German psychiatrist Hans Berger. Because the EEG was so good at differentiating the different stages of sleep, and so good at detecting the abnormal and quite local activity associated with the global attentional lapses of epilepsy, it was natural to hope that it might be sensitive to fantasy. But its difficulty in discriminating between even such radically different phenomenological states as waking and dreaming was a sure sign that we needed a better tool than the EEG to study consciousness.

Whether we will get what we need by expanding the reach of surface EEG recording remains to be seen. Using computer averaging, it is now possible to monitor and compare the electrical activity of many brain sites simultaneously and to generate spectacularly beautiful maps of the electrical activity at the cortical surface. The time resolution of such maps is impressive. With a large enough computer, successive images can be collected every thousandth of a second and the waves of electrical energy across the brain visualized as a moving picture. But can the surface voltage of the brain, no matter how fabulously elaborated, ever tell us what we want to know? I have my doubts.

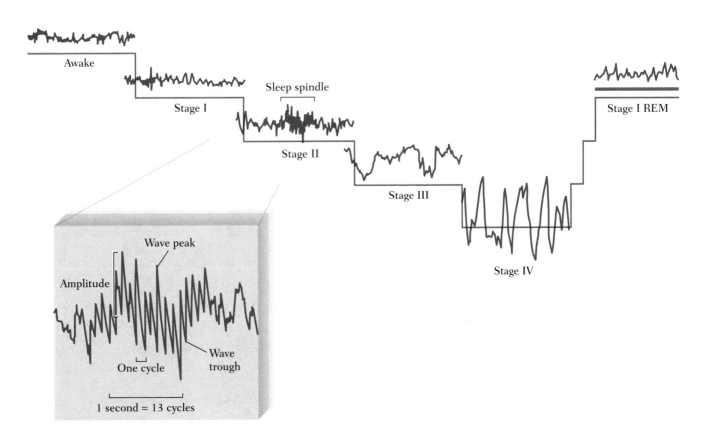

Awake

Stage I

Sleep spindle

Stage II

Stage III

Stage IV

Stage I REM

Wave peak

Amplitude

One cycle

Wave trough

1 second = 13 cycles

Recording Sleep Stages *The EEG tracing undergoes a dramatic transformation as human subjects move through the successive stages of sleep. As the low-voltage, rapid pattern of waking becomes the high-voltage, slow "delta wave" pattern of deep sleep, consciousness becomes less and less intense. This pattern then reverses itself, ultimately reaching a waking-like EEG in REM sleep, when dream consciousness becomes increasingly probable.*

The frequency range of traditional EEG recording can be expanded to record the high-frequency electrical activity that has been shown to be simultaneous in many parts of the cortex when subjects perceive visual stimuli. Does this 40 cycles per second pattern ebb and flow as Walter Mitty floats in and out of foreground awareness? By delivering sensory stimuli that travel through the brainstem and thalamus, it is possible to get a preliminary picture of electrical activity in the depths of the brain. Does the brain become more sensitive to internal signals, such as those related to spontaneous eye movements, when it images fantasies? And does the shift to background processing raise the threshold for external stimuli? Knowing how strong my own powers of concentration can be, my intuitive answer to this question is yes.

As soon as the fishmonger's voice seized my attention, I began unconsciously to reference his voice signals in my lexicon, a part of my internal data source that I was not aware of until it was activated by the external stimulus. If he had said *"Pesche fresco"* only once, I would not have heard it, much less understood the words. Was it the third, or the fifth, repetition that finally registered in my awareness? I am not sure. But sometime between their first and tenth iteration in my brain, the fishmonger's words supplanted those that were flowing into the text that I was writing, and I experienced the delight of recognition. The flash of insight that came when I discerned their meaning followed almost immediately. Like the automatic processing of external data, the translation from *"Pesche fresco"* to "Fresh fish" was automatic and nonconscious. I am happy to report, moreover, that this automatic retrieval procedure now runs in my brain, without instruction, for many hundreds of Italian words.

Topographic Map of EEG Asymmetry *The intensity of the brain's surface electrical activity can be assessed by computerized display as a colored map representing the magnitude of voltages recorded by an array of electrodes on the scalp. Here, the white dots represent the positions of the electrodes. This technique can detect waves of activity as subjects perform tasks, sleep, undergo hypnosis, or simply sit, quietly awake. The color coding of this map reveals that the voltage difference is greatest in the frontal regions of the human cerebral cortex (red, orange, and yellow areas), which are critical to higher mental functions such as thought and volition, and to the individual's temperament.*

Whether such automata as memory retrieval should be considered solely mental mechanisms or physiological mechanisms in the service of mentation is a hotly debated and crucial point. In my book *The Chemistry of Conscious States*, I chose to define the mind as all the information in the brain, and was surprised that no one challenged that assertion. It still strikes me as an arbitrary and debatable choice. I make it in part because I like to emphasize the ambiguity that it highlights: Where does brain physiology end and mentation begin? We cannot say for sure because they are seamlessly melded, as befits a unified system with continuity between its background and foreground levels of operation.

Earlier I used the word *nonconscious* advisedly to foreshadow an important distinction among at least three compartments of the mind that usually are not—and sometimes never are—conscious. The first of these compartments contains the implicit mental automata that can never become conscious no matter how hard we try. My memory search for the meaning of *"pesche fresco"* is an example. I can deliberately set such a search in motion, but the wonder is that it runs without supervision. The second compartment, the cognitive unconscious, contains data like the English words "fresh fish" that I can easily summon into consciousness. The dynamically repressed unconscious contains data that could become conscious, but tend not to do so because their recognition is painful. An example is my sad awareness that today is the birthday of a lost friend with whom I visited these islands several years ago.

I admit to the enormous difficulty of confidently differentiating the cognitive unconscious from the dynamically repressed unconscious. But I tolerate the ambiguity for heuristic reasons. If you are a Freudian, virtually all forgetting—including amnesia for dreaming—is a function of dynamic repression. If you are a cognitive scientist, forgetting is at least as likely to be physiologically determined. Who is correct? We can't yet say for sure. So how can we decide the matter fairly? Only by experimentation, not by clinical anecdote.

Cognitive neuroscience approaches the memory problem experimentally. Since Freud's concept of the unconscious as dynamically repressed has been so difficult to investigate experimentally, and since so much of the unconscious is in any case not dynamically repressed, cognitive science continues to focus upon learning and memory, the mental faculties that have been central to the interests of experimental psychologists from the very beginning.

The essential methodology still used today, reaction time measurement, was developed by the German experimental psychologist Wilhelm Wundt as a way of objectifying subjective responses to tasks.

Reaction time is the delay between the presentation of a stimulus to a subject and the completion of the prescribed response. When driving an automobile, we must sometimes make wheel corrections or apply our brakes to avert collisions. Our reaction time, or speed in doing so, is the sum total of the times taken for stimulus recognition, signal processing, and response generation.

Reaction time is determined by many factors, including our level of alertness, our attention to foreground as opposed to background data, and our exposure to drugs that affect brain functions. No wonder fatal accidents peak late at night when drivers are most likely to be drunk, drowsy, and distracted. In laboratory settings, experimenters design artificial tasks to measure different aspects of the signal processing sequence. If attention is being assessed, the time taken by the subject to shift his consciousness from one stimulus array to another may be the variable of interest. If vigilance is being assessed, then the time it takes the subject to extract a signal from noise may be measured. To assess verbal memory, the subject might be asked to signal recognition of a word in a list to which he was previously only subliminally exposed.

The strengths and weaknesses of reaction time measurement are clear: The experimenter collects enormous amounts of quantitative data, but can interpret them only inferentially unless, as has recently become possible, other explicit measures of brain physiology such as EEG frequency and amplitude are simultaneously employed.

Two Kinds of Memory

Philosopher-critics of the experimental approach argue that while consciousness is dependent upon memory, it is not identical to it. Our componential analysis is consistent with this position. But among the components of consciousness, memory occupies a place second only to self-reflective awareness, which, as we will see, is itself intimately tied to a specific sort of memory. If, as in dreams, I cannot give an accurate account of my current biographical situation, my consciousness becomes confabulatory rather than veridical. At the same time, I lose self-reflective awareness.

Experimental results from the study of memory have led scientists to make distinctions relevant to theories of consciousness and the unconscious. One is the distinction between explicit memory and implicit memory. Memory is explicit if I can give an accurate and detailed report of data to which I have been previously exposed. To do so I must be able to access information that is otherwise uncon-

Wilhelm Wundt *The founder of experimental psychology was a prodigiously productive writer. To put psychology on the map as a science, Wundt forcibly and effectively opposed those who advocated a more speculative, introspective philosophical approach. He trained a whole generation of psychologist-scientists, published a journal to report their results, and wrote an influential series of ponderous tomes. In the end, however, Wundt was a thoroughgoing dualist who declared that mind and matter cannot be compared.*

scious, bring it into consciousness, name it, and report on it. Memory is implicit if I demonstrate acquisition of a skill (walking, for example) without awareness of how, or even if, I have acquired it. Obviously, each of the many steps in acquiring knowledge or skill might utilize a distinct process and hence be localizable to a particular region or a particular functional state of the brain.

A spectacular and by now familiar example is the differential response to stimuli presented in the left and right visual fields of human subjects whose two cerebral hemispheres have been surgically separated to treat intractable epilepsy. In these split-brain studies, information reaching the right hemisphere is perceived, and even reacted to emotionally (implicit memory), but because the fibers connecting the right brain (which perceives) to the left brain (which names and reports on percepts) have been cut, no report is forthcoming. If the stimulus is presented to the left brain, the subjects are easily able to name the object represented and thus to make their memory explicit. Michael Gazzaniga, the cognitive neuroscientist who worked with the developmental neurobiologist Roger Sperry and these very interesting patients, has come to the conclusion that the narration of our conscious experience is a left brain function.

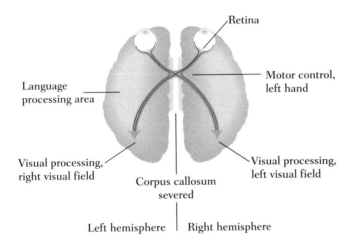

The Split-Brain Phenomenon *The creation of two independent conscious selves is a by-product of surgery to treat epilepsy, which can be ameliorated by cutting the major fiber ducts (the corpus callosum) connecting the right and left hemispheres of the brain thereby creating the so-called split-brain phenomenon. The right hemisphere may then perceive an object and understand its use, but be unable to name it because it is isolated from the language processing structures in the left hemisphere.*

These split-brain experiments make two general points with startling clarity. One is that consciousness, like the brain, is divisible into component processes such as perception, emotion, and memory. The second is that these processes are not only discrete and serial, but also localizable. An even more radical conclusion is that subjects with split brains actually possess two conscious minds, each with its own information and its own capacity for rendering that which is implicit, explicit. It goes without saying that such a conclusion gives strong support to monistic views of the conscious mind: It is the activated brain that is conscious, and the kind of consciousness that the activated brain experiences is determined by its physical structure and its conscious state.

Explicit Memory

There are two kinds of explicit memory. The episodic type represents personal history while the semantic type represents general knowledge. "I was born in Hartford" is one example of an explicit episodic memory. "I am writing this book in Stromboli" is another. "Hartford is the capital of Connecticut" and "Stromboli is one of the six Aeolian Islands lying off the northern coast of Sicily" are two examples of explicit semantic knowledge. In both cases, the data are implicit as they sit in my cognitive unconscious mind, awaiting my call.

I will probably have no problem convincing you that these memories are legitimately mental and that they are unequivocally unconscious unless summoned by my brain-mind into consciousness. And you would agree, I am sure, that to achieve its current status, this information must have once passed through consciousness. To be so well remembered, it has probably passed through consciousness more than once. But have you ever asked yourself the question, in what physical form are such memories stored? To answer this question at all, you must have envisioned some more or less mechanical model of the mind, a tape recorder for instance. That's easy enough to think about even though the brain is really nothing like a tape recorder.

In the Record mode, a tape recorder listens—but does not speak—and lays down a sequence of electromagnetic signals representing the sounds of speech. When I say, for example, "My memory works like a tape recorder," I am implying that as long as no other message is recorded on that particular segment of tape, and the tape is archived so that it does not degenerate or break, the tape can be accessed in the Play mode and heard to say, "My memory works like a tape recorder." To be useful, my tape archive memory would need to be enormous, imperishable, and skillfully indexed. I want all my memory theories to be enduring and readily accessible; that is to say, I want them to be content addressable.

Somewhere along the way you will have realized that the statement I recorded on my tape is false. My memory does not work like a tape recorder. It could not. There is just too much information in my brain-mind to store it all in analog form as a series of statements about the world or my personal history. Furthermore, my memory can record and play back at the same time. When I sit in a lecture and whisper my critique of the speaker's memory theory, I can simultaneously monitor and remember both what is being said and my critique of it. In any case, I trust that you are as convinced as I am that memory mechanisms are brain mechanisms. Although it is a material structure, my brain has little or no physical resemblance to a tape recorder, or even to a digital computer. But if you like the analogy of the tape recorder even a little, you will realize that there is no voice, no sound, inside it. The tape recorder's memory, like that of my brain, must be something like a sequence of electromagnetic states.

Once again, the conclusion is clear. You have no choice but to endorse neuroscience if you have any serious interest in your mind and how it works. And no choice but to follow me to the inevitable conclusion: my cognitive—and even my dynamically repressed—unconscious consists of brain mechanisms with a more impressive information processing capacity and efficiency than any known machine. Opponents of monism may lick their chops at this admission, thinking, wrongly, that the mind must therefore be something else, something transcendent, something spiritual, possibly even something immortal. But all will agree that the translation of the data in my unconscious mind into conscious, explicit messages such as those I now communicate to you is brain-based information processing.

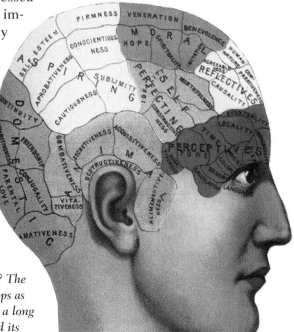

Galton's Map of the Brain *How soon will the new phrenology of cognitive science seem as dated as so many of its famous predecessors? The computer processing analogy may be an improvement over head bumps as character signatures, but we must remember that technology still has a long way to go before it can provide a perfect match to the brain-mind and its conscious states.*

The conclusion that the unconscious mind is a brain state leads us as close to acceptance of the unity of brain and mind as we can hope to get for now. What we need to do next is flesh out this conclusion as best we now can while waiting for the neuroscience frontier to expand so that it can explicitly define exactly how brain states are mental, be they conscious or unconscious.

Implicit Memory

My capacity to walk, to swim or to play tennis depends upon procedural memory. Our motor skills constitute this form of implicit memory with which we are most familiar but tend to think about least. When we think about our motor software—the programs that guide our implicit behaviors—we realize that they must be procedural—at once reliably stereotyped and almost infinitely flexible. We think of mechanical models like wind-up toys and robots. As in our tape recorder analogy, there are wheels, ratchets, and gears that represent muscles and bones. But what about the software programs that run the mechanical parts? Are they tapes? Certainly not.

What are they then? They too are brain states instantiated in neuronal ensembles so interconnected as to be activated—at will or automatically—to drive our bodies in extraordinarily skillful—even beautiful—ways. If asked, you might be able to give an explicit account of how you walk, but the activation of procedural memory that is crucial to actually doing it is so completely unconscious that even a spiritualist would be likely to call it a brain mechanism. Would you, then, be tempted to say that such memory is motor learning and therefore not mental at all? How would you draw such a line? I myself am unable to do so. This seamless meld of explicit, implicit, semantic, and motor mechanisms is to me convincing proof of brain-mind unity.

Procedural Memory *Human beings can train themselves to perform motor acts of enormous complexity and exquisite beauty. The programs for these highly overleavened behaviors reside in procedural memory, a part of the mind that is unconscious. Although they can be called up by the conscious mind, they are so automatic as to remain nonconscious even when they are running.*

The Nonconscious Mind

Are all the neuronal mechanisms that have been influenced by our experience to be considered mental, whether their information content can be brought into consciousness or not? In this view, the mind can be divided into three parts: the small, ever-changing part that is conscious; the much larger part that is unconscious but can be made conscious; and the even larger part that can never be made conscious. I call this third part the nonconscious mind.

All three compartments of the mind show experiential structure in that they contain records of the past. These records, in turn, all share the functional property of adaptability. The information in the unconscious mind is like a personal encyclopedia in that it allows its possessor, at leisure, to look up data and bring them into consciousness for examination and analysis.

The nonconscious mind is adaptable in an even more automatic, reflexive manner. It enables its possessor to behave effectively in moments of extreme demand—in the heat of battle, as it were—without the necessity or the luxury of cognitive reflection. This part of the mind includes what some call intuition, a sixth sense, a "feeling in my bones." The emotional tinge that all these terms connote, of course, may color the content of all three compartments of the mind.

It should also be clear that all three compartments operate by storing representations of experience and calling them into action by voluntary choice or in an entirely reflexive manner. My learning to roller skate—at age 8 1/2—is still a part of my procedural nonconscious mind at age 65, though I am wise enough not to try it now. It is quite enough to watch Luca, my 14-year-old stepson, learning to master his Rollerblades. This example shows too that while my implicit roller skating programs are not themselves conscious, they nonetheless have an important functional relationship to consciousness. I can decide not to use them. And I can actually remember some of the tricks I learned more than 50 years ago and impart them to Luca as he learns and makes at least some of his new skill implicit. An entirely reflexive organism with only primary consciousness cannot teach abstractions that it cannot make. While animal parents can coach their offspring in the execution of those elaborate motor skills that serve instinctual ends like hunting and killing prey, a circus dog that has been taught to roller skate by a human trainer cannot impart that skill to its puppies.

Priming and Associative Learning

One of the key tools used by modern cognitivists to study memory is the semantic priming paradigm. Semantic priming is the process whereby the activation of brain networks containing words like "fish" will simultaneously activate those containing related words like "boat" or "net." Because it entails words, and hence language, semantic priming is a key to understanding secondary consciousness. How we speak, think, and write is related to semantic priming because various parts of our lexicon are represented and become activated in large part unconsciously and automatically.

The basic experimental procedure is to rapidly flash a string of letters on a screen and instruct subjects to indicate, as quickly as possible, whether the string is a word or a nonword. The exposure to these "target" strings is too brief to allow conscious inspection and analysis, but despite this the subjects' responses demonstrate surprisingly accurate subliminal perception. The subjects' speed and accuracy in identifying a word are enhanced if they are "primed" by previous exposure to a word that is semantically related to the target string. Doctor primes nurse. Cat primes dog. Hot primes cold. And so on.

This finding reveals that memory retrieval is largely automatic. Cognitive neuroscientists ascribe it to the activation of neural networks. They further assume that the brain must represent relationships among words in the synaptic strength of the connections between neurons. Some cognitivists deny an identity between this concept of network activation and that of the neurophysiologists. I believe that such disclaimers are both disingenuous and mistaken. I have the same criticism of artificial intelligence models of the mind that claim a functionalism that is independent of neuronal reality. Although it is possible that better ways of processing information than our natural ones exist, it is surely difficult to imagine that we could ever design a brain that would function better than the one provided us by evolutionary eons of trial-and-error tinkering.

Conscious states arise—and change—when the neuronal circuits of the brain are electrically activated and chemically modulated. These circuits are complex, but can be analyzed by a wide variety of anatomical and physiological techniques that specify the multiple influences upon a neuron and its effects upon the many other neurons with which it makes synaptic contact. At each synaptic junction, communication between neurons is achieved by the liberation of chemical messengers, or neurotransmitters. It is by consistent alteration of the mix of neurotransmitters, a process called neuromodulation, that different conscious states like waking, sleeping, and dreaming are regulated.

Back to a concrete example: Although my writing here may not be quite as unfettered as the automatic scrivening of the poet André Breton and his fellow surrealists, it does have an automatic quality. So, now, does my public speaking. All I need is a prime, and my overtrained neural networks do the rest. And, as with the roller skating that I now eschew, I know better, now that my semantic memory is in

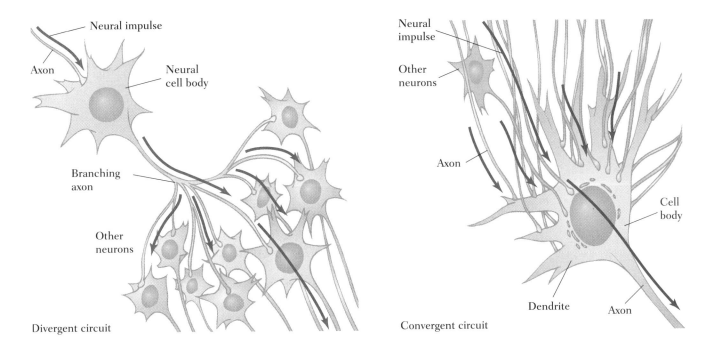

Divergent circuit

Convergent circuit

Neural Circuitry In the divergent circuit above at left, one neuron sends signals to many others through the branching of its axons. In the covergent circuit at right, one target neuron processes signals via the axons projecting from many different neurons. The myriad synaptic contacts impinging on each cell can be directly visualized by the scanning electron micrographs such as this.

decline, than to try—too deliberately at least—to find specific words that elude me.

In his introduction to *Breton's Selected Writings*, Franklin Rosemont asserts that "Psychic automatism remains, and will always remain the golden key to the surrealist quest." Since André Breton began his career as a psychiatrist, it may not be surprising that his work is a bridge between the scientific exploration and the artistic exploitation of brain-mind automata. While trying to fall asleep at 11:00 P.M. on September 27, 1933, Breton's brain-mind spoke automatically as follows:

"Oh no, no, I bet Bordeaux Saint Augustine that a notebook there."

We have recorded equally intriguing nonsense sentences from subjects as they fall asleep. My emphasis here is not so much on the conscious state dependence of autocreative brain-mind mechanisms as upon their utility and their universality. If I need to retrieve a proper name or give a talk, I can give my brain-mind the assignment and it will thereafter do the work unbidden. Semantic priming is just a small and specific aspect of our unconscious ability to elaborate meaning via the unleashing of chains of neural associations.

From Chaos, Self-Organization

Long before the formal institution of psychology as an experimental science in the second half of the nineteenth century, the associative nature of human thought had been emphasized by such writers as the English physician-philosopher David Hartley (1705–1757). John Locke's philosophical proposal that ideas are interconnected, sequential, and descriptive of experience inspired Hartley to propose that all psychological acts might be explained by a single law of association that operates at the level of the brain as well as at the level of the mind. In Hartley's view, even such complex mental processes as imagining, remembering, and reasoning could be analyzed into sequences of elementary sense impressions, and these, in turn, were reducible to brain processes. It was David Hartley who first suggested that dreaming serves to loosen associations lest they become obsessively tight. This genial idea has recently been re-echoed by Francis Crick, who theorizes that we dream in order to forget.

Can it be that within our organic edifice there dwell innumerable inhabitants which palpitate feverishly, with impulses of spontaneous activity, without our taking any notice of them? And our much talked-of psychological unity? What has become of thought and consciousness in this audacious transformation of man into a colony of polyps?   SANTIAGO RAMÓN Y CAJAL, 1885

Even simple and completely nonconscious brains learn associatively. Pair one stimulus with another in space or time, and the lowliest creature will learn the association. Thus the sea slug learns to withdraw its gill mantle even in response to a normally ineffective shock if that stimulus has been presented together with one that reliably and unconditionally provokes gill withdrawal. Both the response and its experimental remodeling are mediated by neuronal networks whose associative interaction is modulated—in a chemically specific way—by experience.

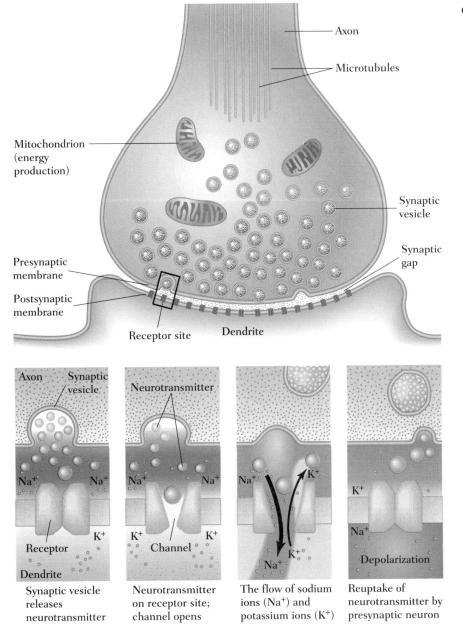

Axon

Microtubules

Mitochondrion
(energy
production)

Synaptic
vesicle

Synaptic
gap

Presynaptic
membrane

Postsynaptic
membrane

Receptor site

Dendrite

Axon | Synaptic vesicle

Neurotransmitter

Na^+ | Na^+

Receptor

K^+

Dendrite

Synaptic vesicle
releases
neurotransmitter

Neurotransmitter

Na^+ | Na^+

K^+ | Channel | K^+

Neurotransmitter
on receptor site;
channel opens

Na^+ | K^+

Na^+ | K^+

The flow of sodium
ions (Na^+) and
potassium ions (K^+)

K^+

Na^+

Depolarization

Reuptake of
neurotransmitter by
presynaptic neuron

Neurotransmission *Nerve cells within brain circuits communicate with each other via the release of neurotransmitters, which alter the cells they contact so that they are more or less excitable. Excitability is mediated by the flow of ions such as sodium, potassium, calcium, and chloride through the pores in the neuronal cell membrane.*

Even more interesting is the fact that one of the essential chemical ingredients of associative learning in sea slugs is serotonin, a neurotransmitter molecule we humans need to stay awake, attentive, and teachable. This means that the associative learning aspect of our consciousness may depend upon chemicals that have been used for learning by many of our evolutionary forebears. Any mechanism that has survived for so long must confer an important competitive advantage on its possessor. In this regard, it is amusing to note that in New York today, those go-getters who are *not* taking Prozac, a drug that boosts brain serotonin, consider themselves to be at a competitive disadvantage.

The associationism of David Hartley was well known to William Wordsworth and his lyrical ballad collaborator, Samuel Coleridge. In writing such immortal poems as "Kubla Khan," Coleridge put his brain-mind on automatic search and did not hesitate to give it a pharmacological kick to get it going when walks in the Lake District didn't do the trick. Wordsworth and Coleridge were going far beyond semantic priming in their poetic embrace of associationism. In their literary experiments, they were even touching on self-organization.

Self-organization is related to the tendency of chaotic systems to spontaneously enter states in which surprising and potentially useful properties arise. This concept is revolutionizing science today by providing an alternative model to Newtonian mechanics.

Chaos is the natural tendency for any multielement structure to develop unpredictable states when activated by deterministic noise. To understand the apparent paradox of a noisy determinism, consider a weather system that is susceptible to spontaneous perturbations from many forces, each of which obeys, at some elemental level, the laws of deterministic physics. At the level of the whole system, however, the interaction of the vast number of elements underlying each of the multiplicity of forces makes the future of the system unknowable from its current conditions. For example, although wind speed is determined by the kinetic energy of air particles, it may unpredictably increase, decrease, or dissipate entirely owing to its interaction with

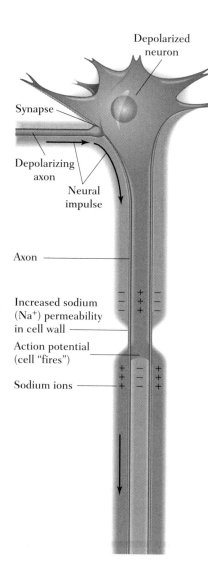

Depolarized neuron

Synapse

Depolarizing axon

Neural impulse

Axon

Increased sodium (Na⁺) permeability in cell wall

Action potential (cell "fires")

Sodium ions

Neural Activation When a sufficient number of sodium ions rushes into the neuronal cell body, a chain reaction—the action potential—progressively depolarizes the entire neuronal membrane, including its axonal endings. This results in the release of neurotransmitters that in turn affect all adjacent neurons. This process, which is both spontaneous and continuous, can be altered by changes in both internal and external signals so as to influence the form and content of consciousness.

water currents of imprecisely predictable temperature. Likewise, the brain may be suddenly and unpredictably "bumped" from one conscious state to another by the escalating activation of one of its many neuronal subsystems. The weather change and the conscious state change are both a function of spontaneous fluctuations (the noise term) in systems whose elements obey strictly causal laws (the deterministic term).

Serotonin may serve to restrain cerebral chaos and may thus be a global organizer of the brain, assuring consistency and stability of conscious state whenever it is available, which is during waking. The degree to which consciousness is unified, single-minded, and predictably associative may depend upon molecules like serotonin.

The unpredictability of complex systems might imply that chaos is undesirable—that, like the id, it is something to be suppressed, repressed, or sublimated. But chaos has its good side too, because all complex systems with chaotic properties can self-organize. If the brain has this natural tendency, then it could be highly adaptive to loosen our single-minded restraint from time to time, let it run free, and see what happens. This is possibly what happens when I put my lexical look-up system on automatic pilot, though in this case I have set it a specific task. When I am harvesting fantasies I let my brain run free and then try to catch the product. Self-organization is thus more likely to be achieved in undirected states, such as meditation, fantasy, or reverie, that border on waking. And it may be best achieved in dreaming.

If this is the case, then we have good reason to accord dreaming an importance that goes far beyond the role of generator of cryptic messages about obscure desire. Instead, dreaming may be our most creative conscious state, one in which the chaotic, spontaneous recombination of cognitive elements produces novel configurations of information: new ideas. While many or even most of these ideas may be nonsensical, if even a few of its fanciful products are truly useful, our dream time will not have been wasted.

The Dynamically Repressed Unconscious

In the Freudian view, my costume at George Vaillant's wedding party in my dream last night—a huge, 3-foot-long, feathery bird hat—could not simply be an expression of my love for exotic dress-up. Especially for corny hats. No. It must rather be a cover-up of my wish to see "the bird"—in Italian, *ucello*—or some other bit of off-limits anatomy, my mother's, for example. There were mirrors too, and photographs being taken for a dream fantasy wedding album. To Freud, this could be the result of regression to the visual domain to conceal my Oedipal mother-lust.

I have already been accused of caricature in teasing the Freudians this way. But any therapist who has read *The Interpretation of Dreams* or undergone clinical supervision with an orthodox psychoanalyst will know that these pseudo-interpretations of my own dreams are not far-fetched. What is the neurocognitive alternative to this id-ridden view of the unconscious? How can the neuroscientist-psychologist account for the visually rich imagery and the flamboyant exhibitionism of my bird-hat wedding dream?

For starters, the volcanic pressure, the flaming gas that drives the system, is neurochemical. One neurochemical modulatory system (the modern equivalent of Freud's censor, but stripped of its prudery) dominates the brain-mind during waking and gives waking consciousness its observational, analytic, and logical quality. When this waking system turns off, its dreaming counterpart (the equivalent of Freud's id, but not nearly so lascivious) turns on. This neuromodulatory system directly stimulates the autocreative visual imagery and the emotional hot stuff so tightly associated with dreaming.

Before I spell out the details of the visual image generation and the correlated emotional activation that occurs in dreaming, consider this emerging picture of the neurocognitive "unconscious." It is not simply a memory file. I have never seen such a bird hat before. It was concocted on the spot, synthesized de novo, by my self-activated, chemically altered brain-mind. Likewise, the wild elation and manic frolic of my emotion was cooked up on the spot. Which came first, the bird-hat or the elation? I used to think that the dream plot inspired the emotion. But recent evidence indicates that it may be the other way around: perhaps the emotion comes first, and the plot is an attempt to contextualize it.

Does this mean that my brain-mind, and yours, is a jack-in-the-box that springs into action when a neurochemical switch is flipped? Yes. Does this mean that dreaming is a kind of madness? A case of consciousness gone wild? Yes again. And this is not a new idea. Can you guess the poet who wrote the following lines 200 years before Freud?

> *Those dreams that on the silent night intrude.*
> *And with false flitting shapes our minds delude,*
> *Jove never sends us downward from the skies,*
> *Nor do they from infernal mansions rise;*
> *But all are mere productions of the brain.*
> *And fools consult interpreters in vain.*

Before telling you the poet's name, let me underline his astute diagnosis of dreams as delusional (hence dreaming is a model of madness), his rejection of religious theories (Pagan gods, like Jove, are discounted as possible agents of dreaming), his rejection of superstitious mystiques ("infernal mansions" could include "ids" as well as ghosts, devils, and incubi), his prescient faith in neuroscience ("all are mere productions of the brain"), and his scorn for superstitious gullibility ("fools consult interpreters in vain").

Who had all these wonderful ideas? The author was none other than Jonathan Swift, remembered today for his satire on eighteenth-century life, *Gulliver's Travels*. Swift was a typical Enlightenment thinker who, like his contemporary David Hartley, developed the rationalist tradition of Thomas Hobbes.

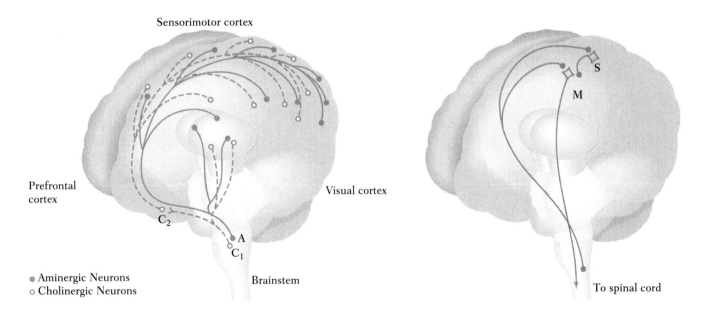

Neuromodulation (Left) Neuromodulatory neurons of the brainstem distribute their axons diffusely throughout the brain. The aminergic group (A), which is most active during waking, consists of norepinephrine- and serotonin-releasing cells that project directly to the cortex. The cholinergic group (C), which is most active during REM sleep, projects to the cortex via an intermediary (C2) in the basal forebrain. (Right) Neuromodulatory neurons of both types exert their effects upon reflex circuits composed of sensory (S) and motor (M) neurons of the cortex and other parts of the brain (not shown). In this way brain circuits, and hence consciousness, are biased toward either external (waking) or internal (dreaming) modes of operation.

Suppose I told you that now, 300 years later, we can prove that Swift was correct. By using our neurochemical knowledge, we can flip the dream switch on and off at will. And so control dream madness. And so control consciousness. You shudder. It sounds like *A Clockwork Orange* or *Brave New World*, with Big Brother dressed up in a bird hat. That's the bad news. The good news is that drugs are not the only way to flip the switch. We can use consciousness itself as an agent to control its own states.

The Cognitive Unconscious

The question remains, how are we to conceive of the unconscious? If it is not the volcanic cauldron of asocial desire that Freud imagined it to be, what is its nature? Is it, as the French Freud, Jacques Lacan, would have us believe, "structured like a language?" Well, maybe. At least the linguistic unconscious must be structured like a language. But what does it mean to voice this slogan? I have an even deeper skepticism about Lacan's contribution to a science of the mind than I do about Sigmund Freud's. My mathematically sophisticated colleagues assure me that his use of topology is entirely inappropriate. Professional linguists say that his use of linguistic concepts and techniques was highly idiosyncratic. And many of his friends and patients regarded him as arbitrary and domineering.

But giving the devils their due, suppose we were to recognize some truth in Freud and Lacan. How much of the unconscious mind would they have recognized? One way to answer this question is to reexamine the thirteen components of consciousness listed in the table on page 16. Assume that each of these modules must have an unconscious component. If we grant Freud limited dominion over the instinct module (because instincts must be represented in the unconscious) and grant Lacan limited dominion over the linguistic module (because our lexicon, our grammar, and our syntactical skills are all largely unconscious), most of the unconscious mind still remains unaccounted for.

Are the brain's perceptual structures unconscious? Certainly. How else could I see, with surrealistic clarity, my dream bird hat with no external stimulus? In waking consciousness, every perceptual encounter is a match between an internal structure and an external stimulus. Without visual experience, the blind do not see—either in their dreams or when their sight is magically restored. In this view the brain is an image file, but remember, it is much more than that, because it can fabricate new images as well as call up old ones. My bird hat is a good example of this novel image-making capability. It is this creative aspect that is at the center of the recent debate between psychoanalysts and cognitivists regarding the nature of the unconscious mind.

As soon as a percept suggests a scene—be it my internally generated bird hat in a dream or the aquamarine Mediterranean Sea shimmering now beyond my vine-covered balcony—my cognitive unconscious seeks to situate the stimulus in a context. The time: What day is today? The place: Where am I? And the personnel: Who is with me? If I attend to any of a myriad details, the answer—in waking—is unequivocally clear, because the context is given by the world. This is Stromboli. The volcano smokes above me. The Miramar Hotel porch with its characteristic Aeolian architecture frames my view. The cast of characters, the blend of my first and second families, has a reassuring unity. My son Ian has brought me the *Gazetta del Sud,* July 23, with its lurid tales of Mafia mischief. The chambermaid strolls by, singing, *"La prima amore no si scordo mai,"* and even though I am busily writing, I know her song means that one's first love is never forgotten.

Without this external structure—and without full access to attention or recent memory—my cognitive unconscious does the best it can in my wedding dream. It creates the context, George Vaillant's house and garden, with a nodding obeisance to certain rules: the house is old, stylish, rambling, and full of antiques. The garden is intricate, full of terraces, walls, perennials, fountains, and hidden places. So far so good. These are the formal features of the Vaillant manse in Dedham, Massachusetts, all right. But they are organized in a completely novel way. So novel, in fact, that when I awake, I will be puzzled, if not downright consternated, by their imperfect fit with reality.

The incongruence between the dream house and the real house is surprising because now, awake, I can visualize the actual house quite easily. I could even draw a floor plan and a map of the garden that I believe would be quite accurate. To account for such a glaring discrepancy, I need to consider factors other than the absence of waking context signals. My cognitive unconscious has clearly different operating properties in dreaming. It is not only inattentive to perceptual detail, but also inattentive to its inattentiveness! I have lost the ability to image accurately. And I have lost the ability to monitor my inaccuracy. What is missing? The superego? I doubt it. A brain chemical? I am sure of it.

But a fair exchange is no robbery, as the saying goes. My cognitive losses are compensated. For my loss of perceptual and orientational accuracy, I have gained autocreative freedom. I could never in waking create so convincing a false scenario as I effortlessly dream.

Conscious Control of Consciousness
All self-directed methods of controlling consciousness during waking share the basic principles of muscular relaxation, reduction of respiratory rate, and introduction of peaceful mental content. The net effect is to move the brain-mind toward the edge of sleep, but not quite over it. At that interface, a wide variety of altered states of consciousness can be experienced. The subjective benefits of these practices may depend more upon their shared physiology than upon the specific mystiques that inform and are supported by them.

My confabulatory powers are enhanced. So are my artistic talents: I paint a more colorful picture of myself than any photograph could possibly record. In my dream, I am a Fellini character costumed in grotesque, comical garb. This is why the surrealists working with André Breton were so interested in dreaming. And it is why even more traditional writers, like Robert Louis Stevenson, for example, so frequently turn to dreams when stuck for a plot solution. Stevenson said he could reliably consult with his dream brownies (or fairies) when he needed a fabulous fiction. His Dr. Jekyll/Mr. Hyde transformation was born of one such dream dialogue.

Memory and the Unconscious

It is precisely this fictive propensity that makes the Freudian unconscious so dangerous a concept: The unconscious is not a reliable repository of memory. As the recent epidemic of false memory syn-

Charcot's Clinic *A century ago Jean Martin Charcot concluded that the symptoms of "hysteria" could not be explained by what was then known about the brain. Today, claims of multiple personality and posttraumatic stress abound. The susceptibility of Charcot's patients to hypnotic trance induction helped him convince others that these states could be suggested and were therefore only functional. Now we realize that all brain-mind states have a neurological basis and that they are all—also—functional.*

drome attests, the worst joke to be played on Sigmund Freud is the use of some of his therapy techniques to suggest to patients the *necessity* of sexual trauma (to explain certain symptoms) and the *necessity* of its recall (to relive and relieve them). Because his theory developed in competition with hypnosis, Freud was scrupulous in his efforts to avoid the conveyance of suggestion to his patients. Sitting behind the analysand and saying little or nothing was supposed to allow associations to run free. But of course, by the time they got to Freud, every turn-of-the-century Viennese knew what kind of memories they were supposed to dredge up. Now, in America, the image of an incestuous father is explicitly incubated by many an overzealous therapist.

The production of egregious and damaging false memories by self-proclaimed ritual abuse and alien abduction victims should sensitize us all to the power of suggestion to cloud our consciousness in ways that are essentially psychotic. And it is not just the survivors of trauma, members of dysfunctional families, or psychotherapy patients who create false memories. We all do.

After meeting Freud and Jung in Worcester, Massachusetts, in 1907, William James warned that the hypothesis of a dynamically repressed unconscious was "a tumbling ground for whimsy." History has certainly proved James correct. It's discouraging, isn't it? If clinical sources of data are so unreliable, what are we to do? Start over. Experiment!

Conscious States and Brain States

After a night of interrupted sleep, I got up yesterday determined to seize the day, even though my brain told me that it needed at least another hour of sleep to function properly. In the morning I had difficulty concentrating. I was therefore happy to accompany my wife and daughter to the beach at midday instead of in the late afternoon as usual. The sun was so brutally hot that the white sand burned my feet. Our friend Pino's beach house, lent to us while he is in Greece, has a gate with a trick lock. When we arrive, we get in easily, but after our swim, we spend 40 minutes wrestling with an iron bar to lift the gate while simultaneously turning the key before we can get in, have a hurried picnic lunch, and drive back to Messina. By suppertime I have done some writing and painting but I am not myself. Instead of my usual gusto for food and wine, I feel sick, tired and irritable. So at 10 o'clock I lay down on the bed, hoping that a breeze would come up and cool the hot room. Within 30 minutes I am effectively comatose.

The Stuff that Dreams Are Made Of, J. A. Fitzgerald, 1858 *This nineteenth-century artist obviously agreed with Shakespeare that it is we that are that stuff. And he further anticipated modern cognitive neuroscience in centering his subject's hallucinatory imagery in her sleepy head, upon which a whole bedful of fairies fix their impish gaze. Now we can go further and look inside. (The Maas Gallery, London. The Bridgeman Art Library International, Ltd.)*

When I am sleep-deprived, I can feel it in my body and even in my brain. I am thus somewhat conscious of my own brain state. I know I need sleep. My brain knows I need sleep. If I give it a chance, it will sleep. How? By changing its own chemistry in such a way that when it self-activates, my consciousness will return, landscapes, plans, writing, and all. But this dream consciousness is entirely spontaneous, entirely internal, and its contents are organized in a dramatically different manner from waking reality. How? And why?

Immediately after falling asleep last night, I was dead to the world. No EEG was recorded, but I could feel my cerebral cortex cut loose from my brainstem and float in the swell of the giant waves of stage IV sleep. My cortex was deactivated, and my brain was flooded with a rush of nourishing molecules that would cure both my fatigue and my flulike malaise. My brainstem was on a chemical holiday. Relieved of the task of keeping my modular brain bathed in waking-state chemicals, the brainstem neurons that make them and distribute them everywhere stopped releasing them. While they let my brain run wild in another way, they stored up the juices I needed to feel alert, well, and refreshed today.

When my brain self-activated about every 90 minutes last night, my comalike state was replaced by dreaming. I did not wake up. I did not move. I did not feel the breeze or the heat. I did not see the landscape or the porch or my text. Instead, I saw my wife Lia, happily telling me about her discovery of a new neurological syndrome called POPI and her plans to present her findings as a poster at an upcoming neurological meeting. It all seemed quite real to me:

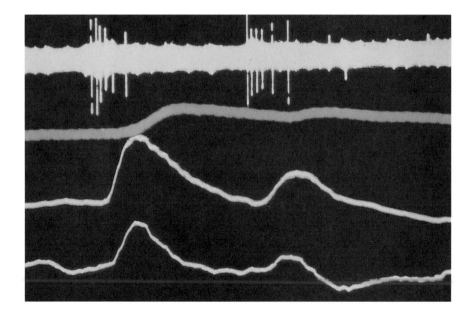

***Brainstem REM-On Cell** When we enter REM sleep and experience dream consciousness, the visions that arise may derive, in part, from the activation and modulation of brainstem neurons (recorded as a green trace) that move the eyes (blue trace) and send signals (orange traces) to the visual centers of the upper brain. We no longer need the fairies—or even unconscious wishes—to explain the visions of dream consciousness.*

There she was (visual perception), in all her youthful, feminine glory (emotion, instinct), telling me, in words I clearly heard (auditory perception), about POPI (this neologism is language, but it is confabulated) and her decision (volition) to give the poster (writing, drawing, and speaking).

Actually, now that I think about it (recent memory loss), I am not sure whether her new syndrome was called POPI or POMI. Since I had never heard either word before (autocreativity), it hardly matters. But this fact should have made me suspect (self-reflective awareness) that I was in an altered state of consciousness instead of assuming, as I did, that I was awake and normally conscious.

The Brain Basis of Conscious States

My dreaming brain doesn't need signals from the world or my body to create a fair replica of both. To create a fair replica of waking consciousness, all it needs is self-activation and inhibition of its external sensory inputs and motor outputs. It can then turn on the modules of sensation, perception, emotion, instinct, volition, and even action. All fictive, to be sure, but good fiction. These aspects of consciousness are all activated brain functions, pure and simple. They need only experience of the world to contain, retain, and marshal representations of external reality.

What's wrong with dream consciousness? Recent memory, attention, orientation, self-reflective awareness, insight, and judgment are all impaired. Why are they impaired? Because of the subtraction from the brain of the neurochemicals necessary to maintain these aspects of waking consciousness. It is the chemical microclimate of the activated brain that determines the quality—the state—of consciousness we will experience. The modular brain performs the several subfunctions of consciousness optimally only when adequately activated and appropriately modulated.

The living brain is always chemically modulated. Changes in neuromodulation are experienced by us as shifts in our mode of perceiving, thinking, and feeling. The relative neuroelectrical activation levels of the brain's many parts may also shift as I move within the conscious state of waking from looking at the landscape outside my study window (sensation and perception) to contemplating the tasks I would like to accomplish before leaving Italy in two weeks (visit the Port of Messina to better understand the economics of Sicily). And, of course, I can do both, seemingly simultaneously, while still going on with my writing (language). When the activation level of all those modules, and thus of my consciousness, declines, I need to stop looking at landscapes, making plans, and writing. I need to sleep.

Brain-Mind Isomorphism

Having laid out a paradigm for consciousness and mapped its compartments, we now turn our attention to the brain itself. We will examine that organ in terms of its three major formal features: its global, componential, and graded aspects. In so doing we will also learn about the brain mechanisms that underlie conscious states and the rules that govern the dynamic exchange of information among them. It is the purpose of this chapter to explain how what is known about brain activation and modulation informs the conscious state paradigm.

Remember that while our philosophical position here is monistic, we continue to rely on linguistic dualism. We assume that, in reality, conscious experience is a physical process—a state—of the brain. But because we cannot yet see how this unity is achieved, we do our best to align those aspects of subjective experience that seem most robust with those brain areas and activities that underlie, or perhaps even constitute, them. This philosophy leads to a strategy of brain-mind isomorphism, the search for similarities of form at the subjective (conscious state) and objective (brain state) levels.

Because this strategy has already proved useful in relating aspects of dreaming (hallucinatory visual imagery, for example) to formally similar aspects of REM sleep physiology (internal stimulation of the visual cortex), we want to see how far it can take us in the elaboration of a more general theory of consciousness. To illustrate the brain-mind isomorphism concept, I indicate in the accompanying table correspondences between the phenomenological (experiential) domain and the physiological (experimental) domain.

The Brain Basis of Consciousness

Phenomenological aspect	Physiological evidence
Modularity	Component regionality
Gradedness	Neuroelectrical activation levels
Global binding	Neurochemical modulation and synchrony

Notice that each phenomenological aspect has an isomorphic attribute in physiology. The modular subdivision of consciousness is mirrored by the anatomical and physiological specialization of brain regions. The overall level of consciousness (in whatever processing mode) is determined by electrochemical activation, which is itself graded. The global aspect of consciousness is conferred by chemical modulation and by synchrony, both of which are ubiquitous. It is important to understand the distinction between the words *modularity*, meaning structural subdivisions or components, and *modulation*, meaning the regulation of operating modes.

By discussing the brain's modularity first, we can grasp its general structure and identify those regional components that contribute to conscious experience. Then we will explore those core structures of the brain that give conscious experience its gradedness and information processing its selective nature. We will treat one part of that core system separately because, by its chemical nature, it modulates the brain and thus confers the global differentiation of conscious states that is seen in sleeping, dreaming, and waking. Finally, we will review the evidence in support of the hypothesis that the brain creates the unity of conscious experience via the synchronization of its elements.

The Modular Brain

We begin by relating the components of consciousness identified in Chapter 1 (page 16) to those brain regions or structures that have been identified as necessary and/or sufficient for producing them. The first and last components in the table, sensation and movement, define the inputs and outputs of waking state consciousness. The fact that they can be so impressively simulated during dreaming (when REM sleep physiology blocks both external inputs and outputs) means that they are only the conduits of information into and out of the conscious brain. In reflex action these conduits do their behavioral job quite well in entirely nonconscious ways. In fact, our conscious awareness of stimuli that have already been acted upon at a reflex level may have little or no influence upon the reflex itself. And so much the better. Some stimuli, especially noxious or surprising ones such as extreme heat or loud noises, are better handled automatically than deliberately.

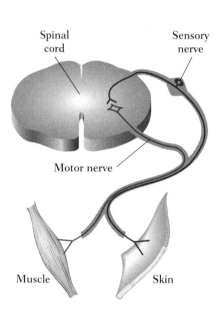

Reflex Pathway *The most elemental operation of the nervous system is the translation of a signal arising in a sensory nerve in response to a stimulus from the outside world into a motor command to a muscle. An example is the knee jerk following activation of a spinal reflex pathway by a sudden stretch of the patellar tendon.*

Brain Structure

For perception to arise from sensation, the brain-mind must analyze the stimulus. Object recognition is accomplished by first extracting the features of a stimulus (say, roundness and redness). Then their likely source is determined by comparing the combined features with records of objects stored in memory (say, apple or ball). These perceptual analyses are carried out in the cerebral cortex, which is anatomically subdivided into sectors for each of the sensing modalities (for example, vision, audition, touch). These sectors of the brain are physically connected to one another and to vast intermediate associative areas where the comparisons are made.

The ball versus apple example allows us to see why the brain-mind requires so many neurons to perform even simple object recognition. And there are many, many neurons in the brain. Although the exact number is not known, educated guesses range from 50 to 100 billion. That means that each of us possesses far more brain cells than there are people on the planet. And all the animals to whom basic conscious awareness has been attributed have very large cerebral cortices.

If the cues for object recognition are ambiguous or obscure, our brains can analyze the existing data more carefully or collect more

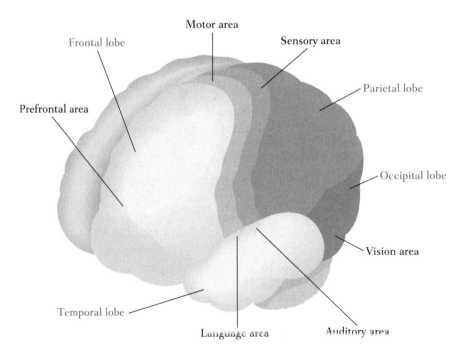

The Cerebral Cortex Scientists subdivide the cerebral cortex (the external surface of the human brain) into four major sectors (lobes) and have identified subsectors where neural processing related to sensation, perception, and thought occur.

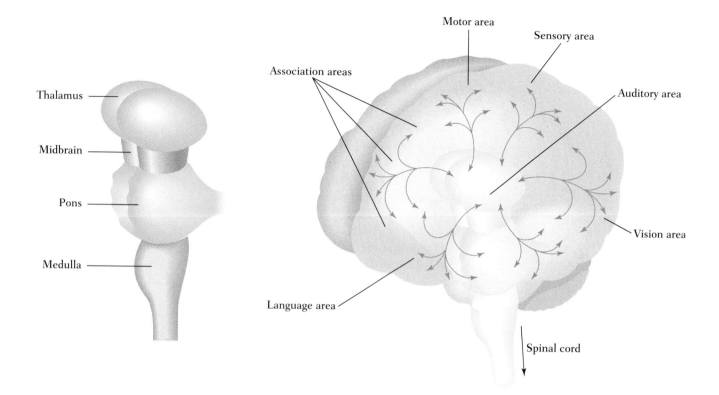

Thalamus

Midbrain

Pons

Medulla

Association areas

Motor area

Sensory area

Auditory area

Vision area

Language area

Spinal cord

The Brainstem and Thalamus *The central position and core structure of the brainstem and thalamus guarantee them a controlling role in determining the conscious state of the cortex and the resonance of information processed by it as well as the nature and fate of any motor commands that it sends to the spinal cord. The sleep-dream-wake cycle is triggered and tuned by neuronal circuits in the pons.*

data via the faculty of attention. If an object is round and red, more careful processing can determine whether the roundness is perfectly spherical (ball) or oblate (apple). The key brain structure involved in attention is the thalamus, a large collection of cells located atop the brainstem in the center of the upper brain. The thalamus receives sensory data from the body via the brainstem, and relays these data to the cortex.

To visualize the brain's structural relationships, make a fist and tuck the end of your thumb under the forefinger. This is what your brain's exterior looks like from the side. The back of your hand, fingers, and thumb form the cortex, the "new brain." Your thumb is positioned as is the temporal lobe, located at ear level. Interior brain structures of the "old brain," the limbic system, the upper brainstem, and the thalamus, lie roughly at the tip of your thumbnail. The remaining brainstem structures extend directly down below the base of your palm.

Each thalamic area is connected to a particular cortical sector. Because these connections are reciprocal, the interaction between these areas is rapid and intense. Consciousness owes its exquisite perceptual intensity and clarity to the capacity of these thalamocortical circuits to represent the world with great fidelity. The system has a built-in propensity to tune (modulate) itself, and that tuning propensity can also be enhanced voluntarily, as when we decide to reduce other sensory inputs the better to concentrate upon those that interest us most.

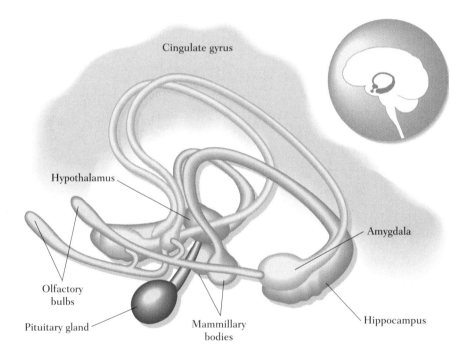

Cingulate gyrus

Hypothalamus

Amygdala

Olfactory bulbs

Pituitary gland

Mammillary bodies

Hippocampus

The Limbic Lobe and Hypothalamus *The horseshoe form of the deep interior brain structures crucial to emotion, instinct, and memory inspired such elegant names as* hippocampus, *while their ringlike aspect is captured in the term* limbic. *The hypothalamus is so named because it sits just below (hypo) the thalamus as the most anterior and superior component of the brainstem. The hypothalamus contains the biological clock that times cycles of rest and activity and gates the sleep-wake cycle in the pons. Its direct connections to the pituitary gland allow hormone secretion throughout the body to be synchronized with the conscious states of the brain-mind.*

The Emotional Brain-Mind

It may seem strange to consider emotion in conjunction with perception and attention, but we utilize our feelings in perceptual tasks whenever we rely on intuition. Our attunement to the world, to our bodies, and to our selves is powerfully shaped by our emotional state. To the degree that it is enduring in us, emotion contributes heavily to what we call personality, or temperament. Some see the world as forever bright and have optimistic thoughts, while for others the world is dark, and their thoughts are of gloom and doom. That these important filters of perception may be largely unconscious is also well known.

In view of the intermediate and shifting position of emotion between conscious and nonconscious processing modes, and in view of its connection to the complex reflex patterns of behavior called instincts, it is not surprising that the brain substrates of emotion lie below the thalamus and cortex and above the spinal cord and brainstem. Taken together, the amygdala, hippocampus, and hypothalamus have been called the limbic lobe of the brain because their conjoint shape resembles a pair of rings or coils sprung from a common, midline junction in the hypothalamus and circling first up, backward, and outward as the hippocampal arches, which then turn forward, downward, but still outward to reach the amygdala in the tips of the temporal poles.

Fight/Flight Response Pattern Road rage, depicted here on a Paris street in the 1950s, is a contemporary name for a behavior that predates the invention of the wheel. Intense emotional arousal prepares the body and brain for defensive action—for fight or flight. Startling stimuli or electrical stimulation of the amygdala may evoke the response. It is significant that two of the three most prominent dream emotions, anxiety and anger, are correlated with spontaneous activation of the amygdala during REM sleep.

The intimate relationship between the hippocampus, which is essential to memory, and the structures mediating emotion suggests that our notion of intuition may be even more valid then we think. By that I mean that an animal without a cortex—or without much of a cortex—and hence without much capacity for the kind of self-reflective consciousness that we enjoy, might do well to tie its experience (represented in its brain as memory) to its fail-safe emotion-and-instinct systems. Such a memory file would, for example, connect all known threat stimuli to fear-flight circuits guaranteeing emotional responses and facilitating escape. By contrast, those stimuli that experience has shown to emanate from innocent or even desirable sources would trigger positive emotions and approach behavior. For us humans, with our elaborate conceptual and analytical brains, these shadowy but powerful shapers of behavior may be not only obscure—requiring our sensitization to them in therapy—but also unwelcome—if we think we can either master them completely or live our lives without taking their effects on others into account.

Memory and the Brain-Mind

If a novel experience is to be recorded in memory, the hippocampus must be intact on at least one side of the brain. We know this because of the devastating effects of surgical removal of both sides of the hippocampus on recent memory. A patient's temporal lobe epilepsy—or schizophrenia—may be ameliorated by such a procedure, but thereafter the brain cannot function cognitively because new data go unrecorded. The fact that memories recorded before the surgery remain intact proves that the hippocampus is not involved in long-term memory storage and retrieval.

Once the hippocampus has processed a new input, the data are distributed throughout the cortex, where they are stored associatively for future reference. The subdivision of recent and remote memory parallels the distinction between the brain's older, more reflexive, mostly unconscious and automatic survival mechanisms—that is, primary consciousness—and its newer, more elective, mostly conscious-cognitive mechanisms, those which constitute a secondary level of consciousness.

The mental faculty of orientation cannot properly be considered apart from memory. Knowing who one is, what day it is, and where one is are, however, such crucial data items as to warrant our special attention. And it is both important and informative to distinguish between this cognitive kind of orientation (which provides an organiz-

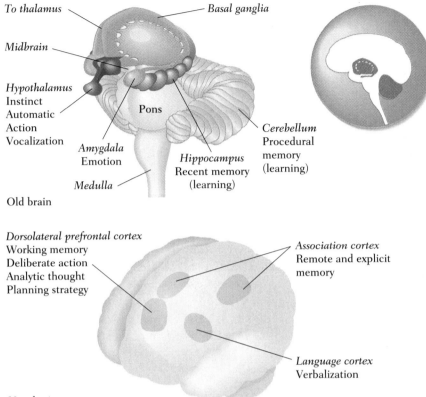

To thalamus

Basal ganglia

Midbrain

Hypothalamus
Instinct
Automatic
Action
Vocalization

Pons

Amygdala
Emotion

Hippocampus
Recent memory
(learning)

Cerebellum
Procedural
memory
(learning)

Medulla

Old brain

Dorsolateral prefrontal cortex
Working memory
Deliberate action
Analytic thought
Planning strategy

Association cortex
Remote and explicit
memory

Language cortex
Verbalization

New brain

Our Dual Natured Brain-Mind (Top) Our phylogenetically old brain, consisting
of the subcortical brainstem and limbic lobe as well as the cerebellum and basal
ganglia, cannot support secondary consciousness but is capable of the primary
mechanisms of learning and recent implicit memory (hippocampus and
cerebellum), emotion and instinct (amygdala), nonverbal vocalization, and
automatic actions (hypothalamus, brainstem, and cerebellum). (Bottom) Our
phylogenetically new brain, consisting of the cerebral cortex, supports secondary
consciousness by storing remote and explicit memories (associative areas); by
thinking analytically, planning strategically, and commanding deliberate actions
(dorsolateral prefrontal area); and by communicating verbally (language areas).

ing set of parameters for the rest of cognition) and the instinctive or
reflexive orienting behavior that is our immediate response to a novel
or surprising stimulus that suddenly seizes our attention.

Here again we see the dichotomy between the deliberate and the
automatic, between the elective and the exigent. And here again we
see the distinction between older brain structures like the upper pontine brainstem, with its direct connections to the amygdala that

mediate startle responses, and the newer midbrain-limbic circuits linking the mammillary bodies to the hippocampus, which underlie accurate orienting in space.

An animal must know its place, how to navigate in it, and how to get to and from it. And it must know who besides itself belongs in — or out of it—and how to monitor the boundaries. The "burglar alarms" that are our high-level invasion detectors are built into the brain at low levels too. Experiments aimed at understanding how the hippocampus works have portrayed it as the map room of the brain, with individual cells tuned to the animal's position in and movement through extrapersonal space.

So although we are largely unaware of it, our brains are full of implicit information about place. It took a great writer like Proust, the literary master of memory, to sensitize us to the way in which place data shape our conscious sense of ourselves. Like Freud, Proust was trying to make the unconscious conscious. By focusing obsessively upon the details of his own conscious experience, he revealed how important orientation is to all of us.

> *Particular attention should be given to the fact that . . . the hippocampal formation . . . forms . . . almost a complete ring around the thalamus.*
>
> JAMES PAPEZ, 1929

Self-Aware Consciousness

As we consider language, thought, and volition, we come to the unequivocally human aspect of conscious experience. The brain substrates for language are all on top (in the cortex) and up front (toward the forehead), signaling both their evolutionary recency and their declarative command contributions to our conscious experience and behavior. Without the capacity to create the abstract, symbolic representations of external reality and internal experience that are encoded as language, there could be no conscious thought. Thought is distinctly propositional and so constitutes an internal language. Without thought, there could be no conscious volition, and no conscious decision to act. When William James said that he had consciously decided to believe in free will, he was exercising these uniquely human faculties.

Language—that is, communication via symbolic representation—is organized in one cerebral hemisphere, which is called the dominant hemisphere if it also controls our preferred hand. There is a strong statistical tendency for humans to be right-handed and left-brained. In this correlation of language and handedness we see the play of evolutionary biological specialization linking our capacity for

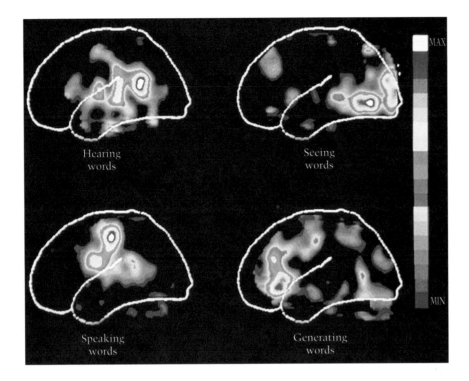

Language Areas in the Cortex
Different language areas in the human cortex are activated by the different tasks indicated below each image of the left hemisphere. As in other PET studies the selective brain activation pattern is inferred from the increased blood flow.

Hearing words

Seeing words

Speaking words

Generating words

propositional thought to our capacity for praxis. We actually move the body so as to accomplish our propositional goals in a more efficient way by virtue of this co-residence of handedness and linguistic laterality.

A receptive area for language sits just behind the executive area for speech at the angle formed by the juncture of the temporal and frontal lobes of the brain. These two areas are named for the European neurologists who described the effects of damage to them. The posterior area is Wernicke's area, and receptive aphasia denotes the inability to understand words. The anterior area is Broca's area, and expressive aphasia denotes the inability to translate the stored language lexicon into speech. Beyond this evidence for localization of language functions, we know very little about the detailed neuromechanics of word storage and retrieval.

How sentences are elaborated, how grammar is managed, and how whole ideas become assembled in the brain when one is speaking and writing are still almost complete mysteries. The failure of neurobiology as yet to disclose how the brain reads, speaks, and sings, and the failure of artificial intelligence as yet to instantiate sophisticated language functions, constitute some of the greatest obstacles to the maturation of the conscious state paradigm.

Without an understanding of language, what hope do we have of understanding those cognitive reflections that we call thought? When we think consciously, we seem almost to talk to ourselves. Indeed, if we are not careful, our thoughts may be heard as articulate speech by others. It is as if thoughts—at least those that can be recorded or reported—must pass to other parts of the brain in order to be recognized by us or read out to the world as speech or action.

Of course it is well known that much cognition—even high-level problem solving—may occur outside of conscious awareness. Einstein insisted that he got his best ideas while riding his bicycle. He suggested that the stimulation arising from his muscles and his movement could generate creative thought production. And there are other spectacular examples of scientific insights arising during daydreaming episodes (Kekule's benzene ring model) and during nocturnal dreaming (Otto Loewi's experimental proof of chemical neurotransmission).

But here we are mainly interested in conscious thought. Attention is clearly involved. To think most effectively, it is best for us to limit external inputs, to restrict movement, and to focus our consciousness upon the problem at hand, be it a technical issue, an interpersonal conflict, or an intellectual puzzle. Experimental evidence regarding how the brain focuses attention remains scanty, but the advent of imaging technology offers promise of great progress in the near future. Among the many phenomena waiting to be examined in the scanner is the change in activation pattern that a subject undergoes when shifting attention from external stimuli to internal ones during hypnotic trance. The ability of highly hypnotizable subjects to concentrate is so exceptional that they constitute an attractive group for cognitive neuroscientists to study.

Once we have analyzed a problem, the brain can act more deliberately. All normal humans are aware of conscious decision making and of the deliberate programming and timing of action. Because volition precedes motor action, it has been possible to study the cerebral preparation for deliberate action in some detail. The prefrontal cortex has been implicated by neurologists for a century as the brain site of volition. Patricia Goldman-Rakic has been able to record the activity of individual brain cells in the prefrontal cortexes of monkeys as

Idea Generator Albert Einstein *reported that many of his most original ideas occurred to him while riding his bicycle from his house in Princeton to his office at the University's Center for Advanced Studies. This observation suggests that thinking is somehow linked to the motor system, and may even depend upon it—perhaps via the shared activation of working memory in the dorsolateral prefrontal cortex, a brain region essential to planning and strategic decision making.*

they wait to obtain a food reward, the location of which they must "keep in mind" during a delay period. Her findings support the concept of elaborate and orderly information processing as the brain accumulates evidence favoring a decision.

The story of the modular brain, like a working sketch, is thus disappointingly incomplete. But a working sketch is at least a design. Fifty years ago we lacked even that. We next consider two factors, brain activation and brain modulation, both of which simultaneously affect the modules of the brain, determining the intensity and the state of consciousness that we experience.

The Activated Brain-Mind

The level of any conscious state in the brain rises and falls in response to the degree of electrochemical activation supplied by the reticular formation in the brainstem core. Whatever consciousness is, and however its components are mediated by the specialized structures of the upper brain, the *level* of consciousness is set by an internal electrochemical drive system that has been called the "nonspecific reticular activating system" (RAS) since its discovery by Moruzzi and Magoun in 1949. The adjective *nonspecific* was applied to the reticular formation because its brain cells were at first thought to project diffusely and distantly throughout the upper brain. This name would be fine if nonspecific activation were its only task. Recently, however, the reticular activating system has shown itself to possess highly specific connections that function in precisely controlled sensorimotor functions such as head and eye positioning and movement that are vital to waking consciousness. And its connections have been shown to be correspondingly more precise and limited than originally supposed.

Enriched by the discovery of its specificity, the Moruzzi-Magoun brain activation concept remains fresh and compelling after 50 years. The main idea is that for the brain to be conscious, its nerve cells must maintain a certain level of electrochemical activity. Intuitively, this is not surprising. However, many sophisticated theorists at the turn of the twentieth century interpreted their unconscious state during sleep as indicative of the complete withdrawal of the activation function: the brain was simply turned on in waking and turned off in sleep. In reality this is far from the case. The overall brain activation level changes as little as 10 percent, or at most 20

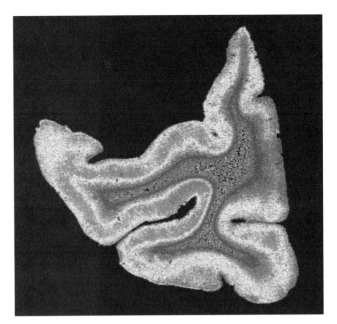

Working Memory Experiment Using behavioral principles first proposed by B. F. Skinner, experimental psychologists look into the brain-mind black box to learn the cerebral mechanics of decision making. Radioactive tracers reveal the metabolic activity in a frontal cross section of the brain of a rhesus monkey performing an object memory task. Neurons in the prefrontal cortex signal sharply in advance of correct guesses by the monkey as to the location of a food reward. The most active areas are displayed in red.

percent, during sleep. Yet consciousness is virtually obliterated during sleep, which leads to the surprising insight that consciousness operates within a very narrow range of activation. Put another way, consciousness is exquisitely sensitive to even slight changes in activation level.

One surprising implication of these findings is that the activation of the brain is automatically maintained at a high level even when we are unconscious. This is consistent with the idea that a significant amount of information processing occurs even while we are completely unaware of it as we sleep. Thanks to this spontaneously high level of activation during sleeping and dreaming, such processing is not only automatic but potentially self-organizing and autocreative. Our brains never turn off, and we should neither devalue our unconscious states nor overvalue our conscious ones.

A second surprising implication of the brain-mind's sensitivity to activation level is that in being so finely tuned, the reticular formation has an exquisite sensitivity that can be altered at will, as anyone who has practiced any of the many forms of consciousness manipulation can attest. Our highest attribute, consciousness, works at the top level of a wide activation range. If we change the activation level even a little, consciousness will respond with a wide variety of states.

In fact, the reticular formation works its magic on the conscious mind not only by changing the level of activation but also by modulating the neural inputs and outputs, especially those arising in and emanating from the spinal cord. In this sense too, the reticular formation is anything but nonspecific. By altering the tension in our muscles and by focusing our internal awareness on one channel of data or another, we can navigate into the more peaceful harbors of the conscious world. When we do this, we bring our reticular formation partially under the control of our will, probably via the prefrontal cortex. The power of positive thinking is finally more than a set of homespun nostrums. It is a neurobiological reality.

The reticular formation is strategically situated between the spinal cord, which mediates rapid and automatic reflexes, and the upper brain, which can take forever to make up its mind. It thus mediates the traffic between our most conscious and our most unconscious brain sectors. The reticular formation got its name from the intricate networklike appearance of its cellular interconnections, which seem to receive messages from and send them everywhere in the brain.

Among the reticular formation's crucial targets are the thalamus, with its vast and variable set of interactive connections with the

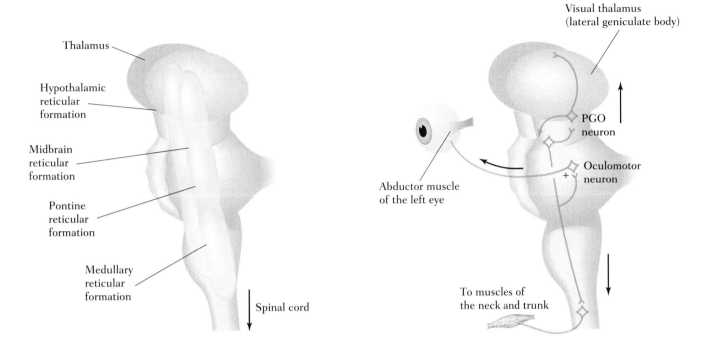

Thalamus

Hypothalamic
reticular
formation

Midbrain
reticular
formation

Pontine
reticular
formation

Medullary
reticular
formation

Spinal cord

Visual thalamus
(lateral geniculate body)

PGO
neuron

Oculomotor
neuron

Abductor muscle
of the left eye

To muscles of
the neck and trunk

The Reticular Formation (Left) *The reticular formation, like a pair of sausages, occupies the central core on each side of the brainstem as it ascends from the medulla upward through the pons and midbrain to the hypothalamus. By contacting one another and specific sensory and motor nuclei of the thalamus, brainstem, and spinal cord, reticular formation neurons serve an internal bookkeeping and integrating role that is essential to conscious and unconscious mental processes. (Right) A particularly cogent example is the coordination of eye position, which involves visual processing centers of the upper brain and spinal circuits mediating head and body position.*

cortex (mediating sensation, perception, attention, and remote memory); the hypothalamus, hippocampus, and amygdala in the limbic lobe (mediating emotion, recent memory, and instinct); and all the sensorimotor data collectors (mediating sensation) and emitters (mediating movement) of the brainstem and spinal cord. The reticular formation keeps all these brain modules at the ready and helps to select among them by resetting the relative levels of activation in each module.

The reticular formation begins in the medulla, just above the level of the spinal cord. The medulla programs many autonomic functions essential to consciousness as well as organizing posture and controlling head and neck position so that we can navigate in our

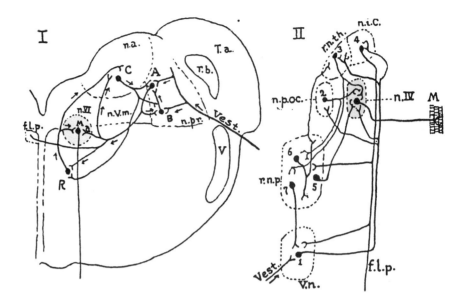

Reticular Formation Circuitry *Some idea of the complexity of the reticular formation's integrative function may be gained from this 1933 drawing by the Spanish neurobiologist Rafael Lorente de Nò, showing the convergence of fibers from reticular and other sources on neurons that move the eye (nVI in I and nIV in II). Each neuron and pathway shown in the drawing represents an entire network of neurons that share similar connections.*

world. At the next higher level, the pons and midbrain are the very center of the reticular system because they so clearly coordinate activation of the higher brain structures. Some neuroscientists also include the hypothalamus and thalamus in the reticular formation. This central core of the brain is a system that supports consciousness and maintains significant levels of activation during nonconscious states. It is the heart of the brain. And upon this heart our thoughts and dreams depend.

Neuronal Rhythms: Synchrony

The thalamus has its own "reticular" structures too. A thin shell of nerve cells surrounds it. Their processes penetrate its core to exert powerful inhibitory control over the principal thalamic neurons, those that relay specific data to and from the sectors of cortex with which they are connected. In this way information flow can be selectively gated.

The reticular nucleus of the thalamus is as close to an on-off switch for consciousness as we have yet found. When the activation level of the brainstem falls, even a little, the thalamocortical circuits begin to oscillate, beating to an intrinsic rhythm that is a function of their own excitatory and inhibitory features. This kind of synchrony contributes to the global loss of consciousness that occurs in non-rapid eye movement (NREM) sleep.

Just let your reticular nucleus relax a bit. You will feel drowsy. Let go a bit more and your eyes will glaze, then close, as you drift off to sleep. For this to occur, the level of firing of the cells in the midbrain and pontine reticular formation must fall enough to allow the thalamic reticular cells to enter their burst-silence mode. As soon as this intrinsic oscillation starts, the thalamic relay cells are no longer available to transmit data from the body and the world to the cortex and back again in an organized way. And consciousness is impaired in the process.

The oscillations of the thalamocortical circuits that occur at sleep onset are robust and so highly synchronous that they cause the characteristic EEG spindles and slow waves of sleep. This characteristic

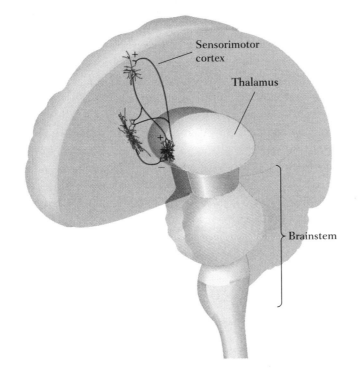

The Thalamocortical System *The thalamus has such specific reciprocal interconnections between its nuclei and the cortical regions that are involved in processing each domain of sensation that it can function not only as a gateway for the simultaneous processing of many channels of perceptual data in parallel but also as a selector of individual channels when attention to detail is called for. Thus the pathway to the lateral geniculate body (the visual thalamus) may be opened and other gates closed when close visual inspection is needed. The visual thalamus may also be triggered automatically in REM sleep, accounting in part for the visual detail of dream consciousness.*

activity has been referred to as "EEG synchronization." The problem with this term is that EEG synchrony has become synonymous with unconsciousness and deactivation of the brain, while the low-voltage, fast EEG patterns associated with activated brain states have been called "desynchronized." But we now are learning that low-voltage, fast, activated EEG rhythms may involve synchronization too. When animals perform tasks calling for alertness and analysis, their brain cells oscillate in unison at a frequency of 35–40 cycles per second. Human consciousness has been said to depend upon such synchronization. But thalamocortical synchrony is sleep. So it cannot be synchrony, per se, that counts.

If consciousness does not depend upon neuronal synchrony per se, what about brain wave frequency and amplitude? In sleep and other unconscious states, the wave frequency tends be to lower and the amplitude higher than in waking and other conscious states. The frequency of synchronous activity in the brain is a function of activation. High-frequency synchronous activity is driven by reticular activation. Low-frequency synchrony emerges when activation falls below a critical level. The table on the facing page categorizes the several EEG rhythms characteristic of various conscious states. The brain structure in which the rhythm is recorded also makes a difference. For example, when rats are most actively exploring their environment, the hippocampal EEG rhythm, called theta, is highly synchronized.

This discussion cannot do justice to the richly detailed neurobiology of brain cell rhythmicity, a topic that is still evolving rapidly as techniques for analyzing both single neuron behavior and EEG phenomena improve. I present it here as one way of beginning to explain the unity of consciousness in the face of the modularity of the brain.

The basic idea is that neuronal oscillations unify the brain's disparate components in the time domain. If all the neurons oscillate in unison, the music of the mind will at least be meaningfully syncopated. Global binding is the term that is used by scientists who puzzle over this phenomenon. And, with the recent discovery of high-frequency synchronization, global binding has become a very hot topic. "Stay tuned" is my advice to the reader interested in knowing whether or not the binding problem is solved by this discovery.

From every point of view—the spatial, the temporal, and the biochemical—the reticular formation emerges as the coordinator, internal communicator, and unifier of activity in the modular brain. As coordinator, it sets a uniform level of activity at points as distant from each other as the motor cortex and the muscles. As communicator, it unifies signaling within the neural system so that behavioral programs

EEG Rhythms Characteristic of Various Conscious States

Conscious state	Wave type	Frequency (cycles per second)
Alert, ?conscious	γ	35–40
Alert, attentive	β	18–30
Awake, relaxed	α	8–12
Drowsy	Θ	4–8
Light sleep	—	15–18
Deep sleep	Δ	1–2

can be rapidly changed, as, for example, when we must move as fast as possible from a state of relaxation to one of readiness for fight or flight if threatened by a real or imagined predator. Finally, the reticular formation as unifier of brain activity sets metabolic guidelines for the brain via its modulatory function. Thus it determines the nature of the brain's two most conscious states, waking and dreaming.

Neuromodulation

Our experience of consciousness is determined by the neurochemical modulatory systems of the brainstem core. These systems change the mode of information processing by altering the chemical microclimate in which the neurons of the various modular components of the brain are operating. They thus confer a second kind of unity on the brain, a metabolic one, which complements electrical synchrony and activation. But modulation also adds diversity. That explains how two strongly activated, high-frequency synchronized brain states like waking and dreaming can be so different.

These differences in chemical microclimate help us to explain the phenomenological differences between waking and dreaming outlined at the beginning of this chapter. They also point to the as yet poorly understood functional difference between waking and dreaming. While the adaptive significance of waking consciousness seems obvious—to interact effectively with the environment—the adaptive significance of dreaming is much less clear. Why do we need to create an artificial world offline and spend two hours a day in it?

Since the Nobel Prize-winning work of Walter Hess, the two main classes of modulatory neurons, the aminergic and the cholinergic systems, have been contrasted as ergotropic, meaning energy-consuming, and trophotropic, meaning energy-restoring. The aminergic neurons, which are most active in waking, are ergotropic. The cholinergic neurons, which are most active in REM sleep, are trophotropic. Hess's functional contrast suggests that the two forms of consciousness seen in waking and dreaming might reinforce each other. They might provide complementary modes of memory processing, for example.

The uniformity of neurochemical background conditions that probably underlies each conscious state is guaranteed by several unique features of the brain's modulatory system:

- The secretion of chemicals with a powerful effect upon the neurons with which they come in contact. All neuromodulators are capable of triggering cascades of chemical events in neurons that control metabolic activity—including protein synthesis. Most neurobiologists believe that memories are ultimately encoded as proteins.
- The system's widespread projection to distant parts of the brain, which ensures that the effects of neuromodulation are uniformly dispersed. This, as much as electrical synchrony, serves to unite neurons within and across modular boundaries and guarantees that all the neurons will operate in a consistent manner in any given state of consciousness. Thus, in waking, the whole brain could be primed to capture data, while in sleep those data might be differentially processed (in the NREM and REM states).
- The multiplicity of neuromodulatory subsystems. On the aminergic (waking) side, at least four different subsystems are involved: the locus coeruleus-based noradrenergic system; the raphe nuclei-based serotonergic system; the midbrain-based dopaminergic system; and the hypothalamus-based histaminergic system. All four appear to energize the brain. How these systems differ from one another is still only partially understood. The noradrenergic and histaminergic systems have been implicated in vigilance, alertness, and attention; the serotonergic system in restraining motor action, helping it to be stimulus- and situation-specific; the dopaminergic system in supporting and facilitating movement, positive emotion, and thought.
- The tendency of all the neurons in any modulatory class to behave consistently and in reliable concert in any particular state. For example, during waking, all the neurons of the noradrenergic, serotonergic, and histaminergic systems fire

Noradrenergic

Serotonergic

Dopaminergic   Cholinergic

***Modulatory Systems** Four modulatory subsystems in the brain of the rat illustrate the widespread neuronal pathways that make up these chemical systems. Only the general brainstem— forebrain projections are shown.*

slowly and regularly. All of them fire more and more slowly in NREM sleep, and all of them stop firing in REM sleep. The coordination of this highly reliable, state-specific pattern appears to be orchestrated by an inhibitory system using GABA, a neurotransmitter that arises in the anterior hypothalamus, where the circadian clock is also located. The only system that does not shut off in REM sleep is the dopaminergic, perhaps to allow motor programs to run offline.

The upshot of this set of neuromodulatory properties is that consciousness can be differentiated automatically, reliably, and consistently so as to resonate harmoniously with the cosmos to which my youthful brain-mind compared it on that starry night in Maine 50 years ago. These features of the brain suggest that the isomorphism of the brain-mind and the cosmos is more than an analogy. It is an intimately synchronous interaction.

chapter 4

Consciousness Emerges

In part because our twins had to share a space usually reserved for one, Andrew and Matthew were born five weeks ahead of schedule. Their premature arrival let us see some of the developmental processes that go on in full-term babies before they are born. It is evident from such observations of premature infants and from the fetal behavior that can be visualized echographically in utero that the primordia of consciousness arise at least as early as 30 weeks' gestation. Of course, sensation and movement are evident even earlier, but only 35 weeks after their conception, our newborns were very reliable conscious state generators. Of the three states they regularly manifested, the one that would become waking was the least frequently seen. The relative paucity of waking and the absence of perception and attention was related to the immaturity of their higher brain structures, particularly the thalamus and cortex. In this sense, Andrew and Matthew were similar to those submammalian vertebrates that function, even as adults, with only spinal cord, brainstem, and basal brain structures. But, unlike those reflexive creatures, Andrew and Matthew were using their brainstems both to survive and to promote the maturation of their higher brains so as to one day achieve secondary, or reflective, consciousness.

The Human Condition, Rene Magritte, 1933 *In choosing this title, was Magritte referring ironically to the fact that vision is always an abstraction made, like the scene painted by an invisible artist looking out his window, by the processing of signals from the outside world arriving in the brain via the eye? Since the resulting ambiguity of image and reality is something that we have to live with, we might as well smile as we realize how easy it is to be fooled by perceptual illusions. (Private Collection. Giraudon /Art Resource, NY. © 1998 C. Herscovici, Brussels/Artist Rights Society (ARS), New York.)*

Among the most convincing bodies of evidence that consciousness is graded, having multiple quantitative levels and qualitatively different states, are those documenting the phylogenetic evolution of species and the ontogenetic unfolding of the individual brain-mind. So closely in step are the co-development of brain and mind across and within species that we can look at these two areas of biology for further insights about what brain structures and functions are needed for what aspects of consciousness. We will see clearly that the brain's pluralistic component structures, their unification, and their graded state differentiation all assume partial, dynamic, and additive aspects as animals develop via speciation over evolutionary time and as each animal develops via growth and differentiation over its individual lifetime.

Our collective consciousness—embodied in our science and our art—is still another level of this process. Even as we speak and sing, read and write, calculate and dance, our collective consciousness is evolving and developing. It may seem odd, in a book linking consciousness to the state of the brain, to refer to culture in this way. But a moment's reflection will convince us that our greatest cultural achievements are brain products too. Each new achievement in the arts, the sciences, and the humanities builds upon cultural memory

Consciousness and Culture *Visual awareness combines with propositional thought and language to create self-awareness and the development of a collective consciousness that we call culture.*

as it is already recorded in works of genius. Like data in the cognitive unconscious, these recorded works lie unnoticed in art galleries, libraries, and institutions of higher learning until viewed, read, or discussed by conscious minds.

Without debating whether this or that animal is conscious or struggling to decide when a human being first becomes conscious, we can use the comparative approach in a strategic way to focus upon some phenomena that are clear-cut. For example, although we may not agree on whether our pet dog—or our newborn child—is conscious in anything like the way that we are, we can agree that each experiences sensation, perception, and emotion via the neural activation and modulation of those component brain structures that have developed sufficiently to support those functions.

In other words, developing animals (whether as species or as individuals) present us with data that can be interpreted within the same subtractive logic that we use in brain imaging experiments. If an animal's brain structure is functionally activated when in any particular objectively defined state, such as attentive waking, we can study that activation function with a view to understanding those aspects of consciousness that we experience in that same state. Animal models are thus not only useful to the conscious state paradigm—they are indispensable.

Synaptic Bootstrapping

Consider vision. To convince you that I am fully conscious, I must first give evidence that I see, and perceive what I see, in an operationally correct way. If the round red object I perceive is an apple, I can eat it safely and utilize its nutrients. This is primary consciousness. A monkey can do it easily, and even a raccoon can do it convincingly. But I must also show you that I know that what I see is operational not only at a behavioral level but also at an abstract level. I can, for instance, imagine other uses of the object. I could use the apple as a ball if I wanted to play catch and didn't have a ball, or even as a projectile to chase a cow away from my orchard if no other more suitable ballistic was at hand. These are examples of low-level secondary consciousness. At a higher level I would understand, as you do, that apples are symbols for attractiveness (the apple of my eye), for rottenness (a bad apple), and for guilt about the awareness of desire (the forbidden fruit). They can even stand for cities, as in The Big Apple, where this book was published. Above all, I can probably

Learning to Represent the World in Three Dimensions (Above) *The elaborate wallpaintings created thousands of years ago by Egyptian artists are flat, two-dimensional representations. (Opposite) During the Renaissance in Italy, artists perfected the technique of linear perspective, which enabled them to depict the world in three dimensions, as embodied here in The Ideal City by Piero della Francesca. By physically depicting the brain-mind's visual capacity for perceiving depth, the human capacity for visualizing hypothetical visual and mathematical constructs took a giant leap forward, as did technological innovation. The Industrial Revolution and the virtual worlds opened to us via contemporary technologies are linked directly to this conceptual breakthrough.*

convince even the skeptic in you by my words that I am aware that I am aware of all these things.

In reflecting on how consciousness emerges, we are really talking about bootstrapping. We start with the simple act of seeing an apple, go on to build mental operation upon mental operation, and end up with the concepts of Adam and Eve, New York City, innocence, and corruption. This additive bootstrapping process is what we see so clearly in both evolution and development. Start off with a limited set of chemical elements like carbon, hydrogen, and oxygen, let them combine to make molecules, build up the molecular interaction until, at some critical point, the molecules begin to operate on the environment in a dynamic way, and life emerges. The molecules self-organize to become cells. Cells unite to form organs, specialize within organs to sense or to see, and you have a brain. Charge up the brain with more cells and chemicals that can view or review the scene, play it back as a scenario, and even describe the process of doing so. The end result is a conscious, creative brain-mind able to write and direct

films for others to see in public theaters and for each of us to enjoy in the private theater of our imagination. The process by which complex functions arise when simple elements interact is called emergentism.

Even while easily accepting the metaphorical moral charge, "pull yourself up by your bootstraps," it is difficult for many people to think of themselves as the product of such a process of functionally guided organic bootstrapping. The idea that consciousness is one of many complex processes that have evolved with the brain over time is difficult to accept. The Darwinian model of natural selection depends so much on chance events that it makes many people nervous. But that's not the worst of it. If we give up the model of an external agent—a divine architect, for example—we must also give up the idea of a little person inside our heads who is watching our neurological movies as they are projected on the screen of the mind. Both kinds of dualism die at the same moment and for the same reason. There may be no God above us, and there is clearly no Little Person inside us. Even though it feels like there must be, this is an illusion.

Free will seems to be on the line here too. If our consciousness is, at any instant, the product of a brain process with a high degree of automaticity, how can it be causal, especially if our awareness of ongoing events is projected backward in time? Causal arrows are supposed to fly forward ($\rightarrow$), not backward ($\leftarrow$). And if consciousness is not causal, what becomes of morality? Is that, too, also an illusion? I think not, as I will now endeavor to explain.

In laboratory and clinical studies involving stimulus-response tasks over the short term, there is convincing evidence that much

A Consultation on the Meaning of Life One of the world's greatest living moral exemplars, the Dalai Lama of Tibet, is a man who has brought mind control to a fine art. On the day that he won the Nobel Peace Prize in 1989, he completely ignored the media storm breaking around him and dialogued calmly, creatively, and humorously about consciousness with a group of six neurobiologists, who seemed more distracted by the announcement than he did. Respectful of and inquisitive about brain science, the Dalai Lama was not about to wait for us to find the neural basis of free will to justify using his.

automatic processing goes on in the brain before conscious awareness arises (if it arises at all). And this is all to the good. Rapid reaction times—in critical situations like automobile operation—may be life-saving. But the conscious awareness that arises after the fact in similarly acute real-life situations can be used in future decision making, as when I choose to make the long drive from Boston to Vermont on Saturday morning rather than late Friday evening because I know that my brain-mind will be more effective in the morning after I have had a good night's sleep. Or when I decide, if I must drive at night, not to drink and so incur alcohol's prolongation of my reaction time on top of that of a sleep-fogged brain. My wife and children will be less at risk.

Part of the reason for believing that moral choice is deliberate comes from comparative and developmental studies. We may learn, by natural and human precept, in an entirely unconscious way, but because we can think abstractly, we can analyze both our personal histories and our social context and so make deliberate choices that significantly change outcomes that depend upon entirely automatic behaviors. It is in this long-term sense that free will is alive and well and playing an important role in our self-reflective awareness as it reviews past events and alters ongoing behavior accordingly.

The Animal Mind

Recognizing that the child is father to the man is no more challenging than realizing that monkeys or snails are our legitimate ancestors. Anything we can learn from them about the genesis of our own behavior, including that virtual behavior that is consciousness, is likely to be useful to us.

Fred Snyder, my mentor at the National Institute of Mental Health in the early 1960s, was such a thoroughgoing naturalist that for some time he raised a pet chimp along with his children in their Bethesda home. Fred just wanted to see how much social behavior could be inculcated in an ape, given equal opportunity. The answer was, not surprisingly, more than you might expect, but not enough so that the chimp would ever be mistaken for a person. And not even enough to tempt me to try to replicate Fred's genial but inconvenient experiment. Other chimp champions have devoted their whole lives to teaching their primate forebears to read, speak—and who knows, even to think?—without much scientifically convincing success.

Language Emerges *Whether the chimpanzee can communicate by using sign language is still a hotly debated topic. But no one doubts the words of linguist Noam Chomsky when he asserts that language has a genetic basis. Like consciousness itself, it seems likely that language has a primary (vocalization) and a secondary (verbalization) aspect. What is at stake is the degree to which abstraction is used in constructing an utterance.*

These heroic and charming experiments force us again to confront the graded nature of consciousness. If such a near relative of humanity as the chimpanzee cannot produce anything that clearly passes for speech or demonstrate by its motor behavior that it can manage abstraction, then we are forced to conclude that even very small differences in brain structure and function make a huge difference when it comes to secondary consciousness. Even the most ardent advocates of primate sign recognition have not suggested that their "Noam Chimpskys" are aware that they are aware, or that they should be appointed as professors of linguistics at MIT.

Is the animal consciousness cup half empty or half full? Pet owners are convinced that their furry friends have conscious awareness, as was the hard-headed research psychologist, Ivan Pavlov. And no one that I know doubts that animals see and feel. They clearly recognize their keepers and communicate their inner emotional states effectively by displaying behaviors of clear meaning. The dog whines and wags its tail when it wants to go out. The cat purrs voluptuously when it wants to be petted. Both stand by their food dishes and call to us when they want to be fed. What clearer evidence could we seek to prove that consciousness is graded and hence necessarily partial across species?

Since all these examples are mammalian, we might wrongly conclude that primary consciousness is an exclusively mammalian brain function. Primary consciousness comprises sensation, perception, emotion, learning, geographic orientation, instinct, and primary intention, and all these can be operationally defined in lower animals. In terms of the conscious state research enterprise, this is all we need to know, since the animals we investigate as models for human states of awareness are all mammalian. We will later examine the implications of this homology when we consider those thermoregulatory and reproductive skills that distinguish the mammalian brain from that of other animals.

Some components of primary consciousness can be found even in much "lower" animals. Consider learning and memory, that consciousness component that is the perennial study favorite of cognitive psychologists. Molluscan creatures such as snails and octopi are justifiably popular with neurobiologists who study learning because their cognitive repertoires are remarkably vast given their remarkably simple brains. And here we see the phylogenetic converse of our Noam Chimpsky principle. With chimps that can't speak, we saw that small differences in brain evolution can yield huge differences in some aspects of conscious capacity. Now we see that small differences in other consciousness components can be observed across vast ranges of brain development.

This paradoxical contrast could be resolved if we could establish the principle that primary consciousness, including sensation, instinct, learning, and movement, is mediated at cellular or subcellular levels while more recently evolved secondary functions like language, memory, thought, and volition are mediated at the intercellular or neuronal network level. This sort of distinction would enable us to bring our notion of graded consciousness into line with the evolutionary concepts of conservation and elaboration. In other words, we could assume that once nature has solved a problem—like retention of experience in the learning example—this function, along with its neurobiological mechanism, is simply "forwarded" to higher neural forms, which then elaborate upon it by building larger, more populous, and more variously interconnected networks of neurons.

In a developmental and evolutionary sense, memory emerges out of learning. Learning may be completely unconscious. Indeed, even when we are conscious of trying to learn—as when we study—the learning itself, the keeping of a permanent record of experience, is an unconscious neurobiological event. When I say "I remember," I mean that I have a conscious recollection of a name, a scene, or a person. Yesterday, when I saw the tall thin trees with their mottled gray-brown striped bark and pale green leaves shimmering in the hot Sicilian sun, I knew I knew their name but could not immediately bring it to mind. I was conscious that the name of the tree that I had previously learned was nonconscious. But it was at that moment only a virtual and potentially conscious activation state of my brain cells.

Back home in the laboratory, my colleagues and I had been studying semantic priming, the process by which a second word is more promptly recognized if the first word is meaningfully related to it. Therefore I began a deliberate experiment in self-priming. Because I knew that doctor primes nurse and cat primes dog in our experiments, I wanted to see if—and how—I could bring the name of the tree to mind. I wanted to see if I could deliberately develop (or evolve) the memory from the learning. Success would not only supply the sought-after word but also demonstrate that an unconscious word search could be consciously directed.

Three clues led to my discovery of the word *eucalyptus*. The first was the word *ypsilanti*, which came spontaneously to mind when I began my tree-name search. I knew at once that Ypsilanti is the name of a city in Michigan, not a tree, and was momentarily distressed by my error. But rather than rejecting *Ypsilanti* as absurdly wrong, I assumed that it must somehow be relevant to the tree name I sought and consciously instructed my brain to keep it activated while consciously letting it fall back into my nonconscious mind. Then I "remembered" or reexperienced the smell of the leaves, which is extracted in the oil that I use to perfume the steam in my Vermont sauna. But while the odor was perceptible as an olfactory image, the tree name still eluded me. My mental sniffing encouraged my detective search even more. I sent my bloodhound memory out on the Ypsilanti trail, that is, to other "places" where I have seen such trees. Greece and Australia immediately came up on my memory screen. And with them came the word I sought: *eucalyptus*. While not exactly an anagram of *Ypsilanti*, *eucalyptus* is certainly its linguistic first

Activating a Network of Associations
Word finding may utilize a variety of pathways through the semantic memory networks of the brain-mind. In the example shown, similarity of syllabic number, sequence, and sound primes Ypsilanti, while olfactory memory is accessed by imagining the scent of a sauna oil, and the place associates Australia and Greece finally add enough activation to bring eucalyptus *into consciousness.*

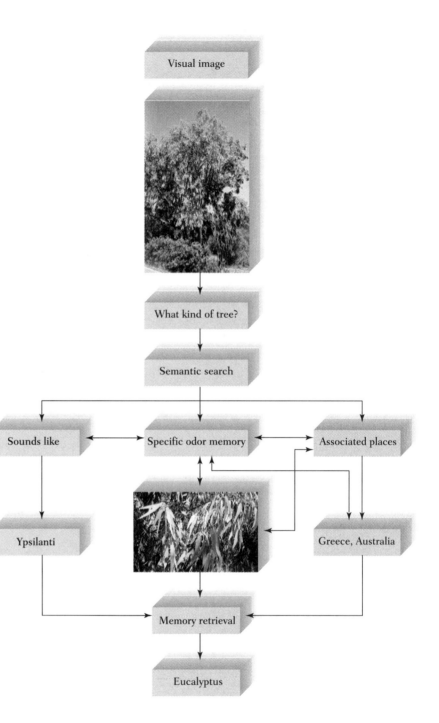

cousin. As is "Eureka!" the triumphant cry of Archimedes when he appreciated the buoyancy of his body in his bathtub.

When I announced the success of my self-priming search to my traveling companions, they all said, "Oh yes, the oil from the leaves has a wonderful smell," indicating that associatively tied to the word *eucalyptus* is the sensation of its odor and that the mind can move in either direction, from odor to word (as in my search) or from word to odor (as in their reaction to my announcement). Similarly, place names like Ypsilanti, Australia, and Greece are tied to *eucalyptus* by two-way streets in the brain's neuronal networks. In other words, priming is not just semantic, but also sensory, and often emotional.

To create a mechanistic model of my eucalyptus look-up experiment, scientists have postulated that the neuronal networks whose activation underlies the word *Ypsilanti*, the odor of eucalyptus, and place names like Vermont, sauna, Australia, and Greece are associatively connected and sequentially activated by one another as the memory search for the word *eucalyptus* proceeds. We will later return to this neuronal network paradigm and to semantic priming, but for now, it suffices to say that my conscious awareness of the trees, my analysis of their distinctive features, my recognition that I knew (that is, had learned) their name, my frustration at not being able to recall (that is, remember) that name, and the instantiation and success of my word search all depend upon neuronal networks and the connections among them.

The eucalyptus example also shows how my own personal history is interleaved with word recognition, with smell, and with place names. "Homage to Marcel Proust" is thus an apt subtitle for any book addressing the associative aspects of conscious experience. For it was Proust who first—and most eloquently—emphasized how place names, like that of his favorite village, Combray, and smells or tastes, like that of his famous Madeleine cake, and feelings, like his love for his grandmother, conspire to create emotionally salient aspects of conscious experience.

Although he was the son of a physician, Proust did not know that taste and odor images were learned by the neuronal networks of his olfactory brain. And Proust did not know that every odor activated his olfactory brain neuronal networks in a specific way, or that other aspects of the context in which he had tasted cake were associatively encoded in still other neuronal networks. While no one believes in "grandmother cells" (single neurons representing complex stimuli), everyone believes that nerve cells learn "Grandmother" and nerve cells learn "soft," "warm," and "loving," and that nerve cells learn these details cumulatively. When Proust writes about his conscious experience, he

Marcel Proust *The literary master of memory, Marcel Proust, was also a keen self-observer. In* Remembrance of Things Past *he emphasized the role of tastes and smells and of places in helping to recapture past moments. As he slept, dreamed, and dozed, he noted the curious play of fear, fantasy, and desire in the shaping of his mental imagery. And, admirably unlike most stay-a-beds, he took the trouble to write it all down.*

does so convincingly because he reports the emotionally salient details of his own development so meticulously. For Proust's animal forebears, these same elements of primary consciousness were even stronger because for them, sniffing was not just a literary nicety, but rather a mechanism of survival—a means of orientation, mate selection, food finding, poison avoiding, territory marking, and the like.

Phylogeny and Consciousness

In using the phrase "animal mind," I am not asking you to ascribe human consciousness—or even human intelligence—to non-human animals. I am not claiming that animals speak or think in anything like the propositional way that we humans do. That would be anthropomorphism. All that I am claiming is that consciousness, as we humans experience it in all its secondary, abstract, linguistic glory, depends upon those primary brain functions subserving perception, attention, emotion, instinct, learning, and action that are the undoubted attributes of all vertebrate animals. And because some of these attributes (such as learning) are reasonably ascribed to invertebrate animals (such as snails), my related assumption is that because the primary brain functions that we investigate in animals are very similar to those that subserve consciousness in humans, they are worthy of our attention.

An extreme example of the link between cognition and the brain can be developed from my previous discussion of my eucalyptus word search and Proust's Madeleine cake evocation. Both are demonstrations of the power of associative learning at the cognitive level. But to understand associative learning mechanistically, we must drop from the cognitive level to the physical level of the brain-mind, then to its component regions, and then to its component neuronal networks. Since even the simplest animals evince associative learning, this building block of memory, of priming, and of word search must be a mechanism shared by neuronal networks at all levels of phylogeny (the evolution of species) and ontogeny (individual development). Besides complexity and abstraction, the only difference between the association of a plant's odor with its edibility by a rabbit (which is always sniffing) and Proust's association of cake-taste with his love for his grandmother is that the animal's association is exclusively automatic and nonverbal, whereas Proust's is in part voluntary, and so compelling verbally as to warrant the word "literary."

But now, another warning: If you accept the seemingly irresistible argument that associative learning occurs in neuronal networks, and

Functions	Brain region or process	Animals evincing				
		H	P	M	V	I
Sensation	Primary sensory nerves	+	+	+	+	+
Perception	Thalamus and cortex	+	+	?	?	−
Attention	Thalamus and cortex	+	+	+	+	−
Emotion	Limbic lobe	+	+	+	+	−
Instinct	Hypothalamus	+	+	+	+	+
Learning	Associative neuronal networks	+	+	+	+	+
Memory, orientation	Hippocampus, cortex	+	+	?	?	−
Language	Temporal lobe	+	?	?	−	−
Action	Motor system	+	+	+	+	+

Note: H = humans; P = primates (monkeys, apes); M = sub-primate mammals (rodents, carnivores); V = other vertebrates (frogs, reptiles); I = invertebrates (insects, mollusks).

if you believe, as I do, that your memory, as in the word search example, is bootstrapped up from learning, then you will be hard pressed to reject the ultimate argument that consciousness itself is neuronal network functioning too. The fact that awareness and awareness of awareness have emerged from brain functions doesn't necessarily mean that subjectivity is reducible to those brain functions, but it comes too close to it for the comfort of those diehard dualists who would still like to believe that the two domains are independent, or at least so essentially different that the study of the one is unconstrained by the study of the other.

The brain-mind link has functional implications as well as mechanistic ones. From the Darwinian perspective, the animal "mind" is that set of brain functions that guides behavior so that innate, fully automatic, genetically determined states (like hunger, fear, and sexual arousal) can be adaptively contextualized by the individual. For contextualized, read integrated with ecological niches; for ecological niches, read environments, climates, conspecifics, food supplies, prey, and predators. Even the simplest animals are so exquisitely evolved as to live out their lives harmoniously and successfully despite a myriad of obstacles and competitors.

Such harmony and success give rise to the imputation of purposefulness, and it is this behavioral quality that most compellingly connotes mind. And just as learning is the primary-level basis of memory, so is purposefulness the primary-level basis of volition. The two levels of consciousness are not the same, but the secondary func-

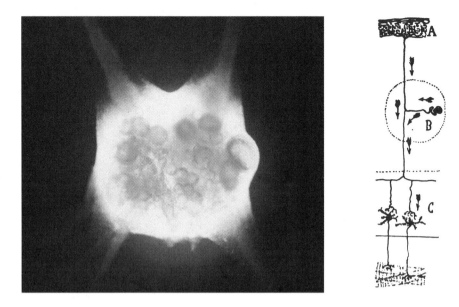

Mechanisms for Learning *(Left)
Aplysia ganglion. Neurobiologist Eric
Kandel has exploited the simple
nervous system of the sea slug* Aplysia
*to gain insights into learning at the
cellular and molecular levels. That the
mechanisms elucidated by these
experiments may be fundamental to
human memory is suggested by the key
role played by serotonin in both the
memory of humans and the learning of
the mollusk. (Right) A drawing by
Santiago Ramon y Cajal, circa 1890,
indicating directional flow in a sensory
neuron.*

tions are causally dependent upon the primary ones. This is all we
need to justify—and to deem necessary—the study of infrahuman
neurobiology.

Eight of the thirteen components of consciousness are present in
lower animals. The table on the previous page is constructed conserv-
atively. I have assigned plus or minus signs only to unequivocal attri-
butions of presence or absence of the indicated function, and used
question marks to indicate areas of controversy or doubt.

Even among the lowest invertebrates, four of the components are
unequivocally present. These primarily reflexive animals have relatively few neurons interposed between those conveying sensory
signals in and motor commands out. But those neurons, organized as collections of collaborative elements called segmental
ganglia, are capable of generating remarkably well-organized behaviors. Like us, snails and worms have neuronal nets constituting
excitatory and inhibitory pathways that allow activation levels to be
controlled and to spread so as to enhance one or another output
function. The ganglia of invertebrates also contain neuromodulatory
elements whose chemicals subserve learning in the nets so that their
electrochemical activation levels and input-output biases accurately
reflect experience. Finally, invertebrate ganglia contain hormone-
producing cells that, by secreting chemicals that induce sexual and
other consummatory behaviors, provide instinctual guidance to the
organism.

The skeptical reader may wonder by now whether I think that the subhuman consciousness cup is half empty or half full. Perhaps only a neurobiologist would believe it to be half full. But while most Western philosophers would still see it as utterly empty, their Eastern counterparts would declare it overflowing. Whatever the tally, it seems unarguable that we will never fully understand consciousness without understanding its components because those components are so clearly building blocks in a bootstrapping process. And there is no doubt that the investigation of the cellular and molecular mechanisms of learning is more efficiently pursued in invertebrates than in mammals. That is because invertebrates have fewer neurons, and many of those few are large and easily identified.

That studying "simple" organisms is relevant to consciousness can be shown by a single example. If an invertebrate ganglionic neuron is to keep a record of its experience, the neurotransmitter serotonin must be released during its training-induced activation. No serotonin, no learning. The same rule applies to humans. During the conscious state of waking, when serotonin is released, we perceive and can remember; by contrast, the conscious state of sleep, when serotonin is not released, allows us to perceive, but not remember. No serotonin, no memory.

The evolutionary coalescence of ganglia into the long tubular structure of the vertebrate spinal cord did not, in and of itself, confer a great neuropsychological advantage. But the associated evolution of a head ganglion, or brain, at the top of the tube was a major design breakthrough. With a spinal cord, much of the input-output processing and its modification by experience could occur at local segmental levels. The reflex machinery of the arm, hand, and finger is at the upper, cervical level of the spinal cord, while the leg, foot, and toe reflexes are in the lower lumbar and sacral spinal regions. It is this segmental processing that Sherringtonian neurophysiology has studied so successfully. But is a ganglion or a spinal cord conscious? Perhaps so in a primary sense, but certainly not in any secondary sense.

For secondary consciousness to be possible, we need another, suprasegmental level of processing running in parallel with the segmental one. The suprasegmental level is "higher" in that it occurs as copies of segmental processing are relayed in parallel to the head ganglion that is the brain. To perform this higher-level processing, vertebrate animals not only evolved more neurons but also moved much of their neuroendocrine apparatus upward. Three important consequences followed from this centralization of neural function.

One was the superordination of automatic reflex action by selective control, a process fundamental to what we call attention. The second was the opportunity to program the sensation of sensations, a process fundamental to what we call perception. The third was the elaboration of automatic processing related to instinctual guidance, a process essential to what we call emotion. All three of these functions—perception, attention, and emotion—are deemed cognitive, and no wonder: they are essential to our knowledge of the world, our bodies, and our selves.

These evolutionary achievements contain the germ of the bootstrapping or emergentist account of secondary consciousness. If an input becomes an output after passing through only one synapse, we call that transaction a reflex. Awareness is neither useful nor imaginable under this circumstance because the transaction happens too fast. Indeed, reflex processing—even by the cerebral cortex—occurs as long as one-quarter of a second before conscious awareness arises. At this reflexive level, learning is useful but memory is not. But if we can imagine making a copy of the input and forwarding it to a higher neural center, where it can be compared with other inputs so that associations between them can be recognized, we can begin to imagine how the stored records of experience could become the content of the continuous iterative processing of those higher neuronal networks that underlie our awareness of a percept, store records of our past, and generate plans for our future.

Thus consciousness is our instantaneous awareness of the act of copying the world, our bodies, and our selves into our brains, and the integration of those copies with all previous copies. It is this integration of perceptions, emotions, and memories that constitutes what we call the self. The self becomes an agent because it can utilize its past to determine its future.

To appreciate the role of emergentism in the bootstrapping of consciousness, consider the following contingencies between the modules of primary and secondary consciousness:

- There can be no perception without sensation.
- There can be no emotion without instinct.
- There can be no memory without learning.
- There can be no reflection without reflexiveness.
- Hence there can be no secondary consciousness without primary consciousness.

The moral of the story is this: Never consider a "lower" animal to be inferior, because everything that makes another animal "higher" depends critically upon the lower level. In this sense we are all lower animals because we recapitulate their structures, their functions, and their evolutionary histories in our own development. This is the essential message of many diverse writers and thinkers who have reminded us of our origins. They include Sigmund Freud (who emphasized the primacy of instinct in his concept of the id), James Papez (who localized emotion and instinct to the limbic region of the brain), and Paul McLean (who called attention to the tripartite organization of the brain).

Having thus moralized, I would not want to be misunderstood by those who assume identity of primary and secondary functions where only interdependence is indicated by the evidence. The principle cuts both ways. Secondary consciousness is not reducible to primary consciousness, however much it depends upon it. And secondary consciousness must not be confused with primary consciousness, however much it may derive from it. This means that while we must be respectful of lower animals and primary consciousness functions, our moral philosophy must be subtle and refined as it takes account of the impressive differences—as well as the similarities—between higher and lower life forms.

> *By introspection we have access only to a limited amount of what is going on in our brains.*
> FRANCIS CRICK, 1994

A Matter of Degree

The difference between the mammalian and submammalian vertebrates is not so much in the number of neural components each possesses as in how they are deployed. Lacking temperature control, submammalian animals are at the mercy of the elements. When it is too cold or too hot, too wet or too dry, too bright or too dark, they just turn off and drop out. By evolving adaptive thermoregulatory mechanisms, mammals became less reflexive, and by increasing the number, size, and variety of their higher secondary neuronal networks, they increased their chance of becoming reflective. And reflectiveness, above all other secondary attributes, is a matter of degree.

Beyond assuring the continuity of function across arid deserts, frigid winters, and dark nights, mammalian temperature control appears to afford optimal thermal conditions for the brain as an engine of cognition. The only animals to which we ascribe awareness and awareness of awareness have exquisite temperature controls. And as anyone who has ever had a chill or a fever knows, even small changes in brain temperature raise havoc with cognition. Reflexes may speed up or slow down with changes in temperature, but reasoning and judgment fall apart. The brain processes underlying cognition operate adequately only within a very narrow range of temperature. Outside of that range, delirium replaces normal waking consciousness.

The mnemonic for cold exposure goes like this: first you fumble, then you bumble, then you mumble, then you tumble. When an intrepid group of my family and our friends hiked from the Lake of the Clouds to Madison Springs Hut in the White Mountains of New Hampshire in a severe storm some summers ago, the cold cost us, first, our fine motor control (we couldn't tie our parka hood strings); second, our motor coordination (we couldn't keep a straight path against the wind); third, our cognitive control (we became disoriented, illusion-prone, and confabulatory); and fourth, our balance (we fell into cracks between boulders). When we finally found the real hut (not the one we had imagined seeing in the swirling fog so many times before), we talked to another climber whose delirium continued for several hours after ours had cleared. He had been out there all alone—and lost—for several days.

Thermoregulation *Human body temperature fluctuates in phase with the biological clock in the hypothalamus, reaching its zenith in the late morning and its nadir in the late evening. In the rising phase, alert consciousness is progressively enhanced and sleep is increasingly unlikely. In the falling phase, alert consciousness is progressively diminished as sleep becomes more and more probable. During sleep—in the nadir of the body temperature rhythm— consciousness fluctuates rhythmically in phase with the NREM-REM cycle. During REM sleep, body temperature does not change, but active control is abandoned.*

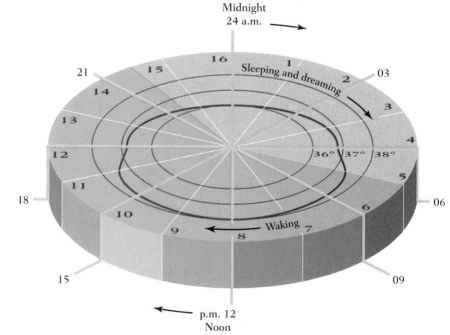

Clock time = 24 sixty-min. segments

Biological time = 16 ninety-min. segments

Because they have a high surface to volume ratio, young children are particularly vulnerable to dramatic shifts in temperature. And because their brain circuits are still developing, they are unstable and so liable to develop seizures when infection drives the brain temperature rapidly upward. These febrile convulsions are called "rum fits" when they occur in adult alcoholics who suddenly stop drinking and have high fevers, especially in the summertime. The delirium that these patients often manifest has all the formal features of REM sleep dreams except that it occurs in waking consciousness. That these two states may share a common causal mechanism is suggested by two facts. First, the recovery sleep of alcoholic delirium is characterized by an elevation of REM sleep duration and intensity. Second, REM sleep is normally characterized by a loss of central temperature control.

It could well be that such crucial cognitive functions as orientation, memory, coherent speech, and stimulus-appropriate perception—which are replaced in delirium by disorientation, amnesia, confabulation, and hallucination—are simply a function of thermally accelerated or slowed transmission within the neuronal nets. In this view, it is simply the temperature change times the number of neurons in the nets, times the number of nets, that determines the degree of dysfunction of consciousness for each increment of change in temperature. When brains get hot or cold they go haywire, fast.

A related point is that temperature control is tied to the state of the brain—and hence to consciousness and cognition—even under the atmospherically controlled conditions of urban interiors at sea level. Thus our body and brain temperatures fluctuate a degree and a half every day as we wake, sleep, and dream in synchrony with an innate circadian rhythm. And although the delirium that is dreaming is not caused by the brain chilling out, as it is when body temperature drops during waking, the REM sleep that causes dream delirium is an internal state that is triggered in part by circadian temperature fluctuations. It seems that the delirium of REM sleep is a cognitive trade-off for the maintenance of body and brain temperature equilibrium in subsequent waking periods. No thermal equilibrium, no consciousness.

The model that we are developing asks you now to ready yourself for a second jump, to the level of language and thought. The first jump, from segmented processing to the associative parallel processing of percepts and emotions, should have convinced you that awareness is possible in animals with complex, well-synchronized secondary neuronal networks. It follows that, given sensation, awareness could emerge simply as the sensation of sensation. With the emergence of vocalization and language capability in higher primates and humans, this sensation of sensation could then be represented abstractly in verbal descriptions and drawings. When we turn next to the development of consciousness in individuals, we will describe this emergence as it is directly observable in children.

Animals, even lower animals, possess a sort of "primordial speech" that they use to communicate with one another. Birds sing distinctive songs by which they identify themselves to conspecifics. They thus attract breeding collaborators onto their territories and warn breeding competitors off them. But we do not usually use the word *language* to describe bird song. Bird song is too stereotyped and limited for that. We need a John Keats to write an "Ode to a Nightingale." The nightingale itself can't do it. Keats's brain contains more networks than the nightingale's. And while Keats may have lost the innate capacity to whistle even a pale copy of the nightingale's lament, he could probably be trained to imitate it. Conscious of his own mortality, Keats created an evocation of sad yearning like the cry of a lover for his long-lost mate, and immortalized both the nightingale and himself in the process.

Language is the transcendent brain function that gives human consciousness its unique character. Human consciousness—and only human consciousness—has this attribute to a significant and convincing degree. But is a complex, polyvalent, multimodal symbol—or a string of symbols—like a language really different *in kind* from any other symbol? Are we really justified to deny bird song the title of language? And if all brain representations are symbolic— as they are—is not language a deeply intrinsic and fundamental brain function?

Vision, we know, is a symbolic process. There are no real pictures in the head, only neuronal patterns isomorphic with external-world structures. From the moment that photons of light excite my retinal ganglion cells, my brain is generating symbols. Each edge and each color in the picture above my desk triggers a symbolic representation in my retina. The millions of retinal signals thus generated spread in an instant to the geniculate body in my thalamus, where the edges are reconstructed and a new set of symbols is sent on to my occipital cortex. And so on in the more anterior cortical zones where image generation appears to be completed.

Now I admit that it would help if we knew more exactly how all these neuronal symbols are organized so that the photograph I took last summer now allows me to see, in my mind's eye, the blue sky, the white house, and the green fields of my farm in Vermont while sitting at my desk in Sicily. We know enough to be sure that even at this

I don't say everything, but I paint everything.

PABLO PICASSO, CA. 1950

descriptive level, the whole process is symbolic. As, of course, is my description of it, in these words to you. The photograph is also symbolic in a personal-literary way because lying on the deck in the foreground of the picture is the lovely woman to whom I am now married. Seated above her is our Italian friend, Fabrizio Doricchi, who knew us both before we met. The picture, like Proust's *Remembrance of Things Past,* is an extension of memory. It calls on the percepts, thoughts, and emotions of a moment in time. It is a representation of representations, utterly symbolic and utterly dependent upon the consciousness of the human brain.

There are, furthermore, two different states of consciousness emanating from the two brains of the two people in the picture. Fabrizio's face is stern and tense, even in the radiant Vermont sunshine, perhaps because he is preoccupied by his career concerns or his wife's health. My wife Lia is simply exhausted and sleeps, as she always does, in the sunshine. Perhaps she is dreaming of her six children waiting for her in Messina, Sicily.

The point of this picture story is to show how consciousness continues to evolve as the representation of representations. What began as mere sensation becomes—in a series of seamless bootstrapping steps—first our sensation of sensations, then our awareness of sensation, and finally our awareness of awareness. The photographer is aware not only of his own awareness but also of that of his subjects at a special moment of time. Literature and art are thus efforts to represent consciousness. The gradual building up of symbol upon symbol as brain circuit is added to brain circuit is as palpable in the development of individuals as it is in the elaboration of species.

Ontogeny: When Do Babies Become Conscious?

The question of when individuals become conscious is as important to a subtle and refined morality as is the question of consciousness in animals. Certainly human infants are born with sensation, with movement, with instinct, with emotion, and with the ability to learn. At birth they possess five of the nine components of primary consciousness. They thus have as many attributes of primary consciousness as animals that have been building up their neural nets for millennia, when only nine months have passed since they were single cells in the bellies of their parents!

But newborns can neither see clearly nor perceive, and hence they can't really attend to the visual world. They show reflexive

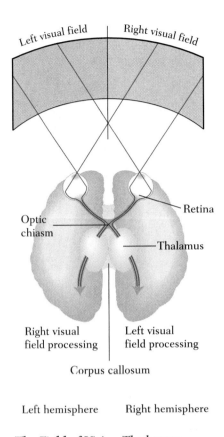

The Field of Vision *The human visual system is organized so that each half retina sees one-half of the visual field and delivers signals representing that space to the geniculate body atop the thalamus and to the occipital cortex on the opposite side of the brain. The right hemifield activates the lateral left retina and the medial right retina, both of whose fibers go to the left side of the brain.*

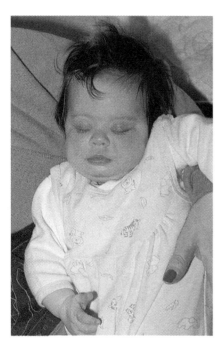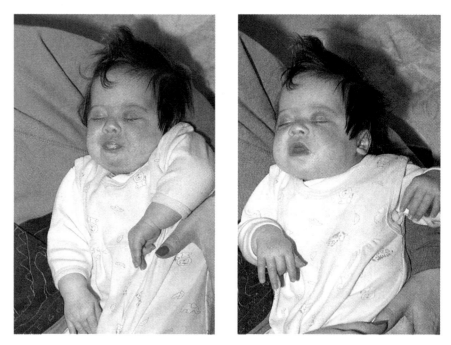

A Human Baby in Active Sleep *By using continuous video monitoring, these facial expressions of an infant were recorded during active sleep, the precursor of REM sleep in humans: (left) smiling; (center) grimacing; (right) surprised.*

orienting responses, especially to cues suggesting food. And if food is not forthcoming, they signal their hunger very effectively by crying, a primitive language system whose decoding is hardwired in their mother's brain. The mother doesn't have to be conscious for her milk to flow in response to her baby's cry. But her reflective consciousness allows her to plan ahead. She may thus adopt a feeding regimen that anticipates her baby's automatic and periodic food-seeking arousals.

Learning to perceive, to attend, and ultimately, to walk, talk, and speak, emerges from these primordial states over the next two years as babies interact with their parents and other caretakers. As we are now in the very center of this trajectory with our twin sons Andrew and Matthew, I will speculate about the dawning of their consciousness.

Since, as newborns, the waking episodes in which they cried and were fed were short-lived (about 10 minutes in duration) and occurred once every three or four hours, they were "awake" only 80–90 minutes per day. Did they sleep the rest of the time because they were tired? Or was sleep a more positive process with a developmental life of its own? The latter possibility seemed very real when we observed their sleep with our scientific curiosity as well as our parental awe. Many parents just tiptoe out of the room and hop into their own beds, hoping to catch up on their own lost sleep, but because Lia and I are both immersed in the study of the brain (and also because Lia is a naturally short sleeper), we spent a lot of time watching our babies sleep. For well over half of that time, they looked as if they might be conscious even though their eyes were closed.

We made that inference because their sleep was motorically active. We observed and videotaped the continuous small movements of their feet and hands and their well-organized facial expressions suggesting pleasure, happiness, fear, doubt, and even anger. It was as if both motion and emotion were being triggered by some automatic mechanism within their infant brains, just as it is in us adults when we are in REM sleep. And the active sleep of the newborn infant is known to be the primordial analog of adult REM sleep.

Neither the movements nor the facial expressions that we observed in the twins' REM sleep had anything to do with what was going on in the environment. Instead, these neonatal REM sleep periods could be thought of as providing a stereotyped activation of the brain. For a total of eight to ten hours a day, they could be facilitating the development of the thalamocortical circuits necessary for consciousness. And each brief awakening could provide the opportunity to equip those networks, little by little, with integrated content. By associating the pleasure of eating with mommy or daddy's smile, they could gradually build up that content into a confident sense of self as their consciousness gradually emerged.

Playing the Trumpet

The developmental psychologist, Jerome Kagan, postulates that consciousness emerges gradually during the second year of human life and culminates at about age 2 with the gaining of awareness of the self as an entity with attributes, that is, the ego, or I. The steps leading up to this achievement began at 7–8 months of age when the infant learns to control movement voluntarily. Since the late nineteenth century this ability has been called "will" by developmental psychologists, Kagan's fellow students of child behavior. Developmentalists assume that the self arises when sensations associated with movement come to be taken as causes of these movements, which they precede. This construct resonates strongly with the idea that mature human thought and consciousness have both motoric and causal aspects.

Three other functions come to be adjoined with these primordial senses of self and will to create conscious awareness during the first half of the second year. To recognition memory, which is already evident at 8 months of age, are added retrieval memory and inference, which allow the 14 month old to detect a logical connection between the past and the present. Each of these functions is at first independent, but all of them are integrated with the emergence of self-awareness.

Experimental evidence that the prefrontal cortex is the seat of working memory and strategically willed action suggests that it may be the substrate where Kagan's five functions of self-aware, deliberate consciousness are integrated. This idea is favored by the fact that whenever, later in life, the functional integrity of the prefrontal cortex is weakened or inpaired, consciousness loses some or all of the five factors identified by Kagan. A prime and universal example is REM sleep dreaming, where the relative deactivation of dorsolateral prefrontal cortex is associated with

- Loss of volition
- Weakening of working memory
- Faulty inferential logic
- Marked deterioration of self-reflective awareness

Now the twins are 14 months old, and the small but exciting changes that we have observed each day have accumulated dramatically. Yesterday, for example, they learned to play their plastic trumpets simply by watching us do it. Today they are playing the trumpets quite spontaneously and obviously enjoying both the sense of mischievous joy that being able to make noise confers and the sense of pleasurable mastery that being able to elicit approving smiles adds to the mix. Although they are not aware of being aware—because, I suppose, they don't yet possess the language necessary for propositional thought—the consciousness cup is by now well over half full. I'd say, as a guess, three-quarters full. And although my judgment is biased, I'd say they have already surpassed their primate cousins, the apes and monkeys.

But, you ask, does this sophisticated imitative behavior denote consciousness? Visual awareness, yes. Motivation driven by emotional pleasure, certainly. And at least an automatic understanding of a mechanism: if I want to make a noise, I need to pucker up my lips

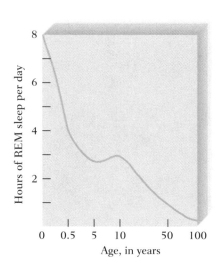

Duration of REM Sleep in Humans over the Life Cycle *REM sleep occupies as much as eight hours a day in the newborn human infant. With brain maturation, this figure rapidly plummets to about one and a half to two hours by age 10. Thereafter it declines gradually over the remainder of the life span.*

and blow! Then a curious inspection of the social surround for our emotional response leads to the strong reinforcement guaranteeing learning. Without language, it is not reasonable to assume that such secondary properties of adult consciousness as reflective awareness, deliberate thought, or episodic memory could yet be present. At the same time, it is impossible not to see that they will soon come, little by little, day by day, in a gradual emergence that will imperceptibly cross a wide, gray threshold zone sometime within the next year.

Now the twins are awake for about half the day. They have lengthened the intervals between feedings from three hours to five and eat only four (down from six to eight) times a day. And their sleep is less dramatically active. Roughly speaking, they have turned ten hours of sleep into waking, and well over half of that conversion comes at the expense of the active REM sleep phase. Over this period their sleep bouts have both lengthened and deepened. All these changes result from the maturation of the neural origin of primary consciousness, the thalamocortical system of the forebrain. The brainstem that ran the show almost completely 14 months ago is still there, but is now subdued, at least part of the time, by the higher centers that it nursed for so long in the dark. Like a child coming to the aid of an aging parent, this is neurological filial gratitude.

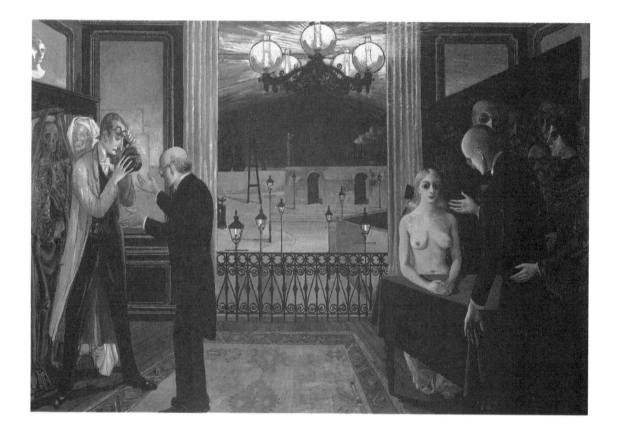

Intellectual Approaches to Consciousness

As I speed west on a flight from Chicago to Tucson, I struggle to focus on editing this chapter. My attention is diverted by the memory of an unsettling experience at the C. G. Jung Institute Conference in Chicago this morning and by the nonstop chatter of a Tucson III-bound psychologist in the seat behind me. In Chicago, the Jungians had made it quite clear that they are not simply uninterested in brain science, but consider it to be so hopelessly inadequate to their quest for holistic union, transcendental spirituality, precognition, and extrasensory perception as to be an obstacle to progress. The media psychologist behind me is talking loudly about the book she is reading and bragging about her own psychic powers. The book is by a psychologist respected for his sophisticated views on sleep and dreams, which he combines with a penchant for meditation in the Buddhist tradition. She boasts that she could tell the sex of each of her children and the exact dates of their births one week after their conception.

L'Ecole des Savants, Paul Delvaux, 1958 *Scientific experts, by virtue of the narrowness of their expertise, often miss the true nature of the phenomenon they are trying to understand. In this painting, Paul Delvaux places a neurologist peering into the brain at the left and a psychiatrist talking with a patient at the right. Neither chooses to look out the centrally placed window and so behold the surreal landscape representing the conscious experience of dreaming. The artist seems to be telling the viewer of the painting that all these elements— phenomenology, physiology, and psychology—must be integrated if we want to understand the big picture that is consciousness. (Museum of Modern Art, Ludwig Foundation, Vienna. © P. Delvaux Foundation, St. Idesbald, Belgium/Licensed by VAGA, New York, NY.)*

What would the great American thinker William James have made of the first two conferences held in Tucson, Arizona, in 1994 and 1996 and formally titled "Toward a Science of Consciousness," but commonly referred to as Tucson I and II? He would probably have been struck by the wild heterogeneity of ideas on the subject emerging from such diverse sources as to defy the very unity upon which any coherent system of thought depends. But, given James's monumental tolerance and his determinedly open-minded eclecticism, he would almost certainly have rejoiced at the pluralistic richness of the proceedings and declared the interdisciplinary communication among philosophers, psychologists, physicists, and physiologists to be intellectually healthy-minded.

As the goal of this chapter is to capture—or at least to convey—a sense of the glorious variety of approaches and ideas now in ferment around the problem of consciousness, I can think of no better introduction than James's own discussion of the "field of consciousness," to elevate his use of this phrase from the psychological to the social level. In his epochal work, *The Varieties of Religious Experience,* first published in 1908, James begins his treatment of the field of consciousness by contrasting the single idea, which many of his predecessors had considered to be the indivisible unit of mental life, with "the total mental state, the entire wave of consciousness or field

Brain Injected with Wax, Leonardo da Vinci, ca. 1500 The interest of Renaissance scholars did not stop at the surface of the body. Dissection of human cadavers, although discouraged by the Church and the law, was practiced by Leonardo da Vinci who made these drawings of the skull and its mysterious contents, the brain. The feeling states and consciousness itself now came to be ascribed to the fluid-filled cavities—or ventricles—and to discrete parts of the brain, like the pineal gland, which Rene Descartes regarded as the seat of the soul. Later, Luigi Galvani (1737–1798) used frog nerves to demonstrate the electrical nature of animal motion.

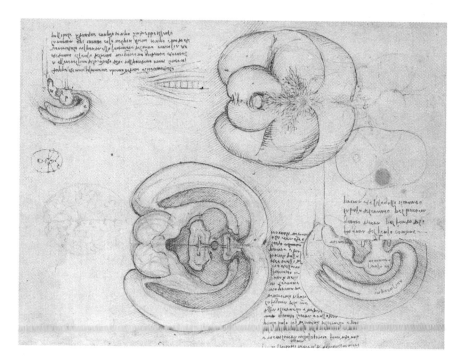

of objects present to the thought at any time." It was this wave, or stream, that suggested itself to James as a more suitable definition of the process that is consciousness.

By analogy, each presentation at Tucson I and II focuses upon a single idea, while the conferences as a whole define the field. But, as James would point out, it is impossible to characterize the whole field of consciousness studies today with specific and particular definitions. The image of the field will therefore be a holistic collage created by the reader from the elements selected by me to represent the field. And let the reader beware: because I so strongly favor the holistic conscious state approach, I am critical of most of the single ideas.

William James moved so freely among the domains of philosophy, psychology, and physiology that he could truly be considered a professor of them all. To deal with the Tucson conferences, he would have had to add a fourth P, representing physics, and the complexity of that field's ideas about consciousness might have daunted even his brave ecumenism. I will try to make sense of the physics via the physiology. But before delving into these topics, let us delight in James' description, from *The Varieties of Religious Experience,* of what it feels like to be conscious.

> As our mental fields succeed one another, each has its center of interest, around which the objects of which we are less and less attentively conscious fade to a margin so faint that its limits are unassignable. Some fields are narrow fields and some are wide fields. Usually when we have a wide field we rejoice, for we then see masses of truth together, and often get glimpses of relations which we divine rather than see, for they shoot beyond the field into still remoter regions of objectivity, regions which we seem rather to be about to perceive than to perceive actually. At other times, of drowsiness, illness, or fatigue, our fields may narrow almost to a point, and we find ourselves correspondingly oppressed and contracted.

From this strong dependency of consciousness upon our state of alertness and our state of health arises the conceptual model that I will develop in the remainder of this book. But here I will try to transcend my own narrow focus on the state dependency of consciousness and sketch the larger frame of reference that James admits is sometimes possible for us humans to achieve. Once again, from *The Varieties of Religious Experience:*

> Different individuals present constitutional differences in this matter of width of field. Your great organizing geniuses are men with habitually vast fields of mental vision, in which a whole programme of future operations will appear dotted out at once, the rays shooting far ahead

into definite directions of advance. In common people there is never this magnificent inclusive view of a topic. They stumble along, feeling their way, as it were, from point to point, and often stop entirely. In certain diseased conditions consciousness is a mere spark, without memory of the past or thought of the future, and with the present narrowed down to some one simple emotion or sensation of the body.

The important fact which this "field" formula commemorates is the indetermination of the margin. Inattentively realized as is the matter which the margin contains, it is nevertheless there, and helps both to guide our behavior and to determine the next movement of our attention. It lies around us like a "magnetic field," inside of which our centre of energy turns like a compass-needle, as the present phase of consciousness alters into its successor. Our whole past store of memories floats beyond this margin, ready at a touch to come in; and the entire mass of residual powers, impulses, and knowledges that constitute our empirical self stretches continuously beyond it. So vaguely drawn are the outlines between what is actual and what is only potential at any moment of our conscious life, that it is always hard to say of certain mental elements whether we are conscious of them or not.

Philosophy

Of the 504 papers presented at Tucson II, 95 were classified as "philosophy" by the meeting organizers. Without wishing to be doctrinaire or categorical, it seems fair to say that what these papers have in common is a concern with logic and with language.

David Chalmers is representative of those who define the so-called "hard problem of philosophy" to be the difficulty of reducing subjective conscious experience to physical brain states. Philosophers like Chalmers insist that it is a category error to equate the qualia of

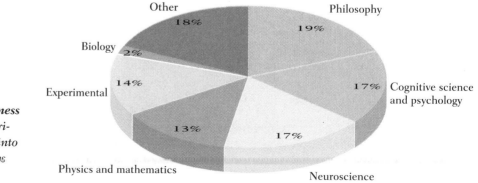

Compartmentalizing Consciousness
This pie chart summarizes the distribution of Tucson II papers falling into each of seven intellectual categories used to subdivide the program.

subjectivity with brain activity and that consciousness can therefore never be fully understood by recourse to neuroscience.

But the explosive growth of cognitive neuroscience has convinced many philosophers that this problem may not be so hard after all. Daniel Dennett is one such thinker. At Tucson II he was the most articulate and colorful of the philosopher critics of philosophy itself. In his recent book *Consciousness Explained,* Dennett takes the position that consciousness is a kind of behavior and as such must be controlled by the brain.

Subjective experience may well depend upon the brain, argues philosopher Chalmers, but it is an essentially different domain from that of neurophysiology. Thus, Chalmers believes that while it is justified and critically important to investigate the neural correlates of consciousness, we must not make the category error of identifying consciousness with brain activity. If we didn't think we knew what consciousness was like from a subjective point of view, we would have no idea what to look for at the neurophysiological level of investigation.

Chalmers argues that since our descriptions of conscious experience are so inadequate and our definitions of consciousness so endlessly disputatious, it is a mistake to believe that neuroscience can be even partially helpful. We must first know precisely for which aspects of subjective experience we are seeking the correlates. The immediate response from thinkers like Dennett is, "Of course, you are right. Now why don't you do something about it?" In other words, why not abandon philosophy and become a cognitivist or a phenomenological psychologist?

This is an understandable reaction to the carping of those philosophers who seem to be saying that no matter how good the neurophysiological data, consciousness will remain unexplained because it is irreducibly subjective. This message is doubly unwelcome to experimental psychologists and neuroscientists because it also contains scolding disapproval of the inadequacies of phenomenology, the one area of natural science that we might expect philosophy to help us develop.

But the philosophers may be justified when they insist that their field is logic, not phenomenology. Phenomenology, according to them, is the responsibility of psychology. Unfortunately, the psychologists

The results add up to a fundamental change in what science has long stood for throughout the materialist-behaviorist era. The former scope of science, its limitations, world perspectives, views of human nature, and its societal role as an intellectual, cultural, and moral force all undergo profound change. Where there used to be conflict and an irreconcilable chasm between the scientific and traditional humanistic views of man and the world, we now perceive a continuum.

ROGER SPERRY, 1982

also deny responsibility for phenomenology because subjective experience is thought to be scientifically unmanageable. And, anyway, what self-respecting scientist would want to study something that is irreducible? The essence of science is, after all, reduction, where *reduction* is defined as explaining the largest number of variables with the fewest assumptions. In the case of consciousness, this reductive quest leads, inevitably, to the brain. But, the philosophers warn, understanding the brain basis of consciousness does not eliminate consciousness itself from consideration.

It is clear that in scientific society the philosophers function as a sort of judiciary, an intellectual police force that reminds us that things may not always be as simple as they seem. Philosophers consider questions such as the following: Is the color red really intrinsic to objects in the world, or is color, rather, attributed to objects by our brain-mind? This is like the schoolyard conundrum, "If a tree falls in the forest and there is no one there to hear it, does it make a sound?" The naive and spontaneous response to both questions is an impulsive yes. Of course red objects are really red. And trees can't fall down silently.

But a moment's reflection reveals that both redness and sound are products of the interaction between the energy emanating from the objects and our nervous systems. The light or sound energy still emanates from the objects even if we aren't there to see or hear it, but it is really consciousness itself that creates redness and sound. Philosophers are persnickety enough to force us to take such ideas seriously. Like William James, they want us, always, to honor the primacy of experience. In the case of subjective experience, which some say is fundamental and not mysterious, we simply have it: the sensation of redness or sound or pain or aesthetic inspiration. And we ought to honor our experience, to investigate it vigorously instead of turning to models like computers or robots that may not really possess the mindful attributes sometimes ascribed to them.

Light Red over Black, Mark Rothko, 1957 *To properly appreciate the power that Mark Rothko's color field paintings have upon the conscious state, it is helpful to sit silently and gaze intently into them, preferably in a darkened room with the only light falling from above on the painted surface. Let the color in, let it spread through your brain-mind, and feel the sensation.*

Are Computers Really Intelligent?

So is framed the debate between such champions of artificial intelligence (A.I.) as Terrence Sejnowski, who has designed a neural network that can make up intelligible words from syllables, and critics of A.I. like John Searle. According to Searle, Deep Blue, the IBM computer that defeated chess champion Gary Kasparov in a 1997 match, cannot be considered to share Kasparov's consciousness simply because it can complete chess moves faster than Kasparov's brain. Searle's critique asks us not to accept as valid the so-called Turing test of machine intelligence. The Turing test posits that if the output of a machine cannot be distinguished from that of a human, then that machine has human intelligence. And if a machine has human intelligence, why couldn't it also be conscious? The Jamesian answer would have to be, of course it could!

But Searle argues that this assumption about machines, while plausible, is by no means proved by their passing the Turing test. Searle asks us to imagine a room occupied by a speaker of Chinese who is taught the rules of translating Chinese into English and learns them well enough to convince observers that he knows English as well as a native English speaker. But this is an illusion. All that the man in the Chinese room knows is the translation rules, not the language itself. And so the attribution of intelligence—or consciousness—to machines may be an error based upon illusory similarity. At Tucson II, this same argument swirled around the concept of zombies, those fabled human automata that, being deprived of free will, may resemble us, but are not really fully conscious humans.

Debate among the philosophers was also intense regarding a second "hard problem," that of defining the evolutionary advantage of consciousness. The fact that graded forms of consciousness are not rare among animals, but rather almost ubiquitous, means to many that consciousness is a major adaptive strategy conferring survival advantages to its owners. If consciousness is not causal and, worse, is a mere epiphenomenon of brain mechanics, why should it exhibit such manifestly robust existence?

On the other hand, if consciousness is not reducible to brain mechanics, have we really escaped the dualism of Descartes? Dennett insists that we have not yet escaped Cartesian dualism, but that we can and must do so. He warns us against the philosophical traps of what he calls the Cartesian theater, wherein the brain, like a movie projector, throws images on a screen for the observational delectation of a homunculus sitting inside our heads. Dennett wants us to take seriously the idea that the subjective experience of seeing is so embedded in brain mechanics as to be both part and parcel of them. He asks us to resist what he calls the "myth of double dissociation," whereby physical signals such as light are transduced by the brain into neural codes (the first dissociation) and then carried to someplace in the brain where they can be further transduced into experience (the second dissociation).

But can we abide thinking of ourselves as brains, or as brain states? There is a lot more at stake in this question than meets the modern philosophical eye. It is, of course, religion, which, while not officially on the Tucson II program, is obviously alive and well there and elsewhere throughout the world.

Psychology

William James was powerfully instrumental in moving psychology away from its exclusive reliance upon subjectivity, speculation, and yes, religion. At Harvard University he founded the first department of experimental psychology in America and recruited Hugo von Munsterburg, a student of Wilhelm Wundt in Germany, to run it. The experimental tradition at Harvard led alarmingly quickly to the behaviorism of B. F. Skinner. Skinner denied scientific legitimacy to the study of mental life, the subject that interested James and many other psychologists the most. Skinner was so radical that he even ruled out the relevance of neuroscience to psychology. To him, the brain-mind was a black box whose operating rules could be effectively discerned only by analyzing its input-output functions as they were manifested in objectively observable behaviors.

Some would say that Dennett is preaching a neo-Skinnerian form of neural behaviorism. And it is certainly true that what is now heralded as the cognitive science revolution is only old behavioral wine in new neurological bottles. This is because the techniques of cognitive science rely heavily—indeed, almost exclusively—upon such behavioral measures as reaction time. These data are used to infer underlying neural network processing. The emerging inferences can in turn be checked against the simultaneously recorded dynamic activity of the brain as subjects perform their behavioral tasks. We will later explain and extol this paradigm. But first let us ask, whatever happened to subjectivity? Where did it go? And can it ever achieve the scientific legitimacy it needs to help us know what aspects of consciousness we expect neuroscience to explain? If not, are we obliged to share Chalmers's pessimism about solving the hard problem?

B. F. Skinner *Probably the most famous behaviorist, Skinner hoped to be a writer and was encouraged to pursue this path when the poet Robert Frost praised some of his college essays. In his three-volume autobiography, Skinner described the "dark year" after college graduation in which he tried to write full-time and discovered that he "had nothing to say." After reading Watson's book* Behaviorism, *Skinner went to study psychology at Harvard. His fame is based not just on his research on animal learning but also on his extensive writings on the implications of a behavioral approach.*

Introspection and Phenomenology

With all the talk of qualia and subjectivity at Tucson II, one looks in vain through the agenda for any systematic study of consciousness itself. William James would despair at this failure of modern students of consciousness to concern themselves much with either the form or the content of consciousness. The symptoms of this marginalization of the study of subjectivity are clear in the defensive, self-aggrandizing tones of those brave few who dared to champion introspective approaches at Tucson. Most have an individual agenda, and whenever that agenda gains prominence, all semblance of science rapidly disappears. Thus the proponents of meditation, of LSD, of yoga, and of lucid dreaming all seem to be proselytizing and advertising as much as they are investigating.

In all fairness, many of these good people have been institutionally marginalized. The swing of academic psychology from Jamesian pluralism and tolerance to Skinnerian narrowness and exclusivity has not completely reversed itself. But the Tucson II program booklet is admirably inclusive and eclectic: the 73 abstracts generously classified as "experimental" and the 93 classified as "other" cover a fabulous variety of exotic subjects from lucid paranormal to cosmic consciousness. Even so, not a single paper reports quantitative data on the substates of waking! Do we really distrust our own ability to give a valid and reliable account of our daily experience as much as this grim statistic—a zero—would denote?

What is wrong? If, as some at Tucson argued, conscious experience is simple, where are the data describing it? Why are the writings on this subject always programmatic and never substantive? The answer to this question must be largely methodological. We simply have not yet developed tools that are adequate to the task. But there are some signs of positive change on the horizon. New methods for studying consciousness in natural settings are taking advantage of modern telecommunications technology.

Experience Sampling to the Rescue

The study of subjectivity can be instrumentalized in several useful ways. One method, experience sampling, asks subjects to respond to a signal, usually emanating from a portable electronic beeper of the sort worn by doctors and plumbers—and which, like theirs, goes off at unexpected times of the day or night. The subjects' reports are usually tape-recorded verbal accounts of the mentation preceding the beep by some brief estimated time period. In addition to these open-ended accounts, the subjects may also be asked to respond to a structured questionnaire so that the investigator can obtain specific information about the context or content of the reports. Was the subject alone, in the company of known persons, or in a crowd of strangers? In what behavior was the subject engaged? Was there a clear relationship or a dissociation between that behavior and the internal conscious experience?

All these questions may seem tediously banal until you recognize that almost all that we know about the quotidian nature of consciousness comes from retrospective recollection, a notoriously unreliable instrument. One already dramatic result of the experience sampling method underscores this point. Their wish to establish the range and depth of emotion experienced over the day led experimenters to design a specific probe of the feelings affecting subjects just prior to beeping. In many cases negative affects such as anger or frustration or irritability, anxiety or apprehension, were rated high in the individual reports. Yet when, at the end of a day, subjects were asked to characterize their own emotional experience, these many instances of discomfort were neither remembered nor reported.

Can this oversight be attributed to conformity with social niceties such as the normalizing response, "Fine," to the question "How are you?" Probably not, because in the heat of the moment, the subjects do not hesitate to say "Terrible" instead of "Fine." And it seems unlikely that the experience sampling technique is biased toward negative affect. We must conclude that memory is the culprit. *Pace*, Proust, *la récherche du temps perdu*, the research of past time, is a fool's errand. It may well be that we do not want to acknowledge how unpleasant much of our moment-to-moment conscious experience seems to be. In that view, we are editing our scripts all the time, making them look good.

The past is hidden somewhere outside the realm, beyond the reach of intellect, in some material object (in the sensation which that material object will give us) which we do not suspect. And as for that object, it depends on chance whether we come upon it or not before we ourselves must die.
MARCEL PROUST, 1928

How much time do we spend alone? How much time do we spend thinking? How much of that time is spent in deliberative problem solving? And how much in escapist fantasy? And what is the nature of that fantasy? No doubt intrinsic individual differences and differences of context will greatly influence these data. But even those influences are of interest, and it seems possible that general rules regarding the form and function of waking consciousness will emerge from such studies. Until such studies are done, we have no database for comparison with all the exotic conscious state data that spiced the margins of the Tucson discourse.

Our laboratory group, under the leadership of Bob Stickgold, has recently completed data collection in a study designed to combine experience sampling by day with objective sleep monitoring at night. We wanted to compare the formal aspects of consciousness in waking with those of sleep in the same subjects over many days as they pursued their normal lives. In addition to carrying beepers for 21 consecutive days, the 16 subjects who participated agreed to wear a portable sleep monitoring system, called the Nightcap, that we had previously developed to assess brain states using an algorithm analysis of head and eyelid movement data.

By attaching the Nightcap analyzer to a computer, it was possible to awaken the subjects at various times after sleep onset to tap the progressive degradation in consciousness that we had previously shown to occur when people fall asleep, and later to awaken them in NREM or REM sleep to elicit reports of their conscious experience in those states. The result was the first longitudinal cross-sectional sampling of the conscious experiences of one subject group around the clock for many successive days.

Because the data set is so large and so rich, only a very preliminary analysis has by now been completed. It took six months just to transcribe, classify, and catalogue the 2124 mentation reports. Judges who were blind to the state from which each experience report was collected were asked to identify it. It is striking that these judges could reliably distinguish between waking and sleep (99 percent correct). This finding alone puts to rest any doubt about the robust validity of the conscious state paradigm.

The judges also achieved surprisingly high accuracy in guessing which reports came from sleep onset (80 percent) and from REM sleep (70 percent). Some errors (27 percent) were a result of confusing REM sleep and sleep onset mentation. This is not surprising from a physiological perspective because these two states share similar EEG patterns. Also not surprisingly, the judges had a much more difficult time (55 percent error rate) in distinguishing NREM sleep reports from those obtained at sleep onset. This finding indicates that the conditions of NREM sleep are instituted quite promptly at sleep onset, and that that state can have waking, NREM, and REM-like features.

So far, then, our findings support the conclusions about the differentiation of conscious states that we had reached by combining disparate data sets. But because our data are so internally homogenous, we can now go on and ask a host of important and specific questions about the vicissitudes of cognitive and emotional processing as the brain changes around the clock over successive days. Does anxiety by day predict anxiety by night? And vice versa? If subjects show a high degree of dream recall, will they be adept at reporting daytime fantasy? And will these two states be differentiable on such scales of bizarreness as discontinuity, incongruity, and uncertainty?

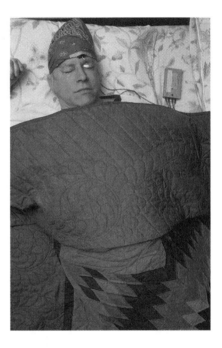

The Nightcap State Monitor *Before going to sleep in their own beds at home, subjects place an instrumented bandanna on their heads and turn on the recorder switch. Thereafter, every head movement and every eye movement they make is recorded. The counts of these movements can then be processed by a computer algorithm that estimates the brain-mind state as waking (both head and eyes move), NREM sleep (neither move), or REM sleep (only eyes move).*

Something was top secret, hm... Someone was trying to find out if I had told anyone anything; they were trying to figure out how good I was at keeping secrets. I think it was related to the sleep study in some way. Uhm... (pause) they had a set of cassettes—yes, it was related to the sleep study, it was that they were listening to the sleep study [microcassettes] and what I was saying to make sure that I hadn't mentioned any of the stuff that I wasn't supposed to mention, cause I had no idea what it was. Uhm... and I hadn't mentioned anything. [15 sec—visual hallucination (0.5), auditory hallucination (0.5), narrative plot, bizzareness, reference to experiment]

Whatever the answers to these questions, we have committed ourselves to a science of subjectivity, and we hope, at the very least, to provide a description of how thinking and feeling fluctuate when accessed intentionally and prospectively.

Cognitive Science Approaches

Even in its pre-Skinnerian form, experimental psychology—now called cognitive science—was facultative. In contrast to the introspectionist approach, which tends to be holistic, cognitivists zeroed in on a single component function of consciousness. The net result is that the field of consciousness studies is divided into several discrete subfields, each concerned with such bounded mental faculties as perception, attention, emotion, memory, learning, and language. The researchers in each of these fascinating realms have their own methodologies, their own language, and their own theories, and they rarely talk to each other. No William James stands ready to give 14 years of his life to writing a one-author, magisterial text like *The Principles of Psychology,* which, when it was published in 1890, summarized all these unitary modules and integrated them into a single story.

At Tucson II, fewer than half of the 87 papers classed as "cognitive science and psychology" were cognitive in the strict sense of the word. And since the strict sense of the word is behavioral, none of them was about thinking, which is what a layperson might suppose is meant by cognition. Come to think of it, thinking doesn't even appear as a topic in such encyclopedic texts as *The Handbook of Cognitive Neuroscience,* which brings together the many wonderful papers presented by scientists who participate in an annual summer program under the auspices of the McDonnell-Pew Foundation.

Thinking, which feels to me like a motor act occurring entirely within my brain, is apparently still too inaccessible a process for cognitive science. In this sense, *cognitive science* is a misnomer. The challenge now is to use behaviorism, the valid legacy of Skinner, to tackle the virtual behavior that constitutes the inner working of the mind.

Cognitive science comes closest to studying thinking when it focuses on working memory, the instantaneous content of consciousness during problem solving. To render working memory experimentally tractable, Pat Goldman-Rakic has trained monkeys to perform a shell-game task in which their job is to recall which of two white cups hides a peanut. She then uses a moveable microelectrode to record the activity in brain cells in the monkey's premotor cortex that encode the memory while the monkey waits for its chance to show how bright it is (see page 66). Using special staining techniques, Goldman-Rakic has been able to determine that the working memory cells of the monkey premotor cortex receive messages in the form of the chemical modulator dopamine, which has long been suspected of mediating motivation and reward. As every student and teacher knows, motivation and reward are critical to cognitive success. And they are also influenced by serotonin, one of the two brainstem mediators of waking consciousness. The point is that every cortical cell involved in the representation of working memory is aided by a variety of chemical helpers that facilitate its job. The beauty of this kind of experiment is not only its clear relevance to the things that interest us most about consciousness but also its successful integration of behaviorism and cellular neurobiology.

Imaging being a near cousin of imagining, the study of mental imagery is another good example of cognitive science closing in on thinking. As I consider how to tell this story, my mind conjures up a vivid picture of my colleague Steven Kosslyn. With comic animation, Kosslyn puts his audience to work by asking them to call up on the screen of their Cartesian theaters the picture of a Doberman Pinscher. If you do this, you immediately grasp the point that Steve is making: When you image, you run your visual system backward, from memory to image, rather than forward from image to memory.

Since Kosslyn works with people, not monkeys, he needs a technique different from Pat Goldman-Rakic's in order to catch their brains at work as they image. Most people would prefer not to have their visual cortex poked with microelectrodes, and they certainly don't want pieces of it to appear under a microscope. To this end, Kosslyn collects images of the brains of people imaging. The development of brain imaging technology such as PET scanning (positron emission recorded by computerized tomography) enables researchers to estimate the functional activity of various regions of the human brain. This works because brain areas of intense neuronal activity are more generously perfused by the blood, which carries whatever radioisotope has been injected just prior to performance of an imaging task. By asking his subjects to image a large *A*, Kosslyn can thus ask their brains if a larger area of visual cortex is activated than when they image a small *a*. It is.

You may have noticed that in these mental imagery studies Skinnerism has been completely abandoned. There is no output in the behavioral sense. No motor act signals completion of the task. The "motor act" is now the calling up of an image, and the "behavior" signaling that act is regional brain activity, blood flow, and all the rest of the cerebral mechanics that are waiting to be revealed by more sophisticated technologies.

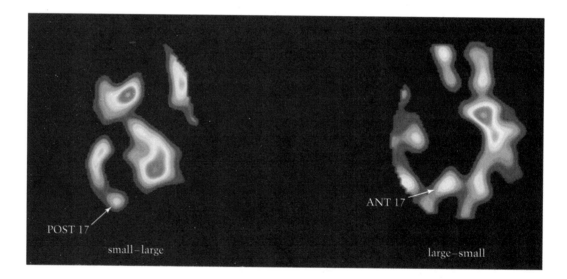

Imagery Research The images compare blood flow patterns when subjects imagine letters at a large or small size. The left image shows supplementary activation in a very posterior portion of the primary visual cortex when letters are imagined at a very small size, whereas the right panel illustrates activation in a more anterior portion of the primary visual cortex when images of letters are formed at a very large size. This difference in mental imagery parallels differences that would be observable in visual perception due to topographic mapping of the primary visual cortex, where each portion of external space is represented by a corresponding portion of the primary visual cortex, smaller central portions of space being represented at the back of the brain's occipital lobe.

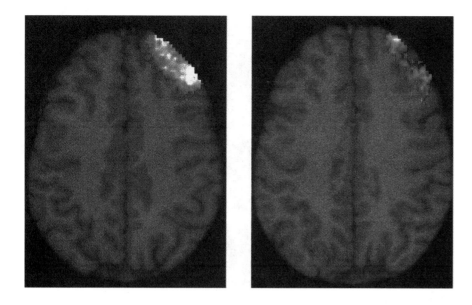

Activation Patterns *Statistical parametric maps displaying the increase in glucose metabolic rate in response to the average of the aversive picture (left) and initial session condition, both of which produced aversive emotion compared with the appetitive picture condition (right).*

Imagery research has cut itself loose on the input side too. There is no systematically controlled sensory stimulus as there is in cognitive studies of perception and attention, only the verbal command, "Imagine a large *A*." And yet imagery research does study perception, and it does study attention. But it does so with an entirely internal focus. Just like thinking. So we must be getting closer. And the closer we get, the more conscious experience comes to resemble virtual behavior, fictive behavior, abstract behavior. Now is the consciousness cup half full? Or half empty? Visualize it and tell me what you see.

Your answer may well depend on whether your left frontal lobe (half full) or your right frontal lobe (half empty) is more active. Optimists, like my colleague Ritchie Davidson, show stronger EEG activation in their left forebrains than in their right forebrains. This lateralized activation pattern can also be detected using imaging techniques. Davidson points out that optimists are people who proceed to action despite risk. This capacity to override fear may be reflected in the tendency of such individuals to show suppression of activation of the amygdala, the fear center of the brain, which is reciprocal to the activation of the cortex. "Full speed ahead and damn the torpedoes" is the motto of these left-frontal-activated, amygdala-deactivated PT boat commanders.

Optimists feel better than pessimists do about the same reality. Their consciousness is constantly brightened by their mood. They thus generate positive emotional responses in other people too. So the question naturally arises: Can a pessimist be converted by the power of positive thinking? Or by cognitive therapy? Or by Prozac? If so, would the brain be converted too? It stands to reason. Using new cognitive neuroscience techniques, such experiments are now possible.

Cruel experiments of nature already show that the converse is true. People who suffer stroke damage to the left frontal lobe are much more likely to become depressed than those whose damage is contained within the right forebrain. This is true whether or not they lose language with left-sided lesions. These curious asymmetries of conscious experience indicate that our minds, like our bodies, are right- or left-handed, and that this brain-handedness decision is taken early in life. Remember the story of development and our twins. Matthew, the impish, outgoing rascal who walks, talks, and throws toys out of his playpen, is left-handed. His brother, Andrew, is more subtle and reflective, but he is also more dependent and cries whenever a caregiver leaves the room. He is right-handed. What about their brains?

We also know that it is possible for some individuals to change what they see, or don't see, on command. The power of suggestion, like the power of positive thinking, can certainly change the mind, and now it seems that it can also change the brain. Those highly

Response to Hypnotic Suggestion
These images record the effect of hypnotic hallucination in blocking the right visual hemifield in four highly hypnotizable subjects. While imagining an obstruction to their view of the stimulus monitor (left), the amplitude of the visual evoked response was reduced in the visual cortex compared with normal perception (right).

hypnotizable subjects who participated in David Spiegel's experiments were able to lower a visual curtain—or wall—and obscure a visual stimulus. When they did this, the electrical activity of their visual cortex was altered. Altering a visual image from color to black and white (or vice versa) also raised (or lowered) the activation of the brain region subserving color recognition in these subjects.

If consciousness can change itself and in so doing change the brain, what other evidence do we need to declare the mind-body problem solved and to elevate the folk psychology assumption of free will to scientific status? The experimental evidence shows that we can imagine, we can feel better, and we can alter perceptions, all as a function of our brain and motivational states. For me, the evidence is already convincing, but I am an optimist. The right-frontal-dominated skeptics must either gather more detailed information about exactly how it is all accomplished or shift the balance of their forebrain activation to the other hemisphere. Perhaps we will be able to show that this is what happens in any conversion experience. This idea calls forth a mental image of Mother Teresa in a PET scanner with rays of faith beaming from her left frontal cortex. When William James suggested in 1908 that neurology was likely to be helpful in explaining religious experience, he was, as usual, about a hundred years ahead of his time.

Learning and Consciousness

B. F. Skinner's innovative operant conditioning paradigm, in which rewards or punishments follow spontaneous behaviors, has powerfully influenced child-rearing and pedagogy. In this view, behavior is determined (or at least shaped) by its consequences. But such associative learning also occurs by means of the pairing of stimuli, like food and the ringing of a bell in Pavlov's classical conditioning paradigm. Much of this learning is automatic and unconscious, which places it outside our control. But whether or not the learning itself is conscious or unconscious, states of consciousness play a role in the acquisition and expression of conditioned reflexes.

One experimental example is fear-potentiated startle, in which an anxiety-provoking stimulus can greatly increase the eye blink and heart rate response to an air puff or electrical stimulus. These and other related psychological tests are now being combined with sophisticated EEG and blood flow measures of brain electrical activity by scientists like Kenneth Hugdahl as a way of tracking the learning process in the brain. For example, Hugdahl has shown that when

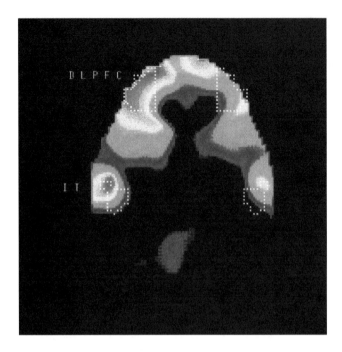

subjects learn a task, the brain activation pattern changes in a distinctive way. In collaboration with our group, he has even been able to demonstrate that the brain discriminates among external stimuli during sleep, when we are subjectively unaware that any stimuli are being delivered.

No doubt it is useful to detect an unexpected signal during sleep: consider the footsteps that awakened me last night, making me wonder if a thief was walking on the tin roof outside my bedroom window. And indeed there was a thief. As I peered into the darkness, I saw the masked face of a raccoon eating the grapes he had stolen from my arbor. Since we are so vulnerable during sleep, it is comforting to realize that our brains are still capable of processing signals that portend possible harm, even when we are unconscious. Those signals awaken us, restoring the consciousness that allows us to evaluate the threat.

Classical Conditioning Five healthy male subjects participated in a classical conditioning experiment, and positron emission tomography (PET) was used to compare regional cerebral blood flow before and after conditioning. Statistical parametric mapping (SPM) analysis of the PET data shows significantly increased activation in the right hemisphere in the orbitofrontal cortex, dorsolateral pre-frontal cortex, inferior and superior frontal corticies, and inferior and mid-middle temporal corticies. The only activated areas in the left hemisphere were area 19 and the superior frontal cortex. The results are interpreted as evidence for the involvement of cortical areas in human classical conditioning.

Just So Stories

One of the major vehicles of human memory is the story, the myth that is promulgated in cultures by oral repetition or by the written word. But each of us also has a personal story—or myth—which is every bit as active an aspect of our conscious experience as are the myths of our culture, whether it is ever shared with others or not. Here we enter a domain that straddles the nonconscious realm of implicit procedural learning of the sort studied by Pavlov and Hugdahl and the realm of explicit conscious recall that was studied by Marcel Proust. We all confabulate in the construction of our personal myths. So one holistic aspect of consciousness is its love of, and quest for, a tidy story. We will believe just about anything if only it is authoritatively and vividly communicated.

Human consciousness depends upon language, grammar, linguistics, and narrative forms. Every sentence contains unproved assumptions, and every paragraph organizes these assumptions into thought structures that are no more than theories. And thought itself, the essence of cognition, has this hypothetical, storylike character. In our ruminations, we constantly tell ourselves stories.

How does this work? Experts on memory, like my colleague Dan Schacter, make a distinction between its implicit and explicit forms. Implicit memories involve recognition, but not recall, while explicit memories involve recollection of specific autobiographical episodes.

In my eucalyptus word search story, I illustrated the way that the sound of the word *Ypsilanti* primed *eucalyptus*. This was an entirely automatic and unconscious process. But when I consciously recognized that I was on the right semantic track, I switched to the explicit, episodic memory mode by visualizing my sauna in Vermont, where I have often smelled eucalyptus extract, and by recalling my visits to Australia and Greece, where I have also seen the trees.

Had I been in the PET scanner, its images would reveal that posterior regions of my brain were activated by the priming task I had set for myself: *Ypsilanti* primes *eucalyptus*. At the same time, my olfactory and auditory areas might be activated. But it was my frontal lobes that were directing the search and piecing *eucalyptus* together for its verbal enunciation after I had instructed my brain-mind to travel to Vermont, Greece, and Australia. And, I daresay, it might have been my left frontal lobe that kept me going despite the difficulty of the search. Both my optimism and my knowledge of the rules of priming constitute autosuggestive, self-hypnotic support for the continued focus of my attention on the search task and for my ultimate success. Now, if anyone out there has any doubt that my consciousness and my free will were both real and functionally significant in this task I set myself, please write me a letter—or another book.

It is disconcerting to see the extreme gap separating neuroscience, which is the main engine of change in consciousness studies, from Chalmers's philosophy and qualia on the one hand and from the physics and quanta of Roger Penrose on the other. Most neuroscientists, myself included, don't know enough about either abstruse field to come to grips with the daunting questions and complex concepts raised by these near neighbors of neuroscience. Yet, just as it is important for neuroscientists to pay attention to philosophy—as logic—it is critical that we pay attention to physics—as natural law. Philosophy is the conscience of the scientific enterprise and hence "above" neuroscience, while physics, with its nitty-gritty concern for the basic nature of matter, is the foundation of science and hence "below" neuroscience.

With this image of neuroscience as the meat in a sandwich of which philosophy and physics are the bread, it is further disconcerting to note the many striking similarities between philosophy and physics. They seem to speak one another's language more easily than neuroscience speaks either of theirs. Are they just ganging up on us, or does each have something important to say? Because the physicists are so numerous—and so obviously intelligent—and because they seem to agree in important ways with the philosophers, let us try to understand their message.

Their first and most important point concerns the classic mechanics to which most neuroscience is still formally bound. By classic mechanics I mean the Newtonian model of the universe with all its assumptions about the orderly relation of space, time, and observation. Most of us still hold this simple-minded view of the world despite the animadversions of quantum physics. Just as qualia do not logically arise from material objects, subjective experience is not easily entailed by classic mechanics. Indeed, it is not at all obvious how subjectivity can arise in brains or, if it does so, how it can possibly act upon them. The easy way out of this one is to assume that subjectivity is, somehow, inherent in the physical structure of the brain—in brief, that consciousness is a "state" of matter.

This leads us to the second point of the physicists' argument, which is that quantum mechanics, and only quantum mechanics, gives any hope of understanding consciousness as a state of matter. The physicists contend that neurobiology can never hope to explain the unity of conscious experience or solve the binding problem on its own. If we want a truly deep understanding of consciousness, we must descend beyond microscopic levels of analysis to that of atoms and subatomic particles, and even beyond that.

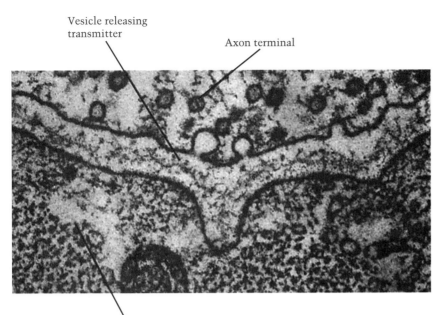

Vesicle releasing transmitter

Axon terminal

Postsynaptic cell

Ionic Basis of Neurotransmission *The Greeks were two and a half millennia ahead of their time when they proposed that all living phenomena, including consciousness, depend upon ionic flux. Nerve cells are excitable because they segregate ions—and hence electrical charge—across their semipermeable membranes. This segregation is an active process involving mechanisms that transport sodium out of the cell. Excitatory neurotransmitters interact with receptors, which alter the size and dynamic properties of the pores on the receiving dendrite so that sodium can rush in and depolarize the neuronal membrane, resulting in an action potential. Action potentials, like telephone messages, travel rapidly, at rates of up to 100 M/sec.*

This is a big jump for the neuroscientist hanging on for dear life to the intrinsic reliability of his observations in a Newtonian universe. The quantum physicist confronts us with such annoying conundrums as Schrodinger's cat (whose life or death is indeterminate) and Heisenberg's uncertainty principle (the location and velocity of particles cannot be determined with accuracy). It feels very dangerous, and even foolish, to embrace Niels Bohr's world if one is doing just fine, thank you, in the world of good old Isaac Newton.

Dangerous and foolish, perhaps, but tempting all the same. Especially if it is really true, as Neils Bohr's Copenhagen assumption asserts, that the wave function of particles has an ontological status equal to that of matter, and especially if, as some physicists hold, the wave function is intrinsically mental and hence capable of qualia. This would seem to be exactly what we are looking for, particularly if there is a two-way street between mind (the wave function) and matter (the particles themselves). That way, both consciousness and causality can be intrinsic properties of the natural world.

As far as I understand this language, it means that matter is composed of discrete particles whose movement is manifested as waves of energy. Light, for example, has both continuous and discontinuous properties. By analogy, the electrical property of nerve cells depends upon ions (discrete particles moving back and forth across membranes), and this activity is also immanent in voltage waves that propagate through the cortex and even punctuate the scalp so that they are recordable as an EEG.

Quantum Theory Meets Neuroscience

One of the brightest notes at the Tucson conferences was struck by the collaboration between the conference organizer, Stuart Hameroff, and Roger Penrose, the distinguished physicist who has written so extensively on the relevance of quantum theory to the understanding of consciousness. Their sincere and sustained effort to tie quantum mechanics to the specific workings of the brain in a manner permitting possible experimental tests is laudable and provides us with a chance to better understand how these seemingly disparate approaches might be unified.

Before attempting to sketch the Penrose-Hameroff theory we should note that Hameroff's research is aimed at understanding the mechanism by which general anesthetic agents ablate consciousness. This effect, which is observed every day in hospitals around the world, is of inestimable social importance even though we don't understand its mechanisms. And it is to Hameroff's credit that his experiments are designed to explore the consciousness question at the molecular level, where the considerations of quantum physics have at least potential empirical relevance.

Hameroff's theory of anesthesia proposes that those gases that are effective anaesthetics cause structural changes in brain proteins that disrupt consciousness by limiting the electron mobility deemed essential by his physicist colleague Penrose. Here, at least, a common mortal like me has a hope of getting the picture. Brain proteins are concrete. Their molecules are composed of atoms and ions whose behavior is linked to brain function. Hameroff further specifies that some proteins have structures that are particularly sensitive to dysfunctional alterations because the anesthetic gases reduce the energy of hydrophobic pockets in their molecules. So far so good. We can all easily imagine how reducing the available energy in a protein that might be an enzyme critical to normal brain function could impair consciousness. In fact, we would be surprised if changing the protein structure of every cell in the brain did not radically alter consciousness.

But now the going gets tougher, because to take these hypotheses to the quantum level, we need to confront the concept of superposition and imagine that it is the state of atoms and subatomic particles that we can't see or even measure in functioning brains that determines the state of the mind. It's a big, big jump, raising the anxiety level of even the most daring neurobiologist. Consider quantum theory as expressed in this quotation from Hameroff: "Startlingly, when isolated, atoms and subatomic particles can exist in coherent superposition of different states (i.e., *simultaneously*—[emphasis mine]—having different or opposite spins, locations and/or momenta)." This is tough. We are being told that one particle can, at the same time, be in two different places, move in two different directions, and exert two different forces. Being confronted with such paradoxical assertions makes me more sympathetic with the Jungians who cherish their holistic world view.

But hang on. That's not all. According to Penrose, it is this coherent superposition of particles and a newly proposed quantum wave function called self-collapse, otherwise known as objective reduction (O.R.), that constitute the quantal basis of consciousness. Exactly how and why these abstruse hypothetical mechanisms are important has not yet been made clear. Does the supposed superposition of states solve the mind-body problem by means of a deep quantal dualism? Does the self-collapse of the wave function have something crucial to do with quantal subjectivity? Is objective reduction at the quantal root of brain-mind identity? The mind boggles at such questions. Perhaps this is just evidence that complex information can itself cloud our consciousness.

Back to Hameroff and the brain. According to his theory, the structural locus of the quantal consciousness dynamic is the microtubule, an intracellular circulation system possessed by all neurons. The microtubule is a candidate for quantal election because of its crystalline lattice form, its hollow inner core, its importance to all neural function, and its capacity for information processing. To many critics of the theory, this choice sounds as arbitrary as it is abstruse. If you will pardon the pun, the microtubule-based consciousness theory may be just a "pipe dream." But at least it is explicit and articulate.

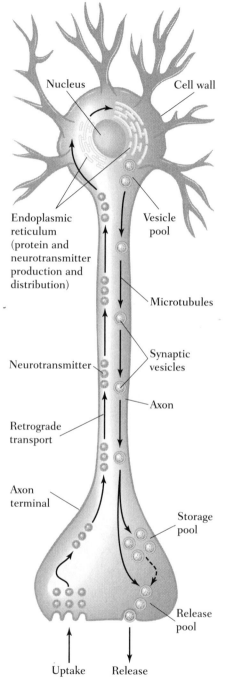

Nucleus

Cell wall

Endoplasmic
reticulum
(protein and
neurotransmitter
production and
distribution)

Vesicle
pool

Microtubules

Neurotransmitter

Synaptic
vesicles

Axon

Retrograde
transport

Axon
terminal

Storage
pool

Release
pool

Uptake   Release

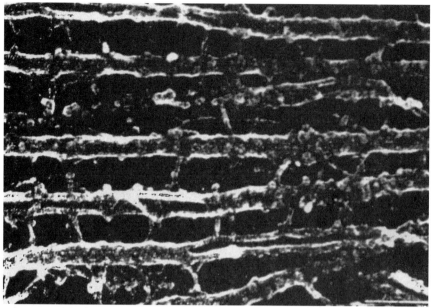

Microtubules *Neurons contain circulatory systems, shown in the micrograph above, by which proteins can be transported from nucleus or cell wall to axon terminal and back again, shown at left. These protein transport mechanisms, like river barges, are quite slow. It may take as long as 24 hours to move the cargo from warehouse to port. But microtubules are very effective, and may alter neuron excitability significantly, because they can deliver enzymes that can manufacture or degrade neurotransmitters.*

Penrose and Hameroff are eloquent as they go on to explain how the quantum coherence of microtubular protein could be synchronized throughout the brain, thus solving the problem of global binding and explaining the unity of conscious experience. In their own words:

We equate the emergence of the microtubule quantum coherence with preconscious processing which grows (for up to 500 milliseconds) until the mass-energy difference among the separated states of tubulins reaches a threshold related to quantum gravity. According to the arguments for OR . . . , superpositioned states each have their own space-time geometries. When the degree of coherent mass-energy difference leads to sufficient separation of space-time geometry, the system must choose and decay (reduce, collapse) to a single universe state. In this way, a transient superposition of slightly differing space-time geometries persists until an abrupt quantum classical reduction occurs. Unlike the random, "subjective reduction" (SR, or R) of standard quantum theory caused by observation or environmental entanglement, the OR we propose in microtubules is a self-collapse and it results in particular patterns of microtubule-tubulin conformational states that regulate neuronal activities including synaptic functions. Possibilities and probabilities for post-reduction tubulin states are influenced by factors including attachments of microtubule-associated proteins (MAPs) acting as "nodes" which tune and "orchestrate" the quantum oscillations. We thus term the self-tuning OR process in microtubules "orchestrated objective reduction" ("Orch OR"), and calculate an estimate for the number of tubulins (and neurons) whose coherence for relevant time periods (for example, 500 milliseconds) will elicit Orch OR. In providing a connection among (1) preconscious to conscious transition, (2) fundamental space-time notions, (3) noncomputability, and (4) binding of various (time scale and spatial) reductions into an instantaneous event ("conscious now"), we believe Orch OR in brain microtubules is the most specific and plausible model for consciousness yet proposed.

Penrose and Hameroff *Progress in modeling consciousness depends upon experts in different fields working together. The English quantum physicist Roger Penrose (left) and the American anesthesiologist Stuart Hameroff (right), shown here at Tucson II, are one such team.*

Specific, yes. And bravo for that. Plausible, perhaps. Let's take its plausibility on faith from these two very bright, hard-working, and co-operative colleagues. But is it testable, and if so, how? Can the theory be disproved? Is the quantal state directly discernible? Can it be manipulated without simultaneously disrupting higher-level neuronal functions? In particular, do anesthetics work only at the level of the hydrophobic pockets of enzymatic proteins, or do they also directly interfere with neuronal membrane dynamics, synaptic transmission, and the electrical organization of large groups of neurons? However bedazzled we may be by the scientific imagination of Roger Penrose, and however impressed we may be by the empirical skills of Stuart Hameroff, it is not at all clear whether and how this beautifully constructed theory can be tested.

What would our mentor, William James, have said about orchestrated objective reduction theory? Would it, I wonder, have inspired in him—as it does in me—something like his reaction to Sigmund Freud speaking on psychoanalysis at Worcester in 1907? Recognizing Freud's genius and keen rhetorical skills, but wary of Freud's arrogance, James pointed out that the concept of a dynamic unconscious that could not be seen directly was exceedingly dangerous for psychology.

Like James, I will remain open to the answers to our questions because we very much want to believe in coherence across all levels from the philosophical to the psychological to the physiological to the physical. But the assumptions, at each level, demand skepticism and experimental proof every bit as much as do the mappings between them.

Everyday Consciousness

I was standing in a courtyard recounting my experiences with lucid dreaming to a group of students. "To get off the ground in the old days," I began, "I used to run and flap my arms like a bird in my dream flights. But once I learned to recognize that I was dreaming—when I was dreaming—I realized that such exertions, however imaginary, were completely unnecessary." I then proceeded to demonstrate how easy it was to levitate simply by assuming a recumbent posture in the air three feet above the ground. "You see," I said to the students, "I can float here effortlessly as for long as I want. Or I can soar to thirty feet simply by willing it." And I promptly did so, while continuing my didactic discourse. When I awakened, I was both proud and amused because I had accomplished this feat of levitation that I attributed in my dream to lucidity without ever having the faintest idea that I was dreaming while it was happening.

The Mysteries of the Horizon, René Magritte, 1955 Magritte's bowler-hatted man is not the usual sort of self-portrait. He is, of course, Magritte, but only in the sense that Magritte is Everyman, the essential person with all the unessential details left out. The consciousness of the bowler-hatted man is generic, having the same formal features every day and—by the light of the moon—every night, in a reliably state-dependent manner. (Giraudon Art/Resource, NY. © 1998 C. Herscovici, Brussels/Artist Rights Society (ARS), New York.)

While the anesthesia that Hameroff and Penrose study causes a potentially irreversible loss of consciousness as the brain responds to an external chemical, sleep causes a *reversible* loss of consciousness as the brain responds to changes in its *own* intrinsic chemicals. Sleep thus constitutes an entirely natural experiment that permits the scientist to investigate the mechanisms by which consciousness changes dramatically every day and every night of our lives. And sleep presents us with the opportunity to understand not only how consciousness is lost at sleep onset but also how it is reactivated and altered during dreaming. Dreaming is a state of normal brain consciousness whose form and content are both quite independent of the outside world. This pure culture of consciousness that is dreaming can teach us the essence of the conscious state at the level of brain mechanisms, and its study constitutes a strategy for understanding how consciousness is altered by changes in brain physiology and chemistry.

Common sense might lead us to object to calling dreaming a state of consciousness at all, because when we dream we are oblivious to the reality of the outside world. But this is the point exactly: without any help from the outside world (except, of course, its representation in memory), the brain is capable of creating such a remarkably faithful simulacrum of waking conscious reality that we are quite regularly fooled into taking it for the real thing—as in my nonlucid, lucid levitation dream. This must mean that the brain has all the hardware and software it needs to create a virtual reality of remarkable verisimilitude. This observation, in turn, implies that one function of consciousness is to create a largely autonomous model—a map of the real world within the head—whose parameters—its latitude and longitude—can be updated by our daily excursions in the real world even as we sail on the deep sea of sleep.

Was it a vision, or a waking dream? Fled is that music:—Do I wake or sleep?

JOHN KEATS, CA. 1815

We begin in this chapter to build the conceptual model of conscious states on which the remainder of this book will rely. Here we contrast the features of waking, sleeping, and dreaming consciousness and set up the strategy of subtraction by which we can analyze the brain substrates of each of the graded components of consciousness that we have discussed in earlier chapters. For example, we explore how many of the distinctive formal features of dream consciousness reflect the subtraction of recent memory from the componential mix. And sure enough, when we then look at the physiology and chemistry of the dreaming brain, we discover that specific brain chemicals and brain regions known to be crucial to memory are likewise functionally subtracted from the operational mix. We thus conclude that amnesia for dreaming is caused by alterations in neural activation and modulation, and specify how this might occur.

The Comparative Psychology of Waking and Dreaming

The accompanying table summarizes how each conscious state component behaves in sleeping and dreaming as compared with waking. By grouping the components according to their functional relationships and then determining whether these groups undergo enhancement or impoverishment during sleeping and dreaming, we can organize our examination of possibly relevant brain mechanics in a more principled way. One of the major points revealed by this

A Comparison of the Modules of Consciousness during Waking, Sleeping and Dreaming

Component	Waking	NREM Sleep	REM Sleep
Input level	High	Low	Blocked
Attention	Selective	Poor	Poor
Perception	Strong (external)	Weak	Strong (internal)
Memory			
Recent	Good	Poor	Poor
Remote	Good	Poor	Good
Orientation	Good	Poor	Unstable and Imprecise
Thought	Directed	Perseverative	Illogical
Insight	Good	Poor	Delusional
Narrative	Good	Poor	Confabulatory
Emotion	Episodically strong (reactive)	Weak	Episodically strong (spontaneous)
Instinct	Moderated	Weak	Strong
Intention	Deliberate	Weak	Confused
Volition	Strong	Poor	Episodically strong
Output	High	Low	Blocked

exercise is that while the subject who dreams is ostensibly unconscious, many aspects of conscious experience are actually improved or enhanced.

In my levitation lecture I used the dream logic gambit called ad hoc explanation to justify the impossibility of my weightlessness. But I had no idea whatsoever—even as I hoodwinked myself and my students—that I must be dreaming. For anyone interested the brain basis of either self-reflective awareness or goofy logic, a waking-REM sleep comparison is thus very much in order. One is subtracted and the other added in a tightly linked, reciprocal manner that is reminiscent of waking madness, in which delusion and loss of insight so frequently go hand in hand.

This conscious state comparison approach contrasts in three ways with what I call the needle-in-the-haystack search for a single deep mechanism for altering the state of consciousness—such as the electron isolation in the hydrophobic pockets of proteins in the microtubules that Hameroff hypothesizes to be the basis of anesthetic unconsciousness. First, the level at which explanatory hypotheses are developed is accessible, well-defined, and experimentally manipulable, since it is the level of the neurons and those of their network interactions that are engineered by well-known chemical signal mediators. Second, the concepts used and the data collected are simple, quantifiable, and straightforward. Third, the quest is more modest since it assumes a multiplicity of causes and seeks only partial explanations.

This last point, of course, is a potential shortcoming of the comparative approach. One objection is that it is not bold enough. And it could be argued that some single deep mechanism undetectable by the techniques of current neurobiology indeed underlies all the described changes, which could then be dumped into the intellectual trashbin of epiphenomena. As we saw at Tucson, it is a pluralistic universe: you pay your money and you take your choice. Time will tell which strategy ultimately proves most useful.

Dreaming's Enhanced Conscious State Components

As employed in the conscious state paradigm, the strategy of subtraction, or withdrawal of chemical modulation in the brain, isolates four components of waking consciousness that are enhanced in dreaming. In each case we must suppose that neural activation and information are somehow added to the system.

Sensory Imagery

While we are capable of bringing visual images to mind during waking, we are never able to image as sharply, vividly, and completely as we do in dreams, where complex visual worlds spring to life behind our closed eyes. Only in the abnormal waking conditions of mental illness is such hallucinatory experience possible. To explain this enhancement, we would therefore expect to find that the visual brain is somehow excited in dreaming and that some internal stimulus source is activated.

Fictive Movement

Not only do we see images clearly in dreams, but we find ourselves moving actively through this imaginary world just as we might in waking. The imagined movement of dreaming may manifest occasional intensifications of speed and may follow decidedly unique trajectories, which may twist, turn, or even leave the ground in hallucinatory flight. Sad to say, I myself have never had the illusion of

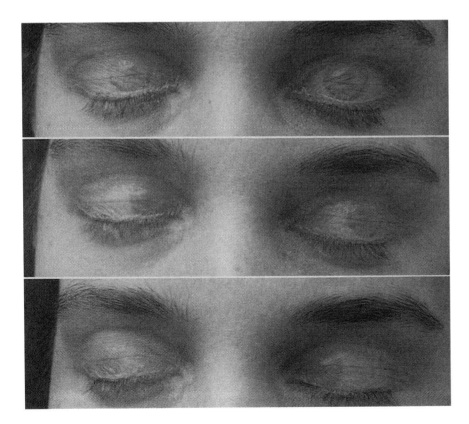

Seeing in the Dark *The movement of the eyes behind the closed lids of REM sleep is simulated by these double-exposure images. The neural activation process that moves our eyes in REM sleep also illuminates our vision so that we see things in our dreams that aren't actually there.*

levitation during waking. That may be a personal shortcoming, but I easily overcame it while dreaming. To explain this convincing fictive movement, we hypothesize that the motor systems of the cerebral cortex must somehow be turned on but inhibited, and that their commands must somehow be turned into the sensations appropriate to responses to them.

Emotion

Dream emotions may not always exceed the emotional peaks that are possible in waking, but fear, anxiety, surprise, and elation levels are much more consistently enhanced in dreams than in waking. Sometimes dream fear reaches such nightmarish intensity as to demand a terrified escape reaction strong enough to interrupt our slumber by breaking through the motor inhibition of REM sleep. To explain this aspect of dream consciousness, we predict excitation by stimuli originating in the brain's emotion centers in the amygdala and surrounding limbic structures.

Confabulation

The waking mind of anyone but a talented artist would have difficulty concocting the elaborate, fantastic, and completely convincing scenarios that are regularly and automatically cranked out by dream consciousness. Is there, then, a narrative organizing function, perhaps in the language area of the brain, that is supplied with visual, motor, and emotional data and knits these strands into dream fables? Or does the linguistic narrative brain play a more active role in commandeering the brain's sensorimotor and emotion networks so that dream experience can fit a plot outline with sufficient credibility? Because we know so little about how the brain constructs narrative, and because it is unlikely that nonverbal animal models can provide the evidence we need, these questions must remain open. But we will look at Wernicke-Broca areas of the cortex for evidence of activation.

Dreaming's Diminished Conscious State Components

On the debit side of the ledger, four quite different components of consciousness are severely impaired during dreaming. And the first three are strongly related to dreaming's fourth diminished component, memory.

Orientation

In a normal waking conscious state, without having to think much about it, we are aware of where we are, the date and approximate time, who is present in our surroundings, and the goal or direction of our behavior. Not so in dreams. We may be topographically lost, unsure even of the era in which we fictively act, confused about the identity or even the gender of our dream companions, and at a loss to know what purpose our strongly driven dream actions might have. Orientational instability during dream consciousness is at the root of dream bizarreness, and it feeds the confabulation that produces dream phantasmagoria.

One factor contributing to dream disorientation is the blockade of external sensory signals, which deprives the brain of the time, place, and person cues that constantly update waking consciousness and maintain orientation in all spheres. But sensory deprivation can't be the whole story. In sensory deprivation experiments, subjects do drift in and out of orientational coherence, but their open sensory gates and intact memory are usually able to remind them that they are still "in the tank." Even an information-deprived brain can stick to one set of orientational assumptions simply by updating itself via its intact memory. That this doesn't happen in dreams indicates that dream consciousness has lost its mooring to itself as well as to the outside world. What is that mooring? How is it slipped in dreaming?

Self-Reflective Awareness

Waking consciousness has a double aspect. We know not only who we are and what is going on, but also that we know it. We know, for example, that the conscious state of the mind is waking. Only rarely do we pinch ourselves in wonderment, asking "Am I dreaming?" And even then we promptly and confidently answer, "No, I am awake." And, deep philosophical doubt to the contrary notwithstanding, we are right. Indeed, we are often all too painfully aware of our selves as we scrutinize our actions, our physical appearance, and our thoughts. We may sometimes monitor ourselves to a neurotic fault. Insight can be painful, as the exquisite self-in-exile poetry of Emily Dickinson reveals.

> Sleep is supposed to be,
> By souls of sanity,
> The shutting of an eye.

Dream consciousness, by contrast, is almost always wrong about itself. In dreams we mistakenly assume that we are awake. Only rarely

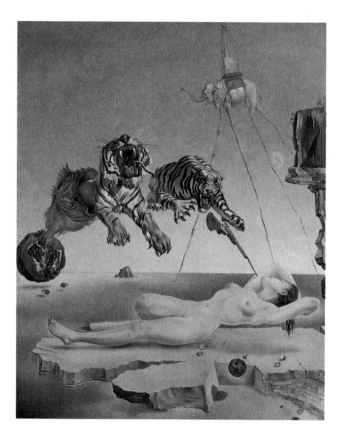

do we correct this error despite the evident improbability of dream events. Even physical impossibilities, like flying, do not usually suffice to give us insight into our conscious state. Remember that I was telling my students that I needed to be aware that I was dreaming in order to levitate effortlessly. But even as I said that in the dream, I thought I was awake! I was utterly without insight about my state. This defective insight is a first cousin to personal disorientation. Although we always correctly assume it is we and not someone else who is having our dream consciousness, we are consistently deluded about our true conscious state. Jean-Paul Sartre called this deficit the most definitive aspect of dream consciousness. How do we lose our selves in dreams?

Dreams Caused by the Flight of a Bumblebee Around a Pomenegrate a Second before Awakening, Salvador Dali, 1944 Many of the formal features of dreams have been represented by modern artists. The exotic visual detail is so compelling as to make us believe the impossible. While dreaming, we normalize nakedness, accept our insertion into fantastic settings, float or fly, experience hyperassociative tasks of imagery, and feel by turns elated or terrified.

Directed Thought

The human animal may well rise above the beasts simply because of the directed thought with which our waking consciousness is endowed. Just as we are able to monitor ourselves in that state, we can also manipulate ideas, solve problems, examine the logic of propositions, analyze the accuracy of observations and assumptions, and even create surreal scenarios, not just experience them as we do in dreams. But during REM sleep, no sooner do we have some unbelievable dream experience than we attempt to explain it by illogical and incongruous ad hoc thinking. And these bogus explanations, which we would see through in a minute if awake, satisfy us when we are dreaming. In dreams we are cognitively adrift. We have no mooring to time, place, or person, no self-awareness, and no critical thought. What do all these defects have in common, and what is their cause?

Memory

It all boils down to this: If our dream consciousness cannot keep a running account of its own operations, how can it be oriented, self-aware, and thoughtful? To perform any of these feats, I need at any instant to be able to ask, what day is it today? and to answer unhesitatingly "July 4" and add "Happy Independence Day!" Where am

I? "Dublin, Ireland." Doing what? "Writing Chapter 6 of *Consciousness*." In what state? "Lucid waking. Thinking to myself critically, 'This chapter will need reorganization, but the building blocks of the story are there.' Hurrying because I need to check out of the hotel in five minutes and meet my wife and her cousin for lunch."

I am sitting at a small table next to the bed in which, only hours before, the same brain that is now writing these words thought it was in Sicily, talking to people, some of whom looked vaguely like family members, friends, or colleagues and some of whom don't really exist. From one instant to the next in that dream I was incapable of remembering much of anything. This made it impossible to update the events of dream scene II in terms of the parameters of dream scene I. Hence my disorientation. And because I couldn't remember one set of dream events long enough to compare it with another, I couldn't assess my state accurately. And I couldn't stop the action by an act of volition so that I could access memory and critically analyze what was going on.

At this juncture it is clear that such enhanced features of dream cognition as the hallucinatory perceptual vividness, the motoric rush, the strong emotion, and the confabulatory synthesis all conspire with memory deficit to make reflective self-awareness and autocritical thought impossible. My poor little brain boat is not only unmoored but also buffeted by the waves of new data driven upon it by the high winds of activation. Before I have a chance to think, I am overwhelmed by new incongruities and discontinuities whose sensorimotor and emotional verisimilitude is so strong as to wash away any doubt I might begin to harbor about their reality.

What Is Subtracted from the Brain during REM Sleep?

Studies of learning and memory indicate that nerve cells keep a trace of stimuli if and only if they are exposed to certain chemical mediators quite different from those that represent the stimuli themselves. To emphasize this difference between the chemicals responsible for the evanescent neurotransmission of stimulus signals and those responsible for the more permanent storage of mnemonic records, we use the term *neuromodulators* for the latter.

Among the neuromodulators thought to be crucial to memory, norepinephrine and serotonin are conspicuously diminished during dream consciousness. We know this from animal experiments, in

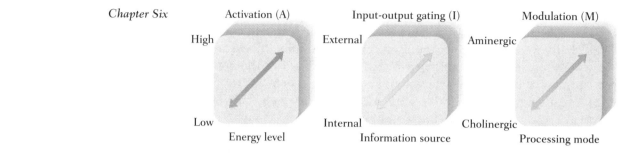

Three Neural Processes that Influence Conscious State *The brain-mind is controlled by three neural processes that influence consciousness. The first is activation (A), which determines the energy level of the system and the intensity of conscious experience. The second is input-output information gating (I), which determines the relative balance of external to internal information that is processed. The third is the ratio of aminergic to cholinergic neuromodulation (M), which determines memory capacity.*

which the neural cells that manufacture these chemicals fall silent during episodes of the kinds of brain activity that, in the sleep of humans, are associated with prolonged and vivid dreams. During waking these same cells are continuously active, whether or not they are excited by external stimuli. We also know from direct measurement that the overall concentration of neuromodulators in the brain falls as a result of this arrested cell firing during deep sleep.

Apparently the brain *becomes* conscious in proportion to its energy or activation level, but the *content* of consciousness changes as the sources of information shift from mainly external ones in waking to internal ones in dreaming. This is one important cause of the difference between dreaming and waking: external data are subtracted. Finally, the state of consciousness—whether it is self-reflective, thoughtful, and oriented—is a function of its ability to remember what has just happened to it. During sleeping and dreaming this mnemonic capacity is subtracted from the brain, but the mechanism is neurochemical demodulation, not information exclusion.

To better appreciate the radical differences between waking and REM sleep consciousness, and to illustrate how the subtraction paradigm plays itself out as the sleep cycle proceeds, we consider first the changes that occur at sleep onset, then go on to describe the brain-mind dynamics that ensue in NREM sleep, before returning, at the end of the chapter, to a reconsideration of dreaming. Along the way, we discuss the relative contributions of three factors to the continuously changing state of the brain-mind: activation (A), input-output information gating (I), and modulation (M).

Pinpointing Sleep Onset

As we all know only too well, the first objective signs of sleep onset are an inability to focus attention, a decline in sensitivity to external stimuli, and an inability to maintain the postures necessary to waking. This drowsiness results in what are politely known as lapses in consciousness. These lapses may result in our missing crucial cues (if we doze off while driving) or committing social gaffes (if we droop over our soup). Of course, it is impossible under these circumstances to produce appropriate motor output, so waking behavior is effectively abolished.

This grouping of signs immediately suggests two underlying mechanisms that can be intuited by anyone. One is a failure of simple brain energy, which we know firsthand as tiredness and fatigue. From our observations of animals that are drowsy, we have reason to believe that another deep component of falling asleep is a decrement in aminergic modulation, represented as factor M in our conscious state model.

Sleep Onset Dreams

Already, at sleep onset, we see the interaction of the brain's intrinsic activation level, A, and its input-output information gating bias, I. As activation falls, the sensory and motor gate thresholds rise, causing a further fall in activation, and so on. But a further complication arises immediately, because information arises not only in the outside world in the form of sensory stimuli, but also as signals arising within the brain itself. Certain neural circuits may remain sufficiently active to trigger pseudosensory stimuli, resulting in visual imagery, brief dreamlike experiences, and sometimes associated spontaneous twitching of the trunk and limb muscles. At any given activation level, then, a dynamic trade-off exists between external and internal information sources, and there is a corresponding oscillation between real and fictive behavior. This means that factor I must be expressed as the ratio of external to internal information inputs and of fictive to real motor outputs as well as the level of sensory and motor gate thresholds.

Unless we wake up, we are unlikely to recall these sometimes quite vivid sleep onset dreams. So memory is already impaired, perhaps simply as a result of the plummeting activation level but also probably because the waking state modulatory neurons in the brainstem have started to miss their beat. Subjects can learn to wake

Dozing in High Places *Sociopolitical prominence is no antidote to the power of sleep as these photos of Pope John Paul II (top) and former Japanese Prime Minister Hiyakawa (bottom) illustrate. In fact, high-powered snoozers may have a greater tendency to doze because of the combined effects of jet lag and sleep deprivation.*

139

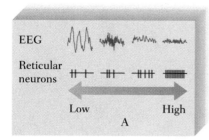

The Physiological Basis of Activation *Activation can be measured in two ways. One is via the frequency and amplitude of the EEG (in humans). The other is via the neuronal firing rate of the midbrain reticular formation (in animals).*

themselves up, however, and thus repeatedly reexperience sleep onset changes in their conscious states. This technique was used by such nineteenth-century French pioneer experimentalists as Alfred Maury and Leon Hervey de St. Denis, who sometimes recruited accomplices to help them track their subjective experience across the narrow but deep waking-sleep divide. As a reference point, external stimuli were delivered so that stimulus thresholds and information transformation could be documented.

Today, the accomplice may be a sleep laboratory technician who also records electrical signals from the brain, eyes, and muscles. Or it can be the simple, self-applicable Nightcap device, which feeds head and eyelid movement signals to a bedside computer and performs the awakenings automatically.

The results of our own study of 850 sleep onset experiences reveal that consciousness undergoes a stereotypical sequence of transformations at sleep onset. Each step in this sequence correlates with a step in the rapidly declining activation level of the brain.

In these studies, activation—factor A—is assessed as the inverse of EEG power because EEG power increases progressively as we fall asleep. At the physiological level, we know that waking depends upon the active suppression of the tendency of the thalamocortical circuits of the brain to go into their oscillatory mode. This oscillation is outwardly detectable as the characteristic spindle and slow-wave EEG patterns of sleep. The lower the intrinsic activation level, the more frequent the spindles, the higher the voltage of the slow waves, and the higher the power of the EEG.

Since the thalamus is the final internal gateway for external information entering the cortex, where it is analyzed and can be made conscious, it is immediately clear why external information fails to enter consciousness when the thalamocortical system is deactivated. The strength of its own oscillatory signals simply swamps those representing the outside world via the sensory pathways. So factor I declines, at first slowly, but then exponentially more rapidly until external stimulus access is ultimately obliterated. Along the way, enough internal information may invade a still sufficiently activated cortex to generate a sleep onset hallucination, or even an evanescent dream. These brief, fleeting sleep onset dreams have been called dreamlets, or microdreams.

Many neurobiologists assume that the thalamocortical system, in its fully activated state, is the very organ of waking consciousness. One of the reasons for accepting this idea is that dream consciousness also depends upon activation of the thalamocortical system. It is the brain mechanism that both states share. But in dreaming, the source and fate of the information that is processed and the chemistry of the activated system are completely different from waking. Indeed, it is these two physiological differences that enable us to understand the phenomenological contrasts between the two states.

But exactly how, you ask, is consciousness mediated by the thalamocortical system? If you insist on knowing the answer to this question very exactly, I will probably disappoint you. But if you will accept a rough explanation, my answer may not seem entirely useless. The thalamocortical system is, in a sense, the Cartesian theater of the mind. In its activated state, information is rapidly and efficiently processed by its circuits. That information can either be online data from the real world or data about the real world that are stored in the brain. In other words, the world, the self, and the body are re-represented in the network activation of the thalamocortical system.

Now, the thalamocortical system is *not* the Cartesian theater in the sense that there is a little person inside my head watching the images on a thalamocortical screen. Instead, my consciousness is the images (and thoughts, and feelings) that are represented in the activated neural networks. How and where does it all come together, you ask? The answer is nowhere and everywhere, simultaneously and always. My consciousness at any instant is simply the integrated product of the information represented in the activated thalamocortical networks at that instant. That includes my sense of self, my awareness of my body, and my awareness of the world, be it real or fictive.

More specifically, we can now define consciousness at any instant as the information that is then represented in the working memory circuitry of the dorsolateral prefrontal cortex (DLPFC). That information implicitly reflects my past in its representation of me as the agent of my motoric actions (volition) and includes my reflective sense of strategy for those actions (thought) and their motivational appropriateness (emotional context). Are all three components (volition, reflection, and emotion) simultaneously present—as a whole—or does working memory multiplex its inputs so rapidly as to create a semblance of wholeness? We don't know. And this question becomes important when we try to decide whether the so-called stream of consciousness experience is smooth or choppy, or both. For Marcel Proust, as for William James, the emphasis is upon continuity of flow. For James Joyce and modern scientific phenomenologists like

> *The brain is waking and with it the mind is returning. It is as if the Milky Way entered upon some cosmic dance. Swiftly the head-mass becomes an enchanted loom where millions of flashing shuttles weave a dissolving pattern, always a meaningful pattern though never an abiding one; a shifting harmony of subpatterns. Now . . . the waking body rouses. . . .*
>
> CHARLES SHERRINGTON, 1940

John Antrobus, the emphasis is upon discontinuity. My position is inclusive. Consciousness is both continuous (in the overall direction of its flow) and discontinuous (in its sampling of the myriad eddy currents of its multifarious inputs).

NREM Sleep

The disabling of the thalamocortical system proceeds apace once sleep has gained a firm hold on the brain. This tends to occur only at night because it is then that the overall levels of body energy and temperature fall precipitately. And it is then that a collusion between the brain and body occurs that is properly captured by the vernacular phrase "falling asleep." We say "I slept like a log" or "I slept like a stone" to convey the feeling that some almost gravitational pull is dragging us down.

Consciousness plummets as the neural activation level falls and the sensory gates clank shut. As the EEG recording becomes dominated more and more by high-voltage slow waves, consciousness becomes more and more obtunded. We move very close to the coma zone, are difficult to rouse, and when aroused, take many minutes to regain our waking conscious faculties. Reports of antecedent mental activity elicited following awakenings from deep sleep are rendered unreliable by the brain fog through which they must pass. The tape-recorded voices of subjects in this state are slowed and garbled. Dream reports, if any can be gleaned, are short, incoherent, and fragmentary, and despite their unreliability, convincingly denote marked diminution in all consciousness components.

Because sensory thresholds are raised, sensation is dulled in NREM sleep. Without sensation, external perception is impossible, and—after the initial sleep onset phase—the brain is insufficiently activated to produce even internal percepts. Attention and memory also fail as activation declines. These functions are further disabled by a progressive decline in the output of the neuromodulators norepinephrine and serotonin. Even if the deeply sleeping brain were truly capable of the low-level ruminations sometimes implied by experimental reports, it is unlikely that they would survive the inertia of awakening. It may even be that the tumult of the awakening process triggers the chaotic and fragmentary mentation that is reported. And even when deep sleepers are sufficiently aroused to be interviewed, they may still generate huge slow waves in their EEGs, indicating that they are in a semistuporous state quite different from either sleeping or waking. Indeed, they may even hallucinate, become

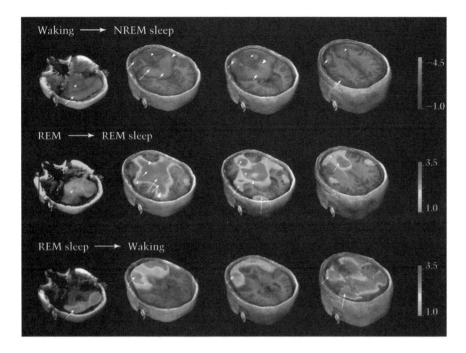

Waking ⟶ NREM sleep

REM ⟶ REM sleep

REM sleep ⟶ Waking

Consciousness and the Brain Blood flow decreases in most brain regions when the level consciousness declines as we fall asleep (wake-SWS) and increases again when we enter REM sleep and experience dream consciousness (SWS-REM). The differences between waking and dreaming may relate to the fact that the regional patterns are quite different (REM-wake) in those two highly activated states.

anxious, and confabulate as if they suffered from delirium. This is precisely what happens in the night terrors of children.

The marked decline in the level and richness of content of consciousness that is experienced by deeply sleeping humans is caused not only by the disablement of neuromodulation in the thalamocortical system, but also by a widespread decline in neuronal activity throughout the brain. We know this from several evidential sources. First, there is a 20 percent drop in overall cerebral oxygen consumption during deep sleep in humans. Second, there is an up to 50 percent decrease in the activity of individual neurons during deep sleep in animals. Third, and most important, there is a dramatic reduction in regional blood flow through the brain during deep NREM sleep in humans.

All three data sources reinforce each other in supporting the conclusion that the decline in consciousness during deep sleep is caused by a decline in neuronal activity. The brain regions that mediate this Dark Age of the mind can now be tied together in a specific theory as follows:

- Huge areas of the prefrontal cortex, which we suppose to be the seat of reflective awareness and goal-directed thought, become inactive during deep NREM sleep.

143

- Inactivation of the frontal cortex is associated with inactivation of the pontine brainstem, leading us to suppose that the decline in brainstem output may be a principal cause of the decline in cortical activation.
- Among the brainstem neuronal groups that decrease their output are the reticular formation, thought to provide energetic and specific informational inputs to the thalamocortical system, and the three neuromodulatory subsystems that supply the upper brain with the neurotransmitters acetylcholine, norepinephrine, and serotonin.

In deep sleep, then, the consciousness cup is, quite literally, half empty. Its electrochemical activation level, its sensory input level, and its neuromodulatory control are half gone. But consciousness itself is much more than half gone. How much more? Quantitative estimates are hard to come by when we want to measure exactly what it means to be "dead to the world," "completely gone," or just "out of it." One objective index is the word count of dream reports given by subjects who awaken spontaneously from deep sleep as compared with dreaming sleep. By this measure, the consciousness level, owing to the 50 percent reduction in reticulo-thalamocortical activation of the brain, is seven times lower. Now, a sevenfold decrease is 700 percent, which means that a 50 percent decrease in neuronal activity causes a sevenfold decrease in mental content. Thus the brain gains enormous control over its mind. A small decline in brain activation, stimulation, and modulation can cause surprisingly large declines in conscious capacity.

Systems characterized by such large gain ratios are usually nonlinear, meaning that the functional decline in conscious capacity may be exponentially related to brain function. Another possibility is that consciousness is a discontinuous process. At, or above, a certain threshold, its strength, focus, and content are the joint product of activation level, input-output gating, and neuromodulation. Below that threshold, nothing. In this view, deep NREM sleep is a physiological condition akin to coma. As we will see, NREM sleep borders on the coma domain in our conscious state model, and so may be expected to share its properties. But whether consciousness has a linear, nonlinear, or discontinuous relationship to brain activation, it is clear that it is a delicate, fragile, and highly tuned process that suffers greatly from even small defects in brain function. When we discuss dreaming next, and when we discuss pathology in Chapter 8, we will strongly emphasize this point.

The sevenfold increase in dream report length that differentiates NREM from REM sleep consciousness is achieved, as pointed out above, by a full recovery of the 50 percent decline in activation level alone. I say "alone" because the sensory input level remains low compared with waking. This means that the information source is exclusively internal during dreaming, an experimental inference that is firmly supported by our subjective experience: dreams are not only not caused by external stimuli, but represent them with difficulty—even if they are strong—and then, the external events are likely to cause awakening. Like the dreaming brain itself, dream consciousness is active, but almost entirely offline.

The shift in activation level (from low to high) and information source (from external to internal) that accompanies dreaming is engineered in a complex and ingenious way by the brainstem control system. The activation level resumes waking values because the reticular formation excites the thalamocortical circuits so that they are pushed up and out of the oscillatory mode of deep sleep. At the same time, the cholinergic modulatory influence of waking is also restored—and then some. The brainstem cholinergic neurons actually become hyperexcitable in REM sleep. They then fire in clusters and so come to constitute not only activation impulses but also pseudosensory stimuli to the posterior thalamocortical circuits that mediate vision and to the limbic areas that mediate emotion. Hence the intense visual imagery and intense emotion of dream consciousness. These mechanisms give a specific brain-based account of two of the four enhanced functions of dream consciousness. We see internal images more clearly and feel emotion more strongly because of the increase in brainstem cholinergic excitation.

Neuroscience can give a less explicit account of the fictive motion and the confabulation of dreams. All we know is that the motor pattern generators that control our gait in walking and running are in the immediate vicinity of the cholinergic neurons and that they can be experimentally turned on by acetylcholine. So we hypothesize that the fictive movement of dream consciousness is caused by cholinergic activation of brainstem motor pattern generators.

What about confabulation? Are the cortical language areas selectively activated in either a regional or chemical sense? We don't know. But we do know that the limbic and paralimbic cortices are selectively activated. These same regions, when electrically stimulated during surgery, give rise to bizarre and dreamlike conscious

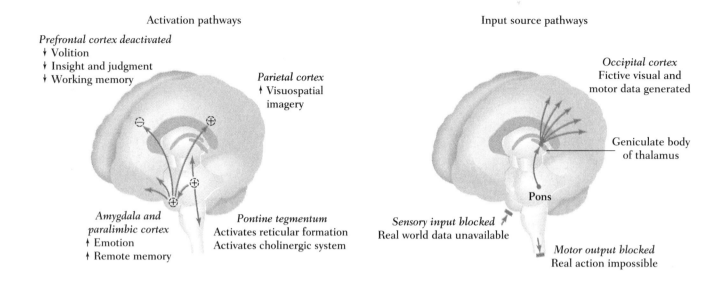

Activation pathways

Prefrontal cortex deactivated
↓ Volition
↓ Insight and judgment
↓ Working memory

Parietal cortex
↑ Visuospatial imagery

Amygdala and paralimbic cortex
↑ Emotion
↑ Remote memory

Pontine tegmentum
Activates reticular formation
Activates cholinergic system

Input source pathways

Occipital cortex
Fictive visual and motor data generated

Geniculate body of thalamus

Pons

Sensory input blocked
Real world data unavailable

Motor output blocked
Real action impossible

experiences. Perhaps we will achieve a better understanding of confabulation by further exploring the consequences of activating the cholinergic circuitry linking the brainstem to limbic areas of the forebrain.

Why does the brainstem cholinergic system become hyperexcitable? And how do we account for the deficits in such components of consciousness as orientation, self-reflective awareness, directed thought, and memory? To answer these questions we need to know what has been subtracted from the brain. The answer is norepinephrine and serotonin, the two pontine brainstem neuromodulators of the upper brain that have been strongly linked by other studies to attention, learning, and memory.

As a consequence of the near complete arrest of firing by the norepinephrine-containing neurons of the locus coeruleus in the lateral brainstem and the serotonin-containing neurons of the raphe nuclei in the brainstem midline, the brain becomes aminergically demodulated during dreaming. Returning to our nautical analogy, it loses its chemical bearings as well as its mnemonic mooring. Three major consequences of aminergic demodulation thus transform our conscious state:

- The energetic activation of dreaming itself arises owing to the removal of inhibitory restraint on the reticular formation neurons that excite the thalamocortical system and stop it from oscillating. Thus, the cortex is reactivated to a level that can support dream consciousness.

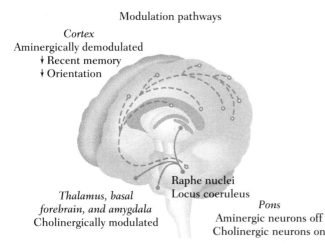

Modulation pathways

Cortex
Aminergically demodulated
↓ Recent memory
↓ Orientation

*Thalamus, basal
forebrain, and amygdala*
Cholinergically modulated

Raphe nuclei
Locus coeruleus

Pons
Aminergic neurons off
Cholinergic neurons on

Activation, Input, and Modulation during Dreaming
These diagrams combine the neurophysiology with recent imaging and brain lesion data to illustrate how the three factors A, I, and M affect various regions of the brain in REM sleep dreaming.

- The input-output operations of the brain shift in balance. At the same time that the cholinergic neurons that enhance motor pattern generators and autostimulate visual and emotion networks are activated, the reticular system that inhibits motor output is turned on. This means that internal stimuli causing virtual vision, emotion, movement, and confabulation are released, but real behavior is actively blocked. Dream consciousness is therefore a closed-loop state.
- The aminergic demodulation itself contains the key to understanding the deficit functions. While the visual, motor, emotion, and synthetic narrative circuits are all buzzing, none of them can keep an accurate record of their proceedings without norepinephrine and serotonin. Without a record, they—the neurons—and we—the dreamers—are up consciousness' creek without a paddle. We see wild animals, feel terror, and struggle forcibly to get away, but we are lost, confused, and cognitively helpless. As in the 1950s song about the consciousness-clouding power of love, we are, in our dreams, "bewitched, bothered, and bewildered."

Our aminergically demodulated brains are thus relatively disoriented, unreflective, thoughtless, and amnesiac in dream consciousness. In waking consciousness these functions are conversely intact, thanks to aminergic modulation. How does modulation work its wonders on the brain? By means of a mechanism called the second message system. The first message is the one conveyed from one neuron to another via synaptic transmission. The second message is conveyed

147

Cellular Messengers When an action potential depolarizes the presynaptic terminal, neurotransmitters pop out of the vesicles into the synaptic cleft and are bound to specific receptors in the postsynaptic membranes. This binding causes second messenger neurotransmitters to be released from the cell wall into the cytoplasm of the receiving cell. When they reach the cell nucleus, they influence the synthesis of gene products, such as the enzymes essential to neurotransmitter production and destruction.

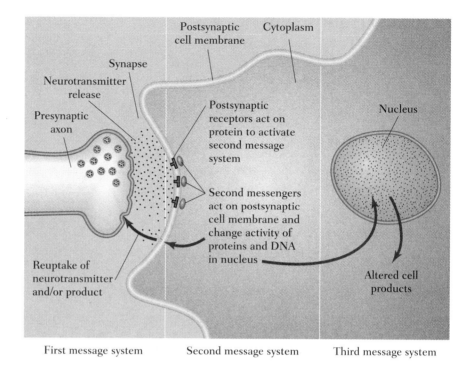

First message system   Second message system   Third message system

from the cell membrane of the recipient neuron to its nucleus by second messenger neurotransmitters—if, and only if, the first message is accompanied by parallel modulatory influence. And it is only the second message that is capable of influencing neuronal memory via changes in the DNA of the nucleus. Some scientists now refer to these genetic mechanisms as the third message system. In waking consciousness, both first and second message systems are working. In dreaming, the first, but not the second, message system is working. Second messengers have been subtracted as if the brain obeyed the adage, If you don't like the message, shoot the messenger!

This modulation/message concept will be important to remember as we construct our three-dimensional state space model of consciousness. It helps that M also stands for memory, without which consciousness would never be more than a dream—and an unremembered dream at that. That dream memory is so short is ascribable to the limited persistence of neuronal activation in working memory. If our conscious state were not changed to waking, restoring aminergic neuromodulation, we might not be able to recall any of our dreams, or even the difference between dream consciousness and any other kind.

How can we account for the exceptional differences between waking and dreaming consciousness? Not by differences in activation strength, because factor A is about the same in the two states. To a degree, by differences in factor I, because external reality cues are excluded and the brain-mind processes only internally generated data. But if that internal data were generated and processed as it is in waking, the difference between waking and dreaming would be no greater than that between the background fantasy scenarios and the foreground behavioral transactions that we have already discussed. And that confabulatory element is not enough to distinguish them. We would still have to account for the hallucinatory imagery, the orientational instability, the anxiety, and the memory loss.

Let's examine how and why changing the neurochemistry of the brain has so potent an effect. To help you think with me about these normal neurobiological details, recall what everyone already knows about abnormal brain-mind states: that enhancing or interfering with brain chemicals like norepinephrine (with cocaine or heroin, for example), serotonin (with LSD or selective serotonin reuptake inhibitors), or acetylcholine (perhaps with atropine or nerve gas) produces just those sorts of modulatory changes that distinguish dreaming from waking.

Factor M is the ratio of the concentration of the aminergic chemicals norepinephrine and serotonin to that of acetylcholine. Because as the former drop, the latter rises, factor M has a very wide range. In the transition from waking to deep NREM sleep, factor M does not decline greatly because both terms of the ratio fall together. Thus

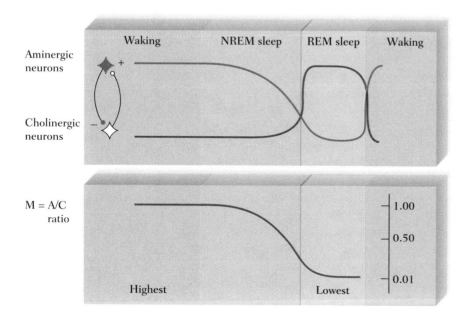

The Physiological Basis of Factor M
The concentration ratio of aminergic to cholinergic neuromodulatory chemicals is highest in waking, declines slightly in NREM sleep, and plummets to a very low level in REM sleep.

NREM sleep is demodulated—as it is deactivated—across the board. As a result, cognition is profoundly impoverished.

But as the value of the aminergic numerator of the ratio drops to near zero with the advent of REM sleep, the value of the cholinergic denominator goes sky high. The consequence is a huge change in the way that information is generated and processed by the dreaming brain-mind, even though the activation level is not much different.

This radical shift in neuromodulation during dreaming is another potential basis for the dreaming brain's capacity to generate and store data so as to simulate the instantaneous experience of waking without it being recognized as a simulacrum. This failure of recognition must be mostly due to the change in M because the brain has lost its ability to track its own state of consciousness. And this, after all, is the essence of self-reflective awareness, of insight, and of critical thought. In dreaming there is no longer a self-observing self because the "I," the first-person experience, has been reduced to a point moving fast-forward in time with no ability to look backward or ahead. This is perhaps the most dramatic subtraction of them all. Without memory—factor M—we are, quite literally, lost souls.

The Neuropsychology of Dream Consciousness

Two new sources of data have greatly enriched our understanding of the brain mediation of dream consciousness components. One is a study conducted by Mark Solms in England of stroke patients who retained the verbal ability to describe changes in their dream experience. The other is a series of PET imaging studies showing selective activation (and inactivation) of various human brain structures in REM sleep and in waking. These studies were performed by teams of scientists led by Pierre Maquet (in Belgium), Eric Nofzinger (in Pittsburgh), and Alan Braun (at the National Institutes of Health in Bethesda, Maryland).

Obviously, to be able to survive their disease and have good enough waking consciousness to describe their dreams, Solms's stroke patients could not have suffered extensive damage to their core brainstem and thalamocortical networks. Indeed, extensive damage to those structures causes coma or even brain death. If the visual centers of the upper brain were damaged, dreaming became less vivid. This means that dreaming does not absolutely depend upon

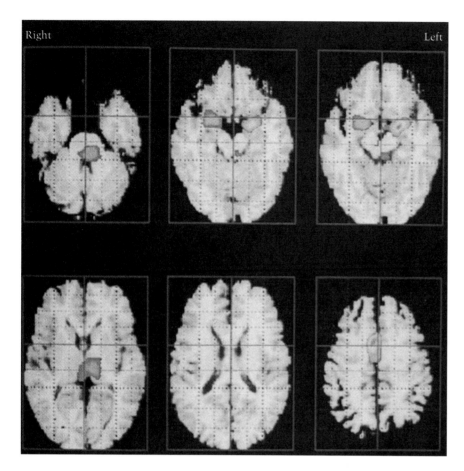

Right   Left

PET Images of the Human Brain in REM Sleep *These images of virtual "slices" through the human brain were created by computerized translation of radioisotope concentrations following injections of isotopes given during REM sleep. The colored regions are those showing greater isotope concentrations in REM sleep than in waking. Dreaming consciousness is distinct from waking consciousness as a function of these regional differences in brain activation pattern.*

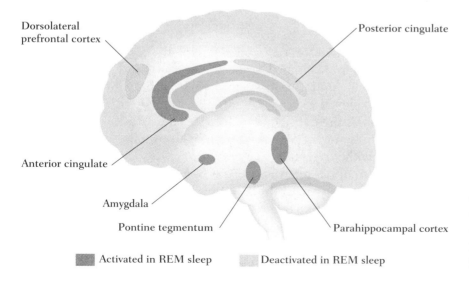

Dorsolateral prefrontal cortex

Posterior cingulate

Anterior cingulate

Amygdala

Pontine tegmentum

Parahippocampal cortex

☐ Activated in REM sleep   ☐ Deactivated in REM sleep

Schematic of the Human Brain in REM Sleep *The dreaming brain shows activation of the pons, the amygdala, the paralimbic cortex, the anterior cingulate, and the right parietal operculum. The dorsolateral prefrontal cortex is deactivated.*

151

visual imagery. But dream consciousness ceased altogether if the limbic, deep frontal, and parietal cortical areas were damaged.

Now, it is precisely the limbic area that has been found by PET imaging studies to be selectively activated during dream consciousness. This means that a crucial set of networks in the temporal lobe—the seat of emotion-tinged memory—must be turned on for dreaming to occur. Other cortical regions, such as the visual cortex, might then be activated secondarily and perhaps associatively by the limbic area. These findings support the hypothesis that emotion has a primary role in determining the content of dream consciousness.

Our group at Harvard reached this same conclusion by the psychological route: when we analyzed dream consciousness reports, we found a surprising consistency between the reported emotion and other aspects of the plot, such as persons, places, actions, and thoughts, none of which were internally consistent. In other words, dream bizarreness resides in discontinuity and incongruity among dream plot elements, but not between those plot elements and emotion. Dream consciousness is thus strongly emotion-driven, and the loss of dreaming following deep frontal lobe destruction may also be due to impairment of this emotion link between the brainstem generator and the upper brain.

In Solms's study, the one cortical region whose destruction caused a complete loss of dreaming was the parietal lobe between the visual centers of the occipital lobe and the language area of the temporal lobe. This finding has been attributed to impairment of the capacity to organize conscious experience spatially and/or to a disconnection among the visual, spatial, and narrative language centers, all of which would be expected to collaborate in dream plot scenario construction.

When these new findings are integrated with the cellular and molecular data from animal studies, the picture of dreaming that emerges is of an initial process occurring in the pontine brainstem that triggers activation, cholinergic autostimulation, and aminergic demodulation of the entire brain. Because the cholinergic autostimulation selectively engages the limbic lobe, a crucial second stage in the process is the triggering of emotions, especially fear, elation, and rage. These emotions then constitute organizers for the third stage, dream plot elaboration, a process that involves the visual imagery centers of the associative cortex, the spatial centers of the parietal lobe, and the narrative organizing centers of the temporal lobe. In this third stage, all superficial cortical areas respond relatively independently and faithfully to directions from the limbic region, but are only loosely faithful to one another. This model explains dream emotion, hallucination, and bizarreness quite well. The memory loss is due to the altered neuromodulation.

Why is directed thought impossible in dream consciousness? What is going on in the frontal lobes? PET studies reveal them to be among the few cortical areas that are *deactivated* during REM sleep as compared with waking. So just as there is a shift from aminergic to cholinergic modulation of the entire brain, there is a shift from frontal to limbic activation. The net result is both impaired memory and impaired reasoning capacity. And no doubt a deficit in either of these functions impairs the other even more. No wonder dream consciousness is so confused, so disoriented, so irrational, so unreflective, and so thoughtless.

Interestingly, the other cortical area reported to be deactivated in human REM sleep studies is the primary visual cortex. This result, which awaits confirmation, was not predicted by cellular-level animal studies, which indicated strong recruitment of primary visual cortex neurons. If substantiated, this finding will constitute suggestive evidence that visual image formation in dreaming consciousness does not proceed, as it does in waking, from decomposed features of the external visual world to an elaborated construction of the scene. Rather, it may bypass this assembly line and tap directly into more highly organized cortical image banks (such as those responsible for faces, movement complexes, and rooms) in an effort to synthesize a scenario consonant with whatever emotion is acting as film director at the moment.

Lucid Dreaming

While dreaming and waking consciousness are generally discrete and distinct states, instructive hybrid mixtures of waking and dream consciousness elements do exist. One is waking fantasy, in which any one of the dream consciousness components can become an internal stimulus source for dreamlike processing by the waking brain. Its reciprocal counterpart is lucid dreaming, in which such usually deficient components as self-reflective awareness and directed thought and action are restored to dream consciousness. This state has thus also been referred to as waking dreaming (not to be confused with dreaming waking, a psychotic condition in which fantasy proceeds to frank hallucinosis).

Lucid dreamers become aware that they are dreaming by "noticing" the bizarre features of their dream consciousness. This recognition may occur spontaneously, especially in young dreamers, and it can be cultivated, presumably by anyone who takes the time and effort to overcome the natural delusion that dreaming is waking. Training consists of a pre-sleep autosuggestion procedure that primes subjects to be observant by saying, simply, "When I dream tonight I will know it is not waking because of the bizarre features." Subjects use a bedside notebook as an instrumental aid and tell themselves, "When I dream tonight, not only will I notice it, but I will also wake myself up and record my experience." Success with this induction procedure can be followed up by subjects training themselves in a variety of diverting practices such as changing the dream plot from walking and running to flying, changing dream emotion from anxiety to elation, enjoying sex with imaginary partners, walking through walls, or even waking up and directing their consciousness back to the same dream or some other dream.

While we know that lucid dreaming occurs in REM sleep, we do not yet know what happens to the regional activation of the brain when subjects wake up while dreaming. We can only speculate as follows. Normal dream consciousness is caused by chemical and regional brain activation shifts. These shifts are, of course, only relative and quantitative, not absolute. And all brain systems are dynamic, not static, so statistical likelihood aside, any combination of variables is theoretically possible. For example, my self-reflective awareness is

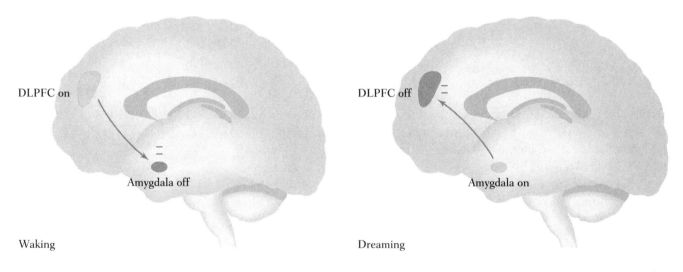

DLPFC on

Amygdala off

Waking

DLPFC off

Amygdala on

Dreaming

The Battle for the Mind *The war waged between the aminergic and cholinergic forces in the pons is mirrored—and amplified—in the forebrain skirmish between the emotion squadron of the limbic lobe and the reason battalion of the dorsolateral prefrontal cortex. In waking, the DLPFC usually wins. In dreaming, it's the amygdala's victory.*

not always dulled. Sometimes I say to myself, "This experience is too crazy to be real (that is, wakeful), so it must be a dream." This glimmer of critical thought might reflect my persistent activation of my frontal lobe networks, whose strength could conceivably grow and spread by recurrent self-activation, especially if those circuits were repeatedly primed by pre-sleep autosuggestion. In this process, I have loaded the networks—"trained them up," as the engineers would say—so that when they are later automatically activated in REM sleep, the self-awareness "program" has a better chance of emerging.

Such spreading activation in the frontal lobe could counteract the strength of signals from other parts of the brain—the cholinergic brainstem-amygdala highway, for example—and could even tip the chemical balance in favor of the aminergic system. Thus memory and attention would be enhanced, exactly as is reported by lucid dreamers.

But the balance among these systems is delicate, and if tipped too far, can result in inadvertent and unwanted awakening. Or, as is more usual, self-activation and self-awareness fade as consciousness is pulled back into the dream state by the natural power of the pontine system. Thus, REM sleep deprivation should make dreaming more intense—which it does—and make lucidity more difficult to achieve—though as far as I know, this has not been tried. Sleep saturation, on the other hand, should make lucid dreaming easier—and in my experience, sleeping in does have this effect.

The beauty of the current status of our science is that all these hypotheses can now be tested utilizing currently available functional scanning techniques. As conscious states are titrated and tilted in one direction or another, I predict the brain regions subserving each consciousness component will light up or go dark together with the mix of subjective experience. That deliberate conscious intervention can alter automatic brain processes is a fact of capital importance for our view of ourselves as agents capable of determining changes in the state of our brain-minds.

A Conceptual Model of Conscious States

When my father read in my book Sleep that people tend to have more shallow, fragmented sleep as they age, he told me that he had never slept more deeply, more uninterruptedly, nor dreamed so outrageously as he did at age 86. Now that I am 65 I am beginning to see what he meant. Last night I slept deliciously deeply. And dreamed—at least once—outrageously. Best of all, after a brief arousal at 5:30, I skimmed playfully over the surface of the sea of sleep for a full hour. Every now and then I submerged into brief, exciting dreamlets. These were either interrupted by blissful deeper dips into unconsciousness, or I would surface again and celebrate my psychedelic success. Even though I knew that I was playing with my consciousness, I had to admit that my consciousness was also playing with me.

Le Gentleman, Joan Miró, 1924 Most definitions of modernism emphasize its celebration of those twin essences of dream consciousness, discontinuity and incongruity. In the hands of the modern visual artists these aspects are often treated whimsically. Miró analyses his gentleman by taking his subject apart and putting him back together again with gently mocking humor. (Oeffentliche Kunstsammlung Basel, Kunstmuseum. Conation Marguerite Arp-Hagenback 1968. Photograph, Oeffentliche Kunstsammlung Basel, Martin Bühler. © 1998 Artist Rights Society (ARS), New York/ADAGP, Paris.)

*T*he twin essences of consciousness, awareness and awareness of awareness, are subject to changes in degree and in kind as underlying brain structures and functions undergo cyclic variation: in the evolution of species, in the development of each individual, and—most proximally—in the course of each day and night. This broad, analytic definition of consciousness further reveals that the intensity and type of awareness the organism experiences is determined by specific physical alterations in the multiple brain systems underlying each component of conscious experience.

To emphasize this state-dependent aspect of consciousness, we now begin to build a conceptual model to serve as a guide to classifying what we already know about normal, everyday states of consciousness. The organizational features of normal conscious state determination reveal how we will measure the model's three major determining factors: activation level (A), information source (I), and mode of processing (M). Each factor has a clear physiological and psychological meaning. The resulting three-dimensional state space model, AIM, allows us to visualize the instantaneous state of consciousness as a point in space whose position is a function of the values of these three factors. The AIM model captures both the dynamic, constantly changing nature of consciousness and its extraordinary qualitative range. The emergent unifying framework will aid our understanding of the abnormal states of consciousness discussed

Virtual Consciousness By visualizing conscious states within a three-dimensional space, it is possible to track the brain-mind as a continuous succession of points. The AIM model plots activation, input-output gating, and modulation as its x, y, and z axes. The cardinal states of waking, NREM sleep, and REM sleep occupy distinct regions of the state space, in which waking and REM are clearly differentiated.

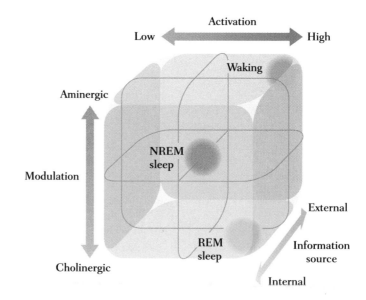

in the next chapter and organize the development of new research agendas for the experimental and therapeutic manipulation of conscious states.

Conscious State Variables

All complex systems, of which the brain may be the supreme example, exhibit states whose properties (for example, stability-instability, unity-multiplicity, uniformity-diversity) are functions of physical aspects of the system's components—its variables. And it is the identification and measurement of these system variables that allow scientists to characterize the states of systems well enough to understand them (at least partially) and even to control them (at least partially).

An example of a relatively simple system is the state of water as a function of its temperature variable. Whether water is a liquid, a solid (ice), or a gas (steam) depends upon how much external energy (heat) is available to its molecules. Knowing this, and ignoring all sorts of fascinating subtleties, such as the influence of external pressure and solutes, we can reliably manipulate the state of the system to heat or cool houses, make tea and coffee, and perform many other functions that enhance our survival and our enjoyment of life. By controlling our environment in this same way, we achieve the most desirable conditions for the natural variation of our conscious states. If this point is unclear, consider falling asleep while camping out in a cold, wet sleeping bag.

At first glance, a system such as the brain-mind appears to have so many working parts, each with so many relevant variables, as to defy analysis using the state concept. If a state is defined as the value of all the variables in a system, as it was in Eric Ashby's 1951 treatise, and the brain is composed of over 100 billion neurons, each firing at rates of from fewer than once to over 500 times per second, liberating well over 100 different chemicals at well over 10,000 contacts with other neurons, hadn't we better give up and go to church and pray? Pray, perhaps. It can't hurt. But give up? No. That won't help.

Why might the confidence of the intrepid scientist be rewarded by a study of brain-mind states? Because, again ignoring the even more numerous subtleties and distinctions of detail, the brain-mind behaves a bit like water in having the three quite different states of waking (akin to liquid water), deep sleep (akin to solid ice), and dreaming (akin to steam). One easily observable, easily measurable variable called activation (A), akin to temperature in the aqueous state example, denotes the energy of the system.

Another reason for confidence is the teleological inference that while the brain-mind is admittedly structurally complex, to function adaptively it must be equipped with a strong and reliable basic control system. To be effective, this control system must exhibit predictable properties that could constitute key variables in brain-mind state determination. Two predictable properties of the brain-mind control system are ubiquity and uniformity. If all the neurons of the brain are to act harmoniously, they must be subject to widespread (ubiquitous) and consistent (uniform) influences that bind them together in the same state at the same time. Otherwise the system would be subject to disastrous dissociations, like the left hand (brain) not knowing what the right hand (brain) is doing.

Michael Gazzaniga describes a split-brain patient with precisely this kind of problem. When a picture of a chicken claw is flashed to his left brain and a picture of a snow scene to his right brain, he correctly selects from an array of objects a shovel (with his left hand, guided by his right brain) and a chicken (with his right hand, guided by his left brain). But when asked to explain his choices, he announces that the chicken goes with the chicken claw and the shovel is used to clean out the chicken shed. The left brain is interpreting the action of the right brain in terms of its own data, not those that guided the right brain's choice of the shovel (to shovel snow).

Much attention has been focused on global binding recently due to the discovery that cortical neurons, when activated to those high levels normally associated with waking or dreaming consciousness, tend to fire in synchronous oscillation at a rate of 35–40 cycles per second. Synchrony, then, is one way of achieving uniformity of conscious state. But this uniformity resides only in the time domain. By what physical structures is such synchrony achieved? And how can temporal binding confer the distinctive aspects that define each conscious state?

These questions force us to ask how the properties of ubiquity and uniformity might be achieved. The a priori answer is a central control system that distributes its variable influences systematically to the entire brain. A posteriori, this control system is the brainstem, whose capacity to activate simultaneously, ubiquitously, and uniformly was described in the last chapter. Let us reexamine the brainstem's control capacities as a prelude to modeling consciousness.

- Central location. The brainstem is positioned just below the thalamocortical system of the upper brain and the cerebellum and just above the spinal cord. The activity level, input-output channels, and processing mode of all three of these structures need to be regulated if consciousness is to access the data it needs to make analytic decisions and command the behavior of the organism.
- The right connections. The specificity of brainstem connections to those other regions of the brain from which it receives and to which it sends information enables conscious state control. The idea that the reticular formation provides only nonspecific activation of the upper brain—of a kind that might underlie, for example, the 35–40 c/s synchronous oscillations of the cortex—has been supplemented by the discovery that reticular neurons have precise connections with vestibular and oculomotor centers and thus contribute to the control of three functions critical to conscious state: posture, head position, and eye position. All these control centers are packed close to one another in the brainstem.
- Decision-making power. The specificity of the brainstem chemical modulatory systems tells the brain-mind what to do with the information it selects. Should a given input be accorded real or only virtual status? Should it enter into critical analytic networks or be short-circuited to reflex circuitry and then, perhaps, canceled? Should the information be regarded as repetitious, hence irrelevant, or as constantly surprising and worthy of note, and if so, what note? Should it be remembered? It is by answering all these questions that the mode of consciousness is determined by the brain-mind.

The AIM model helps to simplify our thinking about how the brain-stem contributes to the organization of consciousness and allows us to visualize the continuous dynamism of conscious states. If the AIM model is represented on a computer screen and the computer is given sets of plausible values, then the dot representing conscious state can be seen to dance. The dance of the AIM data is something like the wave or stream of consciousness that William James and James Joyce alluded to in their metaphorical descriptions of consciousness. But unlike water, the path of the consciousness dot's trajectory doesn't always go downhill, and it doesn't always flow in one direction. Rather, the darting about of the dot allows the vicissitudes of consciousness, with all its sporadic forward and backward, up and down, in and out features, to be depicted more richly and more realistically.

Controller of Consciousness *The three laws of real estate evaluation apply with cogency to the brainstem: location, location, location. Evolution has exploited its strategic position between the forebrain and the spinal cord in two ways. First, brainstem neurons have extensive contacts with other parts of the brain. Second, their chemically differentiated modulatory elements are interconnected, guaranteeing a mode-switching function that allows the whole brain and consciousness to change state simultaneously.*

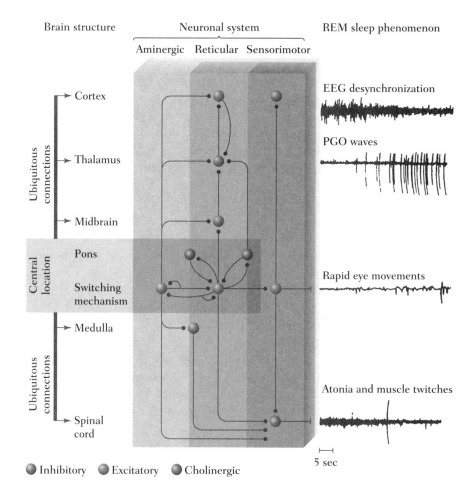

Factor A: Activation Level

How "hot" is the system? What is the "temperature" of the brain-mind state space? How many data is it capable of handling per unit of time? How many neuronal signals are generated per second? These questions pertain to the energy, and hence the throughput, of the brain-mind system. At the neurophysiological level, the answers are obtained by recording the activity of individual reticular neurons one at a time or by assessing the average level of activation in different brain regions using scanning techniques. The single-cell method gives more detail and allows us to tie the activation data to input-output and modulatory operations, but it is time-consuming, inefficient, and inapplicable to normal humans. The whole-brain methods are globally informative but cannot discriminate between neural excitation and inhibition and cannot yet resolve the activity of individual modulatory neurons.

Activation also has meaning at the global level of electroencephalograph recording. We say that the cortex is "activated" if the EEG shows a low-voltage, fast brain wave pattern. So activation can be measured as the power of the high-frequency component and/or as the inverse of the low-frequency power in the EEG spectrum. Activation is also the word used to denote "rate of information processing" by cognitive psychologists, whether they are experimentalists measuring reaction times in subjects performing behavioral tasks or theorists discussing the neural networks presumed to mediate the accuracy and speed of those behaviors. (Note that, owing to the changes in input-output gating discussed in the next section, reaction time is lengthy in REM sleep in spite of increases in all other aspects of activation.) Finally, in the case of experience sampling, the subjective reports issued by subjects in response to the query, "What was going on in your mind just before you were beeped, awakened, or otherwise asked to read out the contents of your consciousness?" are taken to be a measure of activation.

None of these measures is ideal, but because they all tend to run together, activation is an irresistible and indispensable dimension of any model of the brain-mind. Most models, in fact, stop with

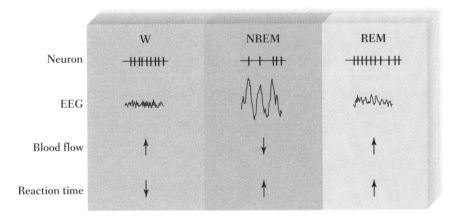

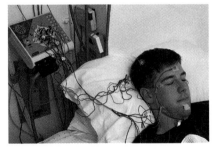

Measuring Activation *(Above) Activation can be estimated in several ways: by recording the activity of single cells (with mean firing rate as the measure), by EEG recording (with frequency and inverse voltage as the measure), by imaging of brain regions (with blood flow as the measure), and behaviorally (with reaction time as the measure). (Right) EEG activation as measured in the sleep laboratory.*

activation. But activation is clearly not adequate to model the complexity of consciousness. Indeed, far more glaringly than in the case of the states of water, the energy dimension is inadequate to explain conscious states.

While activation alone can explain deep sleep and coma, in which it is low or very low—as is temperature in the case of ice—it doesn't work to distinguish waking and dreaming, in which the activation levels are equally high, but we may see either steam (dreaming) or water (waking). In other words, activation level is an adequate measure if all we want to know is how likely consciousness is to be present and how intense it is. But we cannot imagine consciousness as existing without informational content, and we cannot understand consciousness without recognizing that its content differs in kind and in state according to its modulation—the mode of processing currently under way.

Factor I: Information Source

Consciousness can take accurate account of the outside world only if it has the opportunity to represent that world via the transduction of external signals into sensory stimuli, as it does in waking consciousness. But during dreaming, consciousness does a remarkably good job of simulating that world in the complete absence of external sensory stimuli. This observation has four important implications for a theory of consciousness:

1. Consciousness is a brain process with a significant degree of autonomy from the outside world and its signals.
2. Consciousness is designed to represent the world relatively faithfully even when external signals are not available.
3. Even during waking, consciousness may be actively projecting its own perceptual expectations upon the world.
4. One function of dreaming may be to activate the world model in consciousness so as to reinforce or alter its own assumptions.

How the brain-mind arranges these activities is revealed by the data that are used to measure factor I in our three-dimensional conscious state model. Factor I integrates three aspects of information selection: input-output gating, internal and external stimulus strength, and motor output gating.

Input-Output Gating

Information gating is organized by the brainstem. In our discussion of sleep onset consciousness, we saw how the sensory threshold naturally rises when the activation level declines and how the diminution in sensory impulse traffic leads to a further decline in activation level as the process of falling asleep becomes exponential and irresistible. But to achieve effective differentiation between dream consciousness and waking consciousness, the brain must actively exclude external information. This exclusion compensates for the return of thalamocortical activation to waking levels. Otherwise there would be only one state of activated consciousness: waking. Instead, there are two: waking and pseudo-waking—that is, dreaming.

The sensory gates that are closed so that dream consciousness can proceed in its illusory fashion are found at the very first stage of external signal processing. All primary sensory nerves transduce external-world data into neuronal discharge patterns. These patterns enter the brain, where they transfer the data to secondary sensory cells, which relay the data up the thalamocortical networks for conscious recognition and analysis. This first transfer point is the synapse between the primary sensory afferent (inbound) nerves and the secondary sensory relay nerves.

During REM sleep, the endings of the primary afferent nerves are rendered less excitable so that sensory signals have a more difficult time crossing the synapse. This presynaptic inhibition is actually caused by internal excitation from the same brainstem region that is the origin of the pseudosensory internal stimuli that help fool dream consciousness into believing it is awake.

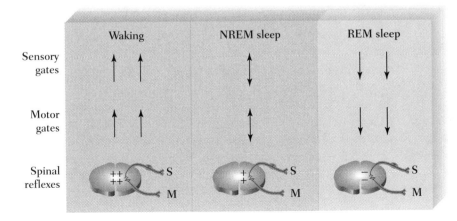

Gating Sensory Signals *Sensory (and motor) gates to the external world are kept open in waking, close partially in NREM sleep as the excitatory level declines, but are slammed shut by active inhibition in REM sleep.*

Neuronal inhibition is usually caused by increasing the membrane potential of neurons so that an increase in excitatory drive is required to lower them to the firing level. This process is called post-synaptic inhibition. Presynaptic inhibition is different in two ways: first, it affects primary neurons, and second, it excites primary nerve endings as if they were being activated by external stimuli. In this way their neurotransmitters are depleted, and when a signal representing the outside world does arrive, it is not admitted to the brain because there is not enough neurotransmitter left to ferry the message across the synaptic gap.

Thus, during REM sleep, an ongoing competition rages between the strength of internal representations of the world and the strength of external representations of the world. This competition, which we observe so clearly in research on dream consciousness, adds a fifth important implication to our list of consequences of the interaction between internal and external stimuli: there is a constantly shifting balance between expectation and observation, a balance that can be tipped in favor of internal stimuli even in waking.

If our internal-world model is biased—or prejudiced—as indeed it is in most of us—then the opportunity to project dangerously false expectations of the world into waking consciousness has a firm basis in the normal workings of the conscious state control system. The hallucinations and delusions of dreaming are harmless—and may even be helpful—but they must be kept in their place because they so devastate consciousness during waking.

However frightening it may be for me to dream of being accosted by a stranger, I can easily, upon awakening, reassure myself, "It was only a dream." But should I be performing a critical vigilance task such as monitoring a patient's physiological activity—as I often did late at night in hospitals—it is distinctly not helpful to me—or my patient—if I am suddenly startled by the entry of an ominously threatening character that I take to be real until he vanishes after having thoroughly distracted me.

Presynaptic inhibition can be measured in animals by placing electrodes in the spinal cord and peripheral nerves. The strength of response in each to stimulation of the other is then measured. Although the central response to peripheral stimulation during both deep sleep and REM sleep declines, there is no increase during deep sleep in the peripheral response to central stimulation, as is seen in REM sleep. It is this paradoxical increase in central excitability that is taken as evidence of presynaptic inhibition during dreaming. Significantly for our theory of consciousness, presynaptic inhibition is most intense during the clusters of eye movements that, in humans,

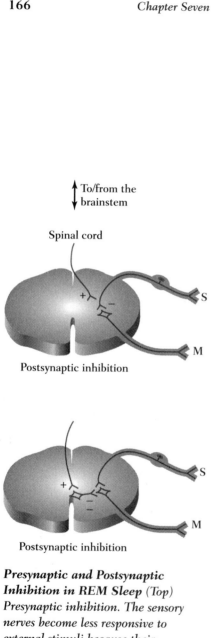

To/from the
brainstem

Spinal cord

Postsynaptic inhibition

Postsynaptic inhibition

***Presynaptic and Postsynaptic
Inhibition in REM Sleep*** *(Top)
Presynaptic inhibition. The sensory
nerves become less responsive to
external stimuli because their
neurotransmitters are depleted by
internal stimuli. (Bottom) Postsynaptic
inhibition. The motor nerves become
less responsive to both external and
internal stimuli because they are
actively inhibited.*

signal the most intense dream consciousness. This means that external signals are most strongly excluded when internal stimulation is at its peak.

In humans, it is very difficult for experimental stimuli to enter and label dream content. This fact has frustrated attempts to study dreaming using the behaviorist stimulus-response paradigm that works so well in other areas of psychophysiology. Visual, acoustic, olfactory, tactile, and even vestibular (rocking) stimuli have all been used during experimental attempts to label dream content, all without conspicuous success. While such stimuli are sometimes incorporated into dream plots, they are more commonly excluded. When their strength is further increased, they cause awakening.

When the threshold to arousal is taken as a measure of the strength of such external stimulus gating, it is clear once again that activation alone cannot account for the findings. While the threshold is highest in deep sleep, as activation theory would predict, it is as high in dreaming as it is in light sleep, which is counter to predictions based only on activation. The external signals do not reach the activated dreaming brain because factor I, in the form of presynaptic inhibition, excludes them.

Internal Stimulus Strength

Factor I would be measured most felicitously as the ratio of the strength of internal to that of external stimulus representation by the brain. While it is possible to record brain potentials evoked by external stimuli in humans, it has not yet proved possible to obtain a good measure of internal stimulus strength when people are dreaming. For that reason, we are forced to settle for an alternative that will seem, at first glance, as counterintuitive as presynaptic inhibition itself. This indirect measure is the frequency of REM sleep eye movement. It is taken as a measure of internal stimulus strength because, first, the eye movements must, of course, be driven by internal stimuli. Second, the internal stimuli that drive the eye movements are likely to be the source of the presynaptic inhibition that blocks sensory input. Third, and most critically, the stimuli that activate eye movements also activate internal signals, called PGO waves, to the upper visual brain.

PGO waves, which can be recorded in animals but not yet easily enough in humans to make their measurement practical on a routine basis, are informative regarding the way in which the brain-mind communicates with itself. Neuroscientists regard them as the best candidate yet discovered for the generators of the pseudosensory internal stimulation of the sensorimotor cortex and the emotional illusions of dreams, for they possess fully ten features of interest in terms of a theory of consciousness. PGO waves

- Originate in the pons (P), a brainstem center for conscious state control.
- Radiate into the thalamocortical system, the proposed essential core structure of conscious experience.
- Activate the geniculate body (G), which is the visual thalamus, and the occipital lobe (O), which is the visual cortex.
- Radiate into the limbic lobe, and specifically to the amygdala, the proposed mediator of dream emotions and especially of anxiety.
- Are difficult to evoke in waking consciousness, although strong, novel external stimuli trigger them, together with a startle reaction associated with subjective surprise, fear, and the interruption of ongoing thought processes.
- Appear spontaneously during dream consciousness and are frequent in that state, indicating a marked, state-specific change in their mechanisms of activation.
- Arise in REM sleep via a mechanism causally related to factor M, summarized here as aminergic undermodulation with cholinergic overmodulation.
- Appear to convey information about the direction of eye movement to the visual brain.
- Simultaneously alert the brain-mind to the emotional salience

The PGO System An internal signaling system links the eye movement control network of the brainstem to the visual centers in the upper brain so that the perceptual apparatus can pan continuously to take account of changes in eye position. When the eyes move to the left, the PGO waves are of larger amplitude in the left visual thalamus and cortex, and vice versa.

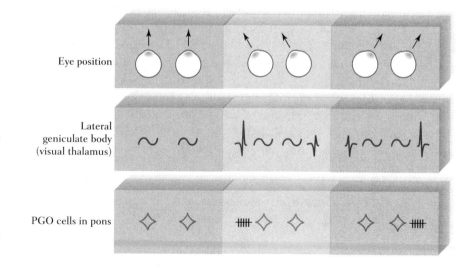

Eye position

Lateral geniculate body (visual thalamus)

PGO cells in pons

of stimuli (whether external or internal) and establish an instantaneous priority for their processing.

• Assume a presumptive priority that precludes both ongoing sensorimotor, emotional, and cognitive activity in the upper brain and the processing of new data from the periphery until their own significance has been evaluated by the brain-mind.

The implications of such an internal stimulus system for a theory of consciousness are obvious. When PGO waves are evoked in waking, they demand that consciousness drop whatever information processing it is engaged in. This is exactly our experience when an unexpected stimulus like an explosion or a scream suddenly demands our full attention. Survival is the big prize, and the PGO system is its gold ring. PGO waves prepare us for fight or flight should these prove necessary. The startle reactions provoked in us by real or imaginary intruders are mediated by PGO-like signals.

Wired for Survival *(Above) Just like this cat, an unexpected external stimulus causes us to freeze and rapidly shift our gaze in its direction as we prepare ourselves for fight or flight. The PGO system mediates these reactions to external threats during waking. During REM sleep, the system is taken over (or parasitized) by internally generated startle responses. This may factor into the orientational instability and anxiety of dream consciousness. (Right) The participant in this study is being tested to measure learned fear in humans.*

Our subjective experience in dream consciousness confirms this model. Our attention is constantly seized by unanticipated percepts. Waves of strong emotion—notably fear and anger—urge us to run away or do battle with imaginary predators. Flight or fight is the rule in dreaming consciousness, and it goes on and on, night after night, with all too rare respites in the glorious lull of fictive elation.

While we cannot yet easily record these spontaneous, internally evoked potentials in humans, further advances in computerized EEG and brain imaging techniques such as fast magnetic resonance imaging (fMRI) will almost certainly soon make the recording of PGO waves possible. Meanwhile, we must make do with the indirect rapid eye movement measure. It is a good measure, however, in part because it is so deeply linked to PGO wave generation.

Motor Output Gating and Conscious Experience

Powerful mechanisms of motor output control render conscious experience consequential (and hence real) in waking, but inconsequential (and hence delusional) in dreaming. Fortunately for our theory of consciousness, this state-dependent output gating is measurable in humans simply by calculating the probability that a given sensory stimulus (a physician's rubber hammer tapping your patellar tendon, for instance) will elicit a reflex response (the brisk knee-jerk response that declares you normal). In experiments with sleeping subjects, electrical stimulation of the skin nerves of the lower leg is substituted for the rubber hammer, and electrical recording of calf muscle activity is substituted for observing leg twitches, but the results are interchangeable: the so-called "H-reflex," along with the knee jerk, is abolished during REM sleep dream consciousness.

This inhibition of motor output obliterates not only any possibility of an upright posture (our muscles all fall flaccid in dreaming sleep) but also greatly reduces any possibility of moving our body parts because our skeletal muscles are as effectively paralyzed as our sensory nerves are anesthetized. This motor output blockade is caused by classic postsynaptic inhibition. Spinal motor cell membrane potentials are raised to levels that cannot be overcome by the excitatory signals calling for walking, running, fighting, or fleeing that the dreaming brain emits. The inhibitory signals arise in the brainstem control center, where the circuitry that issues them is well delineated. Even the chemical molecule that cranks up the membrane potential of the spinal motor cells is known. It is glycine, one of the basic and essential amino acids.

We know all these details because it is possible to measure the membrane potential of individual motor neurons in the spinal cords of cats by inserting microscopic pipettes while the animals sleep naturally. Experimenters have observed that as the brain self-activates and begins to generate PGO waves and rapid eye movements, the membrane potential of the impaled cell gradually increases, making it immune to the excitatory motor commands that would normally result in the movements of guided behavior during waking. By combining this experimental technique with pharmacology, the chemistry of REM sleep inhibition has been doped out.

Are we humans conscious of our motor paralysis in dreaming sleep? Mostly, we are not. We are fooled into thinking that we are actually moving through dream space even though, because of the attendant paralysis, we are immobile. It is only when we are so frightened by a dream threat that we try vigorously to escape or to combat it that we may become conscious of our immobility. We try to run, but our legs are heavy or rubbery or stuck as if in quicksand. This strong voluntary effort to move may overcome the inhibition, breaking the spell of the dream by shifting the brain-mind to its waking state. Under such conditions, dream recall may be quite good.

How is fictive movement created by the dreaming brain? How is dream consciousness so easily fooled into believing that we are moving? The answers are important because they describe mechanisms that must also operate during waking consciousness in concert with the real movements we can then make. Surprisingly enough, every motor command that is issued, in any state of consciousness, not only is sent to motor output neurons but also is copied to the sensory system. This efferent copying process is analogous to a nation's government deciding to declare war and simultaneously informing its citizens that it is going to do so.

In waking the motor act is effected. In dreaming it is not. But in both states the upper brain receives internally generated information about the intention to do so. From this information, and in the absence of any feedback to the contrary, dream consciousness creates the completely convincing illusion of motion. One implication of this mechanism is that many neurons in the upper brain are involved in computing the expected consequences of movement, whether or not the movement actually occurs. Put another way, parts of the brain that are properly considered "sensory" not only provide data relevant to the intention to move but also receive new sensory data describing the aftereffects of that real or fictive movement.

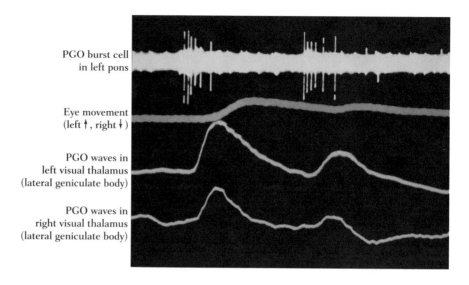

Internal Copies of Motor Command Signals Prior to every leftward REM sleep eye movement (blue), neurons in the left pons fire a cluster of action potentials (green). The left thalamus responds consistently with a larger PGO wave than the right thalamus (upper and lower orange traces).

In this way, and only in this way, can conscious experience maintain a continuous and stable image of the body in the world. As I move my head and my eyes from this page to scan the busy coast of Calabria across the Straits of Messina, every detail of my movement is seamlessly and unconsciously integrated. My consciousness is able to continue the elaboration of the concept I am explaining and take in the idyllic scene at the same time. In other words, movement is both the occasional consequence of conscious deliberation and its constant confidant and informant.

A most practical consequence follows: the beneficial effect on performance of running through a complex behavioral routine, such as a difficult dive, a tumbling act, or a stage performance, by consciously preplaying the moves involved. The commonsense interpretation of this strategy trivializes its astonishing explanation by calling it "studying," as if the plasticity were only conceptual. In fact, it is sensorimotor. Visualization and fictive rehearsal may not substitute for real practice, but they do appear to enhance actual performance.

Eye Movement as a Measure of Internal Stimulus Strength

Of all the body parts that move, none is more continuously active than the eyes. As the collector of visual information, the eyes deliver more information, by far, to consciousness than any other sense organ. The eyes move, often imperceptibly, at rates of up to 20 times per second. Depending upon our distance from a target, even small eye movements have huge effects upon the location of the target's image on the retina.

Suppose, for example, that I hear the doorbell ring as I write at a table to the right of the door. My immediate unconscious response is to swing my eyes about 60 degrees to the left. As this happens the image of the door moves to the center of my vision and is perceived immediately, without any blurring during the movement and without any afterimage of the movement, even though the images from about one-sixth of the room and its contents have been forcibly dragged across my retina.

Visual data are thus folded into consciousness without the discontinuity and jitters that would ensue if the consequences of eye movement were not anticipated by the visual perceptual system. The mind boggles at this monumental computational task, which no computer's artificial intelligence has yet even faintly matched. The evidence indicates that for each and every eye movement that is executed, eye movement command centers in the brainstem send the thalamocortical visual system excitatory signals that help the brain update its image of the world. This happens so rapidly that we are not consciously aware of either the interruption or the blurring of the image that would be the inevitable consequence of eye movement were it not for this correction imposed by the brain upon itself.

While the PGO waves that reflect eye movement cannot easily be measured in humans, eye movements themselves can be detected automatically. The classic technique uses an electroencephalograph to amplify the voltage differences that are generated when the two retinas move together toward or away from a pair of electrodes, one beside each eye. Depending on whether the coupling to the machine is direct or indirect, each eye movement can be quantified in magnitude or simply counted. This method is accurate but expensive, and too cumbersome to be useful in naturalistic studies of conscious experience.

An alternative approach is to measure the movement of the eyelid, the body part that, more than any other, controls the access of external visual data to the brain and to consciousness. The eyelid is a famously objective judge of subjective experience, as anyone who has ever addressed an amphitheater full of sleep-deprived students well knows. But it is not widely appreciated how exquisitely the muscle tension in the eyelid tracks vigilance, and how well correlated with eye movements are twitches of the eyelid muscles. These sensitive eyelid measures can be easily accessed, as they are in the aforementioned Nightcap device, by attaching a Band-Aid—like piece of piezoelectric film to the eyelid and connecting the film to a recording device via a bandanna or headband, which also contains an accelerometer sensitive to head movement.

The Nightcap can reliably distinguish the behavioral and brain level signs of the three cardinal conscious states: waking, sleeping, and dreaming. It is a powerful tool for constructing our model of conscious states for two related reasons. First, the presence of eye movement predicts that a subject is either waking or dreaming, while its absence denotes sleep. The presence of head movement together with eye movement predicts waking, while the absence of head movement with eye movement present predicts dreaming. Using the Nightcap, these predictions have been found to be about 87 percent accurate, an acceptably high correspondence given its hundred-fold increase in efficiency over more elaborate and expensive methods. Second, eyelid movement counts can be used to assess both the vigilance level of waking consciousness and the intensity of internal sensory stimulation during dream consciousness. Both values are indispensable to our three-dimensional state space model.

> *The content of visual awareness is the result of the brain's attempt to make sense of the information coming into the eyes.*   FRANCIS CRICK, 1994

Factor M: Modulation

Knowing the degree to which the brain is activated predicts the intensity of consciousness experienced by subjects. Knowing the frequency of eyelid and head movement tells us whether the provenance of information is external or internal and estimates the amount of information that is being processed. But we still need to know the neurochemical mode in which the information is being processed. Recall that the cognitive essence of modulation is memory. Is the information that is processed being stored or not? Modulation appears to provide the answer: When serotonin and norepinephrine are available, it is yes; when they are not, it is no.

Even in animal subjects, the accurate assessment of processing mode is difficult. The experimental recording of modulatory neurons in the brainstem is an extremely demanding, expensive, and inefficient task. The only alternative, collecting brain fluids and measuring the neuromodulators using chemical means, is even more so. In the past quarter century, the number of aminergic and cholinergic neurons that have been recorded barely reaches 1000, while the number of direct chemical studies stands at fewer than 10. No wonder cogni tive neuroscientists chose to commemorate one of their recent summer workshops with T-shirts proclaiming, "So many neurons, so little time"!

The neurons that control the modulation of consciousness are difficult to access not only because of their position, deep in the brainstem, but also because they are small, sparse, and interspersed with other types of neurons. That's the bad news.

The good news is that, once encountered, these neurons are easily recognized by their characteristic firing patterns and by the dramatic change in these patterns with change of conscious state. The norepinephrine-secreting cells of the locus coeruleus, the serotonin-secreting cells of the raphe nuclei, and the acetylcholine-containing cells of the dorsolateral tegmental nucleus all discharge with metronome-like regularity in attentive waking, indicating that constant aminergic and cholinergic modulation is the reliable and constant mode of waking consciousness. As soon as this modulatory influence subsides, perception, attention, and memory decline. In this sense, factor M tracks activation—factor A—and external information input—factor I—quite well. When all three factors decline together, we experience the progressive obliteration of consciousness that is greatest in deep NREM sleep.

As deep sleep gives way to dreaming sleep, however, the M function diverges widely from the A function as the cholinergic neurons are reactivated and the two aminergic populations shut off completely. This is why we say that dream consciousness is aminergically

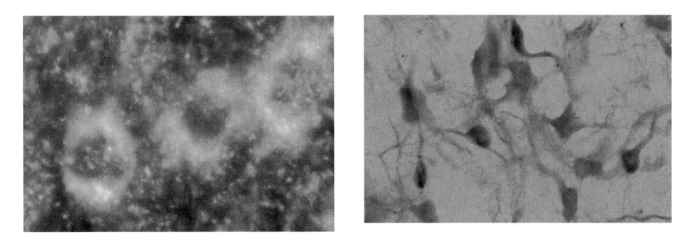

Modulators of Consciousness *Aminergic neurons in the locus coeruleus (left) and cholinergic neurons in the peduncopontine nucleus (right) stained with dyes specifically sensitive to their particular chemistry.*

demodulated and cholinergically hypermodulated. The best way to capture this divergence is by expressing factor M as the ratio of aminergic (*a*) to cholinergic (*c*) modulation. Waking consciousness profits from high levels of both *a* and *c,* deep sleep enjoys only about half of the waking levels of each, and dream consciousness has between a tenth and a hundredth the waking power of *a* but a full complement of *c.* This means that the activated conscious state of dreaming is as different from waking as it could possibly be with respect to the M function—and of course, it is also processing only internal information.

Two external links to this complex set of deep chemical changes can be utilized in constructing our model of consciousness. The first link is the extent of muscle inhibition, which tends to increase as *a* decreases. The second is the intensity of eye movement, which tends to increase as *c* increases. These correlations are strong enough to suggest a causal link and allow us to use the increase in muscle tone as a proxy for *a* and rapid eye movement as a proxy for *c* in our model.

The AIM Model

Having defined the three dimensions of the conscious state control system, we can now lay them out and create our conscious state space model. This model will help us to visualize the state of consciousness as it fluctuates over the course of a night or day.

The advantages of a three-dimensional model over the traditional two-dimensional graphic formula are formal as well as substantive. At the substantive level, the two-dimensional formula plots conscious

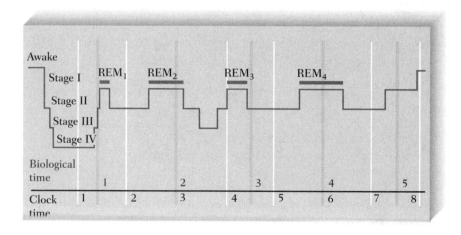

Traditional Two-Dimensional Conscious State Graph *Using the data from a polygraph, the states of waking, NREM sleep, and REM sleep are represented as levels of a staircase-like graph, which nicely discriminates NREM sleep but less clearly differentiates REM sleep and waking states.*

state only as rising and falling in level of intensity. It thus focuses on activation only. While it hints at an internal stimulation factor by showing eye movements as a solid bar above the activated EEG in REM sleep, the two-dimensional model does not address that concept directly, and it does not take eye movement intensity into account. So it cannot come to grips with the obvious importance of information source. And it doesn't even hint at the neuromodulation factor, which, indeed, is only now beginning to be given credence by most sleep psychophysiologists.

At the formal level, a three-dimensional conscious state space model allows consciousness to be described more accurately by adding these two relevant dimensions, I and M, to activation, A. It also provides the description of conscious states with the dynamic mobility it needs to be realistic. Consciousness not only fluctuates in intensity but also moves into and out of contact with the outside world as its own ideational and emotional causes are advanced and

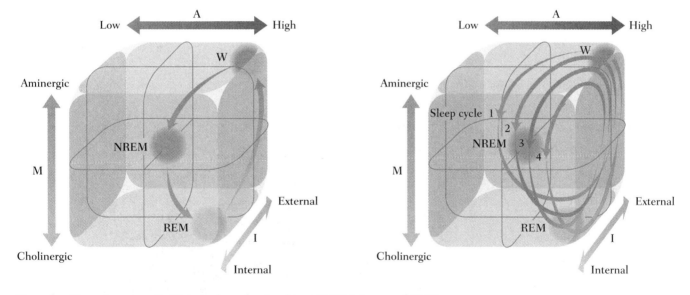

Everyday Consciousness (Left) A single cycle of waking, NREM sleep, and REM sleep. Unlike two-dimensional models, the three-dimensional AIM model clearly differentiates the three cardinal states of consciousness. (Right) Successive cycles of a single night of sleep. Each cycle penetrates less deeply into the NREM domain and more deeply into the REM domain of conscious state space. Notice that the sleep cycles represented in AIM space are ellipses, not circles, because subjects usually spend a longer time in NREM sleep than in REM sleep. Furthermore, the ellipses are asymmetrical because it takes longer to get into REM sleep than it does to get out of it.

withdrawn and as its content is accorded importance (and saved) or discounted (and discarded). In a three-dimensional model, the locus of A, I, and M is a point that can dart about in the state space—forward and back, up and down, in and out—just as our minds do, especially in the waking state. This is surely better than representing waking as a single, straight line!

Not only is the point in space representing consciousness dynamic, but its dynamics can be recursive, both in the short term, as when we go in and out of light sleep while dozing on the terrace after lunch, or in the long term, as when we cycle automatically through NREM and REM sleep at night. Instead of being seen as up and down staircases that our brain-minds solemnly trod, these recursions are modeled as elliptical cycles slicing sleekly through the conscious state space.

The assignment of each function to a dimension of the state space is arbitrary. I have placed factor A along the horizontal axis, factor I along the base of the side wall, and factor M vertically. As a consequence, the energy level of the system is expressed as its width (factor A), its informational orientation as its depth (factor I), and its processing mode as its height (factor M). The fourth dimension of the AIM model is time. If AIM is calculated at regular intervals, the

Altered States of Consciousness
People who wish to induce altered states of consciousness may utilize sleep deprivation (as in some initiation rituals) or drugs (such as peyote or LSD) that interact with the M system so as to enhance the probability of REM phenomena occurring during waking. The intense visual imagery induced by eating peyote cactus buds is captured in this yarn painting. The geometric stereotyping that is common in drug-induced states is not common in REM sleep dreams but may occur at sleep onset.

distance in AIM space between any two successive points is a function of the velocity of state change.

Of course, the "walls" are also arbitrary and should not be taken as setting upper limits on these dimensions, all of which could be pushed beyond physiological limits by drugs or electrical stimulation. As far as we know, however, none of the dimensions can dip below zero. This says nothing more or less than that the AIM model is not equipped to deal with the possibility that consciousness persists after death. It also says that the state space cannot really be a cube. It could have a curved or even a wrinkled surface, and much of conscious life could transpire in a very limited part of the space, whatever its shape. In fact, most of conscious life does appear to transpire in a relatively limited subsection of the state space. Could it be that people seek the dangers of addictive behavior precisely to escape such narrow bounds?

AIM *in Daily Life*

With the conscious state space laid out in this arbitrary way, we see that the AIM parameters of waking place it in the upper rear right-hand corner of the space: upper because modulation (M) is balanced, rear because external information (I) has maximal access to the system and motor output is fully allowed, and right because the activation level (A) of the system is high.

NREM sleep falls in the center front of the space because all three AIM dimensions diminish. As the energy level of the system falls, the A value moves to the left. As the system begins to exclude external inputs and outputs, the I value moves toward the front of the space. As the output of aminergic neuromodulators fall, the M function falls halfway down its axis. Light sleep occurs at the boundary with waking, and a decline in any of the functions will move consciousness in that direction. As sleep deepens, consciousness moves farther and farther toward the left lower front corner of the space. This is waking's opposite pole, and could be defined as death. A zero value of A is, in fact, the legal definition of brain death. Perhaps this is why sleep has been likened to death by poets across the ages.

> *We are such stuff as dreams are made on.*
> *And our little life is rounded by a sleep.*
>   William Shakespeare

Rounded indeed. As if in a state space.

> *Do not go gentle into that good night.*
> *Rage, rage against the dying of the light.*
> Dylan Thomas

Instead of dying, consciousness veers away from its rendezvous with death and turns instead toward dreamland—the REM domain—in the lower right front corner. Why right? Because, as in waking, the activation level (A) is high. But most decidedly unlike waking, factor I goes to its nadir as internal information has exclusive play and motor output becomes virtual, not real. And most decidedly unlike waking, the bottom falls out of the aminergic modulatory function, causing M to reach its own low point, whose depth is amplified by the return of cholinergic modulation to waking levels and beyond.

Now let us imagine the AIM model as it would appear on a computer screen, playing back the conscious states of a normal day recorded, if it were possible, on a second-by-second basis as a point of light. Beginning with a wake-up signal in the morning, the light dot will be driven up into the waking domain, where it will spend its day moving up and down, left and right, forward and back, as a joint function of behavior and time. Within an hour, and especially if we drive or take public transportation to work, it will be driven into the hypervigilance subdomain of waking as activation, aminergic modulation, external stimulation, and motor output all become intense. Hypervigilance is thus to the waking domain as the waking domain is to the whole state space, lying in the very upper, right, rear corner.

These are the AIM conditions that American society has chosen as optimal for the performance of what is called work. In this state, our attention is strong enough to keep consciousness focused on external stimuli and to process them using the linear logic of most real-world discourse. Whether our work task is cerebral or somatic, repetitive or creative, we need activation, input-output control, and balanced modulation to do it well. Should we become fatigued, or should internal feelings or thoughts unrelated to work invade our brain-minds, the AIM meter shows it by moving downward, to the left, and forward in the waking subdomain. Visions of *A Clockwork Orange* spring ominously to mind as I contemplate Big Brother watching my brain-mind wander off the beaten track of practicality into the tempting groves of fantasy.

But I am reassured by realizing that my AIM meter is itself only a figment of my imagination, and that I can usually catch myself daydreaming or napping. Then my self-reflection monitor acts to drive

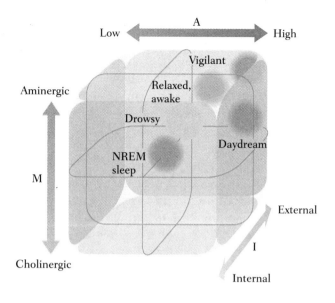

A — Low ↔ High

Aminergic

M

Cholinergic

Vigilant

Relaxed, awake

Drowsy

Daydream

NREM sleep

External

I

Internal

The Waking Subdomain of AIM Space The AIM model accommodates the rich variety of substates of waking in the quite different loci of drowsiness, hypervigilance, and daydreaming compared with relaxed waking.

AIM back to the levels optimal for task performance. This is one of many instances in which the awareness of awareness (or awareness of unawareness) acts in a causal way to alter conscious state. For this to occur, one part of the system must be in one waking subdomain while other parts are in another. This sort of dissociation seems to violate the rule of personal unity expressed in the binding notion, but in fact, such dissociations are so common as to demand recognition and explanation. In the following chapter we will see that these commonplace and entirely normal dissociations form only the tip of the psychopathological iceberg.

We also use external props to help hold AIM where we (and society) want it. "Breaks" divide each half-day of work into two or three 90-minute segments, and lunch does the rest. During these lulls we allow the strongly suppressed internal stimuli out of their box as we converse with colleagues about weekends past and present, rehash the news, anticipate weather changes, and—best of all—exchange juicy gossip. At the same time we pump up the M function with caffeine or by bolstering the output of our own natural stimulants, and ready ourselves for another work cycle.

Most people can hold themselves in the optimal zone of the waking consciousness domain for 6 to 8 hours. Some can even go on for 12 hours, but when we push ourselves beyond whatever our normal limit is, we feel anxiety, stress, and fatigue as the system begins its own natural peregrination toward the center of the state space. Physical exercise, taken as formal sports or walking or even gardening, helps to counter this trend. By allowing motor output to increase, we decrease the demands on attention and thinking while at the same time driving the aminergic system hard. In this case AIM may come forward in conscious state space, but it does not sink, as it later will in sleep.

After 6 to 8 hours of alert, task-oriented waking, we are ready to "kick back," to enjoy leisure activities such as hobbies, family life, social activities, reading, watching TV, or going to the movies. We can even manage to pay attention to and absorb the information of family life if it is not too demanding or demeaning. We hope that interaction with our spouses and children will trigger strong positive emotions and not the fear or anger that inflame, rather than mellow, our conscious states. For many Americans, however, caretaking constitutes a second career, running in parallel and in series with an out-of-home work life. The burden of such dual careers lies heavy, creating both anxiety and stress by day and sleep deprivation by night. Instead of loping through long, lazy orbits that descend and linger in the sleep domain, we are "all wound up" in tight, constricted cycles reluctant ever to leave the workspace of waking.

When we do manage to step off the treadmill, we are pulled downward to the edge of sleep. We may know we have passed the edge when we realize, for example, that we have been reading for three pages and can't remember a word. Here is another dissociation. The eyes are open as they scan the book's pages, but the information doesn't really get through to the brain-mind because the thalamocortical system has deactivated and descended toward its threshold for spontaneous oscillation. Noticing this, we wisely transport our bodies to the bedroom, lie down, and turn out the lights.

This conscious voluntary act massively reduces both external input and motor output so that the AIM system is free to do its own thing. And unless we have a head full of worry, it does. With the sudden drop in external input-output traffic, the A and I functions plummet and consciousness starts its nightly trajectory toward the center of the state space. This long, slow voyage lasts 70 minutes or more, probably because of the inertia of the M function. Aminergic output declines very slowly after sleep onset and does not reach its exponential decay phase until very late in NREM sleep. Meanwhile our conscious state is migrating mostly forward and to the left. As this path is steadily plodded, consciousness staggers and lurches but makes little headway, as it has neither sufficient activation nor much in the way of internal stimulation to work with. Think-

Runner's High *Vigorous exercise produces powerful enhancement of activation (A), external stimulus strength (I), and aminergic modulation (M). This may be why runners experience a high without resorting to drugs and why they feel less fatigued after exertion than they did beforehand.*

ing in NREM sleep is perseverative. Like a decorticated animal, it is capable of only obstinate progression. Keeping your eyes focused on the AIM point in this part of the sequence is trying because it moves so little.

But now the system begins to behave in a most unexpected fashion. The A function stops moving to the left. It has reached its nadir. But the M function is declining ever more rapidly, moving through the middle of its range and heading rapidly toward its own nadir at the bottom of the space. As aminergic modulation more rapidly falls, cholinergic modulation more rapidly rises because their interaction is both reciprocal and exponential. During this time, the A function returns to the right side of the space, pulling AIM with it. Last but not least, the I function begins to shift dramatically, and internal stimuli are generated with greatly increasing intensity. This helps to drive the A function even more rapidly to the right. Motor commands are issued but, except for the eyes, ignored. As the strict censorship of postsynaptic inhibition is instituted, down go the output gates. This is a good thing, because we would otherwise act out our dreams.

AIM has now moved into the lower front right-hand corner of the state space. Consciousness regains its waking intensity, but substitutes exclusively internal data for mixed external and internal sources and exclusively cholinergic for mixed aminergic and cholinergic

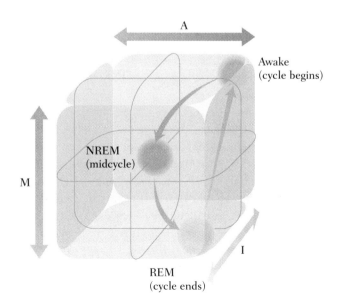

AIM Space Boomerang REM sleep normally takes a long time to develop, but it can be abruptly terminated. This is because the brain-mind is already as activated as it needs to be to support waking and because the inhibitory processes responsible for the I and/or M values can be quickly aborted. When this happens, AIM can move from the REM domain back to the waking domain in seconds or even fractions of a second.

modulation. This corner of conscious state space is the dream consciousness domain. It is a long way from waking in the sense that it normally takes AIM a long time to get there. But it takes only seconds for AIM to return to the waking subspace if the time spent in dreaming consciousness increases beyond fixed limits or the external stimulus strength or the internal motor drive go above threshold. Then the system rapidly resets, and AIM whizzes back to the upper right rear corner of conscious state space. We awaken.

How can we account for the paradoxical difference between the difficult entry into and the easy exit from the REM-dream domain? From an adaptive point of view, survival is favored by waking consciousness and threatened by dreaming. Put another way, one function of waking consciousness is survival. As to the physiological mechanisms, it must be relatively difficult to suppress the aminergic system and relatively easy to activate it. This difference could be related to the pacemaker properties of aminergic neurons, which fire spontaneously unless they are powerfully inhibited. Instantiating the inhibition necessary to shut down the aminergic system is a time-consuming process. This inhibition emanates in part from the hypothalamus and builds its strength gradually as deep sleep proceeds. The same resistance to inhibition is seen in the motor system. It takes a long time to turn it off but it can be reactivated in seconds.

Once instantiated, dream consciousness is its own worst enemy. As both the cholinergic drive that energizes it and the aminergic inhibition that allows it begin to decline, dreaming is gradually attenuated. So the AIM point is actually inching its way back up the right side wall of conscious state space even as dreaming continues. Thus the two interacting modulatory systems first creep—then suddenly spring—back to equilibrium. Like the precarious stone wall in Robert Frost's poem, "Something there is that doesn't love" a dream. It all falls apart so easily.

Another naturalistic analogy ties the concept of gravity to the state space model: the elliptical orbit our conscious state follows as it makes its daily rounds. Just as the earth rotates around its axis, so does our brain-mind state spin with a period of about 24 hours, with the time of sleep corresponding, in most of us, to the dark phase of the day. Then and only then do we definitively leave the gravitational field of waking. But once out of its pull, we cycle more rapidly, making the rounds of deep sleep and dreaming once every 90 minutes. And these four or five orbits change their shapes as, with each successive round, the pull into the deep sleep domain diminishes and the pull into the dream domain increases. Finally AIM is pulled irresistibly into waking gravity again.

Then, instead of basking in the weightless joy of an astronaut tumbling fearsomely but safely in dream space, we lift our heavy bodies from bed and carry them around the earthly world for the next 16 hours or so, until we are launched again from the underground silo of deep sleep into the incredible lightness of dream being.

Abnormal States of Consciousness

Sleeping on the ground floor in the back of the Doubletree Hotel in Tucson, Arizona, did not make me consciously anxious even though the two sliding glass doors that looked out on the pool patio afforded easy access to and from my room. I was excited by my invitation to give a paper at a small but select meeting on Sleep and Cognition. After supper, I went to bed early so as to awaken refreshed for the opening session the next morning. And awaken I did. But the realization that an intruder had managed to slide open the patio door was anything but refreshing. And when I saw that my uninvited roommate was carrying an unsheathed hunting knife, my fear rose up through the terror zone so powerfully that I was frozen on the edge of my bed, unable even to cry out. It was not until my assailant raised his knife high above his head that I sprang into action. In a flash I reared my feet high above my shoulders and kicked at his hand to dislodge the knife. This superhuman effort worked wondrously. As soon as I had powered my legs upward, my assailant vanished into thin air, and I fell back into my bed in a state of grateful relief. I had just survived an episode of hypnopompic hallucination with sleep paralysis.

The Disquieting Muses, Giorgio de Chirico, 1925 *At night the same urban landscapes that are designed to be reassuring by day assume a distinctly menacing aspect. The statues are not where they are supposed to be, and instead of representing benevolent national heroes, they have become faceless, unreachable anonymities ready to judge, reject, or even attack us. (Collection Mattioli, Milan, Italy. The Bridgeman Art Library International, Ltd. Foundation Giorgio de Chirico/Licensed by VAGA, New York, NY.)*

Our daily trajectory through the state space of consciousness is every bit as impressive as a Cape Canaveral rocket launch. With four REM-induced "earth orbits" and a safe return, it is also every bit as limited in extent, since it is restricted from the far reaches of the cosmos. Conscious state space has many corners that we never enter. Woe be to those who, by virtue of some involuntary genetic spin or some injudicious voluntary folly, find themselves in such forbidden zones as waking hallucination (schizophrenia or LSD psychosis) or delirium (alcohol or amphetamine withdrawal), or worse yet, irreversible unconsciousness (the many forms of coma caused by brain disease and trauma). It's bad enough to get stuck halfway between REM sleep and waking, as I did that night at the Doubletree.

AIM *as a Diagnostic Tool*

From a conceptual point of view, each of these conditions can be seen as an exaggeration or aberration of one or more of the AIM factors. Hallucinosis is an imbalance of factor I such that internal stimuli normally held in check during waking are released as they normally are only in dreaming. Delirium is an imbalance of factor M, perhaps as a consequence of the ingestion of drugs that alter the normal metabolism of brain neuromodulatory systems. This causes not only hallucinosis during waking but also such dream consciousness components as disorientation, recent memory loss, and confabulation. Coma is a depression of factor A, with the defective activation arising as a direct result of a loss of neurons from either the thalamo-cortical end of conscious experience or the brainstem systems that energize and modulate it.

When I beheld the Doubletree intruder, my still partially dreaming brain inserted him seamlessly into the real-life set of my poolside bedroom, which I perceived quite clearly with that part of my brain that was awake. My brain was activated (very activated) and the input gates that are my eyes were open, but my brain-mind was still receiving the internal stimulation of a dream, and I was paralyzed by persistent REM sleep motor inhibition.

The AIM state space model is, of course, too limited a construct to offer even as summary an account of the pathological conditions just mentioned as it does of normal dreaming and its dissociative vicissitudes, sleep paralysis and hypnopompic hallucinations. But it does solve one important problem that no other formulation has even approached: the integration of apparently disparate conditions into a unified conceptual framework. Several important advantages attend

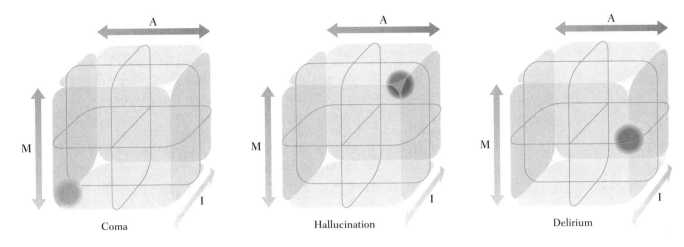

Coma   Hallucination   Delirium

Pathological Domains of AIM State Space *Abnormal states of consciousness can be mapped in AIM space. If activation (A) is deficient owing to traumatic damage to the brainstem, coma may result. If input-output gating (I) mechanisms fail, internal stimuli may be released, causing hallucinations. When toxic chemicals interfere with the balance of modulation (M), delirium may be a consequence.*

conceptual unification, and these are well worth the risk of oversimplification, a sin of which the AIM model is sure to be accused.

One clear advantage of the AIM state space model is functional continuity between normal and abnormal conscious states. Of course, structural defects of either an intrinsic (for example, genetic) or extrinsic (for example, drug-induced) nature can be critical determinants of pathological conscious states. But they act upon and through the same brain systems that mediate the normal states we have already described. Furthermore, such defects act on those systems in ways that the normal vicissitudes of consciousness can help us to recognize and understand. And that understanding can be both technical and phenomenological.

If we physicians, as engineers of conscious states, want to fix a given condition like hallucinosis, we can look at the way the brain itself clamps off internal stimuli and then simulate this process. Most treatments that work, in fact, push factor M in the waking direction. If instead, as psychotherapeutic empathizers, we wish to more convincingly identify with our fellow humans who are, say, delirious or otherwise psychotic, we have only to pay closer attention to our own dream consciousness to know, at first hand, how anxiety-provoking and how disorganizing of the self is delirium.

The strong moral payoff of this approach is that it makes unconsciousness (as in deep sleep) and madness (as in dreaming) universal

189

rather than abnormal. Once we get over the blow that this recognition deals to our pride, we can take satisfaction from the humble acknowledgment that normal consciousness is normally subjected to deformations, dissociations, and distortions of pathological proportions. Gone forever is the false comfort of the "we the sane, they the mad" distinction by which we have isolated, alienated, and confused our disordered conscious state relatives for millennia.

In making this point, I am not advocating the naive and irresponsible excesses of the deinstitutionalization movement. Quite the contrary. I am an advocate for more care, not less, and will even accept temporary restrictions of civil rights in the interest of helping to move people with disabled consciousness into functionally adaptive state space domains. Armed with the AIM model, I can approach my fellows with a sense of true conscious state equity. We are all floating through the same state space with the same relative degree of helplessness. AIM provides a map that all of us lost souls can use. And when we are lost, any map is better than none. Notice how quickly I was able to regroup at the Doubletree. Being a sleep-dream scientist has practical as well as academic advantages.

A second advantage of the AIM model flows from the recognition that conscious state space is both universally open to all and universally continuous and dynamic. Normal and abnormal states of consciousness are seamlessly linked to each other in the state space, and abnormal states are more flexibly interchangeable than the one- and two-dimensional models of consciousness now in common use suggest.

Thus, rather than imagining psychopathology as an endless list of discrete conditions—each with its own particular cause and specific treatment—we can envision a single state space containing within it an infinitude of possible conscious states. And just as normal human beings are neither always in waking consciousness nor always in dreaming consciousness but rather always moving within and between such states, so are those who enter the forbidden zones always moving. I was certainly moving that night at the Doubletree—moving so fast that I crossed the REM-wake boundary without breaking the dream barrier! It was only when my intense cortically initiated effort to move finally overcame my spinal paralysis that I was all of one conscious state again. Thus the mentally disordered may resemble one another more than themselves from one day—or one psychotic episode—to the next.

Here, again, a warning is in order. In advancing a kind of psychopathological universalism, I am not saying that there are no fixed points, no anchorages, within the state space. Indeed, because there

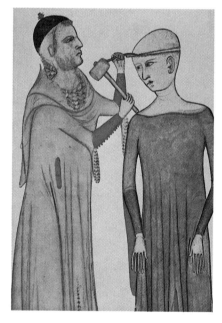

Medieval Therapy "Bats in the belfry" is one of many vivid metaphors for the cerebral infestations that were supposed to cause madness. The obvious remedy? Fumigation, extermination, and extirpation have all been attempted. In this medieval woodcut, the diagnosis is migraine, the therapy, trephination. Today we use talking therapy and medication and assume we have made progress.

are preferred domains, AIM's diagnostic precision can be both valid and reliable, as long as we take the dynamism and fluidity of the brain-mind into account. Because, as we who inhabit the coastal regions of New England say, If you don't like the weather, wait a minute! And, be careful, today's anchorage may be tomorrow's shoal, especially since the chemical interventions that we use to alter consciousness may alter the brain as radically over time as the marine tide alters a shoreline.

A further caveat to the reader of this formulation: The classification of coma as a disorder of neuroactivation, or of depression as a disorder of neuromodulation, is completely arbitrary because it is impossible to change one dimension of the state space without changing the others. The spirit of this discourse is to celebrate the dynamics of this system and the diversity that it ensures, rather than to enshrine a new orthodoxy with the same rigidity as the older structural models of consciousness.

By considering abnormal aspects of consciousness in terms of each of the three dimensions of AIM state space, I intend to turn the usual clinical approach to diagnosis on its head for important heuristic purposes. While single, discernible causes for the disorders that we call neuropsychiatric disease may exist, they all wreak their havoc upon consciousness by disrupting the normal dynamics of brain-mind state control. By viewing the symptoms of these disorders as manifestations of such disruption, the state space model can seamlessly unify normal and abnormal consciousness. My subtext here is moral, and follows Harry Stack Sullivan, who said, "Schizophrenics are more human than otherwise," and John Donne, who cautioned, "Do not ask for whom the bell tolls, it tolls for thee."

> *To know the brain is the same thing as knowing the material course of thought and will, the same as discovering the intimate history of life in its perpetual duel with eternal forces, a history summarized and literally engraved in the defensive nervous coordinating of the reflex, the instinct, and the association of ideas.* — SANTIAGO RAMÓN Y CAJAL, 1885

Disorders of Activation

A deficiently activated brain-mind cannot be awake, as cases of prolonged coma clearly indicate. Whether or not dreaming occurs in these cases cannot be established empirically because reports of dreaming can be given only in the waking state. The AIM model predicts that dreaming will be impossible in coma if activation cannot exceed the level of deep NREM sleep. The assumption that dreaming is lost in coma is supported by the fact that abnormally deactivated states tend to resemble deep NREM sleep in showing a high-voltage, slow EEG pattern more or less continuously.

The most terrible and irreversible destructions of consciousness are the comas caused by structural damage either to the upper brain (by tumors or by vascular insults and strokes), or to the brainstem (most commonly by trauma). In both cases the activation function is lost because the brain cells that mediate it are killed. It is for this reason that such comas can be prolonged, sometimes lasting years or even decades without significant improvement. The brain, so richly profligate in its number of nerve cells and so profuse in the connectivity that links them together into functional networks, does not replace dead cells with new ones, as does almost every other tissue in the body. We are born with all the neurons we will ever possess, though new connections among them continue to develop throughout life.

Brain activation is also exquisitely sensitive to decreases in oxygen and blood sugar levels. And the brain has a fabulously elaborate vascular system to ensure the delivery of these vital fuels of consciousness. The effects of the breath-holding games of childhood, which are designed to impair activation and consciousness by means of voluntary anoxia, are usually reversible because involuntary muscle atonia relieves the strangulation, and oxygen levels return to normal within seconds.

Hyperventilation may also adversely affect consciousness. By rapidly lowering the amount of carbon dioxide in the blood, hyper-

Whirling Dervish One way to alter brain state is to spin around one's vertical axis. Choreographer Laura Dean has been called a "post-modern dervish," for her spinning dancers put audiences in mind of those trance-seeking spiritualists.

ventilation causes a drop in hydrogen ion concentration (respiratory alkalosis) accompanied by a giddy light-headedness experienced as unpleasant by victims of acute anxiety attacks. Gaining control of respiration, a crucial aspect of the relaxation response and related meditation procedures, may alter consciousness at least in part via shifts in blood gases and acid-base balance. Slow down. Take a deep breath. Now don't you feel better?

Even the coma of diabetic hypoglycemia, which may last for hours or days, is fully reversible. "Sugar shock" coma has, in fact, been voluntarily induced in human patients in a vain effort to alter the disordered conscious states seen in schizophrenia. As with electric shock treatment (ECT), the short-term effects may be dramatic, as if the shocked system were shifted to a normal part of conscious state space. But little by little, the system moves back to its dysfunctional position.

Brain cells need be deprived of oxygen for only six minutes to be killed forever. In order to damage the thalamocortical system of the upper brain sufficiently to cause irreversible coma, anoxia must be widespread. This can most easily occur when carbon monoxide, inhaled accidentally from unvented gas heaters or in automobile exhaust suicide attempts, displaces oxygen from its blood hemoglobin carrier. Like carbon monoxide, encephalitis viruses are small enough and numerous enough to go everywhere in the brain and so wipe out the cortex simply by usurping its cells' DNA. For strokes to have

widespread effects, many blood vessels must be closed off, and even when this happens, as in old age, only some aspects of consciousness are lost.

Because the brainstem is smaller than the cortex, and because it is contained in a smaller space, it is easier to deal its neurons fatal blows than it is to kill the vast thalamocortical system that fans out overhead. That is why the twisting and tearing injuries of head trauma are particularly dangerous to the brainstem. And injuries to the brainstem can be aggravated when damage to the upper brain — by tumor, stroke, or trauma — causes acute swelling. Since the upper brain cannot expand upward, it expands downward into the brain-stem's space, causing devastating damage to those smaller, critical state control neurons that occupy it.

Wherever and whatever the pathological process, whenever the capacity for activation is lost, consciousness is altogether and un-equivocally absent. In some cases of brainstem injury, however, the results are not so clear-cut. One of my high school classmates, Sam Vesill, sustained a traumatic brainstem injury in an automobile accident in the late 1950s. Sam remained in a troubling state of sus-pended animation for 30 years thereafter. He lay in his hospital bed immobile but reactive to events in his surroundings. Because he made roving eye movements that often seemed to follow visual stim-uli, his caretakers, his family, and his friends could not be sure that he was not conscious. The disturbing theory that his behavior evoked in all who saw him was that he *was* conscious but simply unable to communicate with us. One reason for taking this idea seriously was that his upper brain showed the activated EEG pattern that is seen in normal waking consciousness.

This upsetting picture of coma vigil (akinetic autism) occurs when the central activating structures (A) are intact, but their links with the input-output system (I) are broken. As with babies and ani-mals that cannot speak, we cannot know what kind of conscious ex-perience coma victims might have. This uncertainty raises moral questions because consciousness is the attribute that we value above all others. Only when we feel sure that consciousness has been lost forever are we able even to consider terminating heroic and costly life support measures.

The evidence that convinces some of us to abandon hope is the patient's failure — ever — to show enough neuroelectrical activation of the brain to make the hypothesis of consciousness tenable. In these cases, when the brain waves disappear from the EEG, we refer to the individual as brain-dead. And we then question the wisdom of keeping the unconscious body alive at whatever cost. Since the evidence is not now and may never be adequate to convince everyone that we have a fundamental right to die, it is essential for individuals to make their own wishes explicit, in advance, in the form of a living will. And it is equally important for society to determine, democratically, whether or not an individual has the right to die.

Overactivation and Hyperconscious States

Our twin boys, Andrew and Matthew, now 15 months old, are as different as any two brothers because each developed from his own special egg fertilized by his own special sperm. Because they are growing up together in the same environment, it is easy to observe the marked differences in inherited activation level that distinguish them. Andrew is calm and docile. He sits contentedly, focusing his emerging consciousness upon the objects and people in his small world. It is easy to imagine him in later life as a scholar content to explore a narrow subject in depth. Matthew is active and demanding. He wants to move. And he so needs attention from others that he vocalizes, makes faces, and hurls objects constantly. It is easy to see him as an athlete, a sportsman, or an adventurer in later life. While Matthew now walks daringly unsupported, Andrew still prefers to play it safe and crawl.

These different behaviors are the presumptive signs of quite different brain-mind activation systems. Time will tell where the boys lie along the continuum that distinguishes normal short sleepers (like their mother, who likes to get six but can get by with four hours of sleep) from normal long sleepers (like their father, who gets by with seven but feels better with eight or nine hours of sleep). How will they use this potential five-hour difference in time spent in waking consciousness—for the contemplation and internal signal processing that their father prefers, or for the external signal processing and interactive work that their mother thrives on?

And time will tell whether the twins will exceed normal limits in the degree or quality of activated consciousness they experience. The inability of some children, like Matthew, to sit still and to concentrate can evolve into the syndrome called attention deficit hyperactivity disorder (ADHD). This disorder is mediated by hyperactivation of the perceptual and attentional modules of consciousness. Because every external signal has easy access to consciousness, none can be easily excluded, and consciousness is a slave to the world and its stimulation.

"Hyperactive" children thus have a disorder of the attention component of consciousness, which the current research of Michael

Posner conceptualizes in his brain region model of attention. The localization of external stimuli is performed by networks in the posterior thalamocortical system, but their identification is made by more anterior circuits. This "Where is it? What is it?" analytic sequence functions optimally when internal vigilance signals are reliably supplied to the upper brain by the brainstem. These vigilance signals are carried by norepinephrine, the aminergic neuromodulator made by the locus coeruleus, which works by toning down the thalamocortical system so that attention can be focused more selectively.

Already, the perspicacious reader will realize that this hyperactivation disorder (A↑) is a product of disordered modulation (M↓) and that it is manifested by an overinclusion of external stimuli (I↑). One implication of this formulation is that both activation level and input level must be tempered by appropriate modulation in order to hold AIM in an optimal position within the waking subspace. Once again, it is not only the overall state of consciousness that is determined by the AIM factors but its microscopic substrates as well. Another, more practical implication is that the overactivation and overinclusiveness of hyperactive conscious states can be counteracted by modulating consciousness artificially. For instance, drugs like amphetamine, which mimic the action of norepinephrine and thus raise the flagging level of M, are the pharmacological treatment of choice for attention deficit hyperactivity disorders in prepubescent children.

A hyperactivation problem that is complementary to overinclusion of external stimuli during waking is the failure to quell internal stimuli at the end of the day, when sleep is desired. The result is an

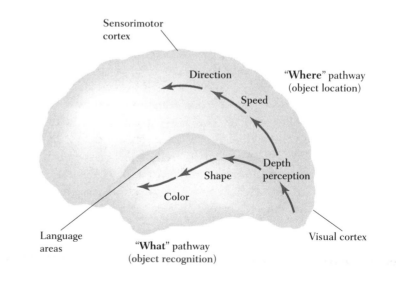

Neural Pathways *External stimulus sources demand localization (Where is it?) and identification (What is it?) by the vigilant brain-mind. These cerebral look-up services are provided by circuits in a posterior system that organizes extrapersonal space and an anterior system that comprises our semantic lexicon.*

Sensorimotor cortex

Direction

"**Where**" pathway (object location)

Speed

Depth perception

Shape

Color

Language areas

"**What**" pathway (object recognition)

Visual cortex

inability to deactivate the thalamocortical system enough to allow it to go into the oscillating mode that pulls the brain-mind into the unconscious depths of NREM sleep. The consciousness of insomniacs, already overdriven by internal emotional stimuli by day, cannot shut down at night. Such individuals take their troubles to bed with them, or fail to go to bed at all, because their internal stimulus processing is never done. They know it will not stop even if they lie down and turn out the lights.

In insomnia, consciousness is overly activated (A ↑), internally stimulated (I ↓), and hypermodulated (M ↑). Relaxation training can

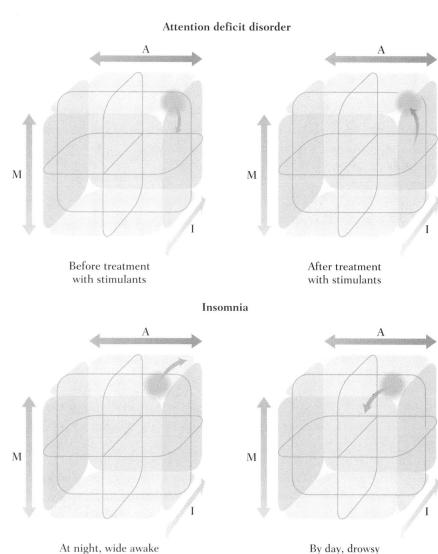

Attention deficit disorder

Before treatment with stimulants

After treatment with stimulants

Insomnia

At night, wide awake

By day, drowsy

Disorders of Activation *(Top) Attention deficit hyperactivity disorder. Congenital deficiencies in aminergic modulation and/or excessively excitable motor systems conspire to abbreviate attention span and provoke perpetual motion as the subject fails to inhibit motor outputs. When a child's aminergic M function is bolstered by a stimulant like Ritalin, his brain-mind can be boosted into the normal waking domain of AIM space. (Bottom) Insomnia. Insomniacs may be wired for excessive waking, but they usually take waking concerns to bed with them. As a consequence, they cannot move down into the NREM sleep domain in the center of conscious state space—until the next day, when they may experience excessive daytime sleepiness.*

substitute neutral information for arousing internal emotional stimuli and thus allow normal deactivation (A↓) to occur. This approach can be abetted medicinally by sedative hypnotics that aminergically demodulate the brain (M↓).

But even when sedatives have deactivated the brain enough for the EEG signs of sleep to appear, they may not completely shut down the engines of internal emotional stimulation. The result for the insomniac is a dissociation of the normal coupling between activation (A) and input-output (I) mechanisms, so that their subjective experience of sleep is not peacefully oblivious but rather disturbed by the continuous cerebral noise of unproductive rumination and worry. This condition has been called pseudoinsomnia, as if the subject's complaint of not being deeply or restfully asleep were invalidated by the evidence of EEG inactivation.

Since we already know that low levels of waking conscious experience persist even in very deep NREM sleep, it is clear that activation level alone is not enough to decide the case. Rather than impugning the insomniac's subjective experience, we should admit the inadequacy of our one-dimensional model. By adopting the three-dimensional AIM model, we are in a better position to understand and respond to the problem of excessive internal consciousness during sleep.

Disorders of Input-Output Gating

In the pluralistic, multidimensional real world of conscious experience, a virtual infinitude of sometimes bizarre substates is the order of the day—and even more so of the night. It is this multiplicity of substates, their often hybrid aspect, and their dynamic interchangeability that the AIM model is designed to address. Insomnia is a subtle and poorly understood disorder of consciousness that is often relegated to the clinical ash-heap over which presides the hypochondriac, *le malade imaginaire.*

When the internal stimuli that invade consciousness are more clearly of physiological origin, we are more easily able to fit the condition into classic models of disease. One such condition is epilepsy. In epilepsy, consciousness is literally seized and held hostage more or less completely by an uncontrolled focus of hyperexcitability in only one of the brain's internal circuits. Another such condition is narcolepsy, in which the normal boundaries between waking and dreaming consciousness dissolve. Like epilepsy, narcolepsy involves the release of normally inhibited neural circuits, which then generate internal stimuli and preempt motor output neural circuits.

Epilepsy has been called "fire in the brain." From the vantage point of the AIM model, this brain fire consumes consciousness in one of two ways. If the seizure arises in the thalamocortical system, it can preempt consciousness completely by driving that system into a sleeplike oscillatory mode. This is generalized epilepsy. It is called "grand mal" to indicate that it is big (*grand*) and bad (*mal*). In petit mal epilepsy, the seizure is more partial and short-lived. This leads to temporary lapses of consciousness, the so-called "absences" of petit mal ("not so bad") epilepsy.

If the seizure focus is in the temporal lobe, it is more likely to invade waking consciousness and contaminate it with internal emotional stimuli that, like the temporal lobe stimuli of dreams, are incorrectly assumed to come from the outside world. Because they so clearly illustrate the basic assumptions of the AIM model, temporal lobe seizures are among the most instructive invaders of the brain and consciousness. Consider the following similarities and differences between normal dream consciousness and the abnormal consciousness of temporal lobe epilepsy:

- Both dreaming and temporal lobe epilepsy involve paroxysmal activation of the limbic brain. They are therefore both characterized by sudden and spontaneous emotions such as fear, elation, rage, and sexual excitement.

- Internally generated emotions are integrated by paralimbic cortical structures. In the case of epilepsy they are integrated into ongoing reality (because the rest of the brain is still awake), and in the case of dreaming they are integrated with recent and past memories (because the entire brain-mind is absorbed in the REM sleep process).

- Both dreaming and temporal lobe seizures are associated with a loss of insight, indicating that consciousness is held hostage ("seized") in both conditions by such strong internally generated stimuli that the brain-mind uncritically projects the synthesis of these signals onto the outside world.

- Both the normal and abnormal states are associated with a suspension of memory for the experience itself, even though in both states the recall of past events may be present. Since both conditions share the paroxysmal takeover of the limbic lobe, the mechanism of amnesia for dreams may arise from factor I as well as from factor M. In other words, the memory system of the limbic brain may be driven so powerfully into the playback mode by internal stimuli that it cannot store the newly synthesized products of consciousness in short-term memory.

Given these striking correspondences, it is difficult to decide whether dreaming is the result of normal temporal lobe seizures or temporal lobe epilepsy triggers abnormal dreaming. One reason for taking the first hypothesis seriously is that the physiology of the internal stimulus generation driving normal dream consciousness to its hallucinatory and delusional experiences is decidedly seizurelike. The PGO waves that arise in the pons and are conducted to the amygdala and visual brain during dreaming have precisely the same spike and wave form as the EEG stigmata of epilepsy. And we know that, at the cellular and molecular levels, both of these EEG signs of internal stimulus generation are produced by failures of inhibitory restraint.

As for the second hypothesis, the use of the term "dreamy state" to describe the consciousness of temporal lobe seizures speaks volumes about the deep correspondence between two conditions that we would prefer to believe are quite different. Subjects undergoing brain surgery for temporal lobe seizures also report dreamlike experiences when the neurosurgeon stimulates the temporal cortex electrically. This means that remote memories, feelings, and sensations can be experimentally induced by simulating the internal stimuli of both dreams and temporal lobe seizures. This classic experiment of clinical neurobiology takes on a new meaning when seen through the lens of the AIM model.

If normal dreaming were seriously considered to be the result of the epileptiform discharge of normal neurons, we might expect to see full-blown REM sleep suddenly replacing waking consciousness. And this is exactly what we do see in narcolepsy, a condition whose very name suggests its seizurelike nature. In narcolepsy, the pontine REM sleep generator is inadequately inhibited. For that reason it becomes possible for external stimuli to trigger episodes (or seizures) of dream consciousness during the daytime, when in most of us they are impossible. Although the fundamental mechanism of narcolepsy is unknown, it appears to involve a deficiency of dopamine, another of the aminergic neuromodulators that are so crucial to maintaining waking consciousness.

While many narcoleptic attacks occur spontaneously, we note with interest that many are precipitated by external stimuli that evoke strong positive emotions, especially surprise, elation, humor, and— our old friend—sexual excitement. Funny? Yes, in a way. But not so funny for the sufferers, because in addition to being plunged into the dream state, they lose contact with the world with embarrassing and annoying abruptness. Muscle tone may also melt away, adding the risks of bodily harm to those of social opprobrium.

Why are these emotional stimuli so potent? Possibly because they activate the limbic circuits that normally participate in emotion mediation. These neural circuits may have intimate interconnections with the pontine REM sleep generator via input gates that are normally closed during waking. This hypothesis makes a three-way link between normal dreaming, temporal lobe seizures, and narcolepsy, all of which are seen as the consequence of unchecked paroxysmal discharges of limbic lobe neurons, and all of which share many specific conscious state features.

Narcolepsy is instructive for a second reason: It exaggerates the normally partial dissociations of waking and dream consciousness. Examples of such dissociations are visions occurring at sleep onset and offset (hypnogogic and hypnopompic hallucinations, respectively) and sleep paralysis, the inability to move upon awakening from

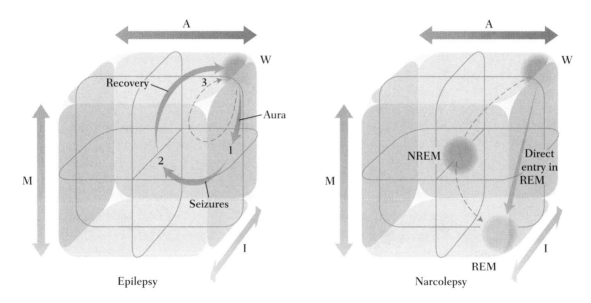

Epilepsy   Narcolepsy

Disorders Related to Input-Output Gating *(Left) Epilepsy. When the neurons of some part of the brain escape from inhibitory control, the subject may experience an unusual sensation (1) called the aura that warns of the coming lapse of consciousness (2). Depending upon the intensity and spread of the seizure, the recovery orbit (3) may be long (grand mal, solid line) or short (petit mal, dotted line). (Right) Narcolepsy. Instead of traversing the NREM domain of the AIM conscious state space (dotted line) en route to REM sleep, patients with narcolepsy are pulled directly into it. They can thus experience all or part of the REM sleep behavioral complex at the edge of waking. This is why they have sleep-onset REM periods.*

dreaming. All three dissociations are more disturbing to some subjects than are full-blown narcoleptic attacks, both because they are more intrinsically frightening and because they raise the specter of mental illness. While having hallucinatory experiences within dreams is analogous to psychosis, having them while awake is *identical* to psychosis.

Because the hypnogogic and hypnopompic hallucinations of narcolepsy are predominantly visual, they are both gripping and terrifying. Subjects may suddenly see people or animals in the bedroom, a place that is usually safe—even sacrosanct—and their vulnerability naturally increases their sense of dread. The anxiety is no less intense when, on awakening from a frightening dream, the subject finds herself unable to move. She is then literally—not just figuratively—frozen in fear. The negative emotions associated with all these symptoms of narcolepsy are again reminiscent of the conscious experience of temporal lobe seizures, as is the insertion of the emotions into otherwise normal waking consciousness. The inevitable conclusion is that one (or more) part(s) of the brain are awake while other(s) are dreaming.

The take-home message of this discussion is that the line between external stimulus "waking reality" and internal stimulus "dream fantasy" is always thin, and always shifting. The line between madness and sanity, however firm, may also be quite thin, as our discussion of disorders of modulation will shortly reveal. Consciousness is a many-splendored thing, but some of its splendors are both terrifying and disabling.

The Psychoses as Disorders of Modulation

We now turn our full attention to the modulatory (M) dimension of the AIM model in an effort to explain the most debilitating disorders known to neuropsychiatry, the psychoses. Because the two major defining characteristics of psychosis, hallucination and delusion, are also prominent features of normal dreams, it is clear that powerful and quite normal processes may be disrupting the perceptual and cognitive components of normal conscious experience. These mechanisms are so commonplace—and so normal—as to suggest that psychosis is anything but the bizarre, recondite, alien state of mind that conventional wisdom has often taken it to be.

Three points should be kept in mind as we move now to consider the three most frequent and debilitating mental conditions that can affect human beings. The first is that the so-called "mentally ill" are

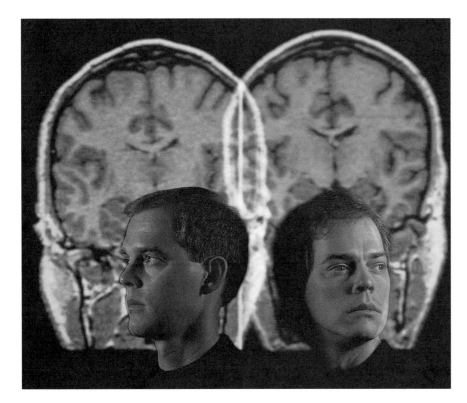

The brains of identical twins may diverge dramatically during development and these developmental differences may contribute to discordant behaviors. Steven Elmore (right) is schizophrenic and has a brain which is slightly smaller than his twin brother David (left), due to reduction in the thickness of the cortex. The fluid-filled ventricles of Steven's brain are correspondingly larger as is common in schizophrenia and other disorders of thinking. Genetics and experience both contribute powerfully to our conscious states.

not qualitatively different from the rest of us. The second is that neither are they so different from one another as our descriptions might suggest. From the vantage point of the AIM model, psychotic patients are simply pulled toward and/or stuck in a part of conscious state space that most of us glide through quite smoothly every night of our lives. And they too can move in and out of these forbidden zones, or move from one to another. The third point is perhaps the most challenging to grasp. It is that the so-called organic psychoses are every bit as functional as the functional psychoses are organic. Whether a disorder of consciousness is triggered by a personal tragedy or by taking a pill, the disorder is mediated at the level of the brain-mind, and the brain-mind is functionally altered by such mediation.

To understand these points, consider the following facts:

1. Organic psychoses, in which delirium is a prominent feature, are clearly caused by chemicals that raise havoc with the neuromodulatory brain systems that confine our dreams to sleep. Thus we can all be rendered psychotic simply by tampering with the M function of the AIM model. And we

don't have to ingest drugs or alcohol to get crazy in this way. Even such a simple and commonplace manipulation as sleep deprivation can produce delirium. And, of course, our dreams are properly considered organic psychoses caused by radical changes in factor M.

2. Affective psychoses, otherwise known as bipolar or depressive disorders, are functional exaggerations of normal fluctuations in mood. Our moods (another M word) fluctuate up toward mania and down toward depression all the time. Fortunately, for most of us, these fluctuations remain within bearable bounds. But we should not ignore the point that it is natural for mood to fluctuate widely. While each of us may have a genetic predisposition to be temperamentally disposed toward the high side (mania) or low side (depression), or to oscillate wildly (become manic-depressive), life events have an impressive power to push even our most stable moods further up or down than is comfortable. But when depression of psychotic proportions is clearly triggered by overwhelming loss, are we correct in calling this a functional as opposed to an organic psychosis? I think not. All psychosis, including that of our dreams, is functional, *and* it is all organic.

3. Schizophrenia, the condition rightly most dreaded, shares with affective illness a border that is often blurred or invisible. The

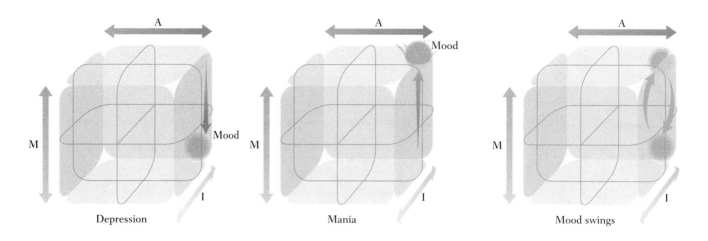

Depression   Mania   Mood swings

Affective Disorders In depression, shown at left, the M function falls, and with it mood. During recovery it gradually goes back up again. But this switch may be rapid, as shown in the center, and M may go through the roof. This is mania. The cycle of manic-depressive illness is represented on the right as successive risings and fallings of the M function.

classic conception of schizophrenia holds that affect is flat
and/or dissociated from cognition. But even this stigmatic
feature is not constant. Many diagnosed with schizophrenia
are, clearly, depressed at certain phases of their lifelong
trajectories through conscious state space. And all of us
so-called normals frequently find it advantageous to dissociate
our thoughts from our feelings. We are all capable as well of
flattening our affect if it gets in our way or is unbearable.

The take-home message, once again, is that consciousness is multifo-
cal and is dynamically regulated by brain processes that are subject to
myriad controlling and disrupting forces. Even normal consciousness
is a balancing act, for madness is never far beneath the surface of our
outward calm. Two insights emerge from this view of ourselves. One
is that to achieve the full glory of rational and creative human consciousness, nature has tinkered up a clutch of delicate brain mechanisms, each of which contains its own risk factors for dysfunction.
This being the case, the wonder is not that so much madness exists,
but that there is so little! Madness and sanity are two sides of the
same coin: heads, you are crazy only in your sleep, and tails, you are
also crazy when awake.

Schizophrenia: Dis-Integration of the Self

We begin our state space analysis of psychosis by considering schizophrenia, clearly the more organic of the two so-called functional psychoses, and the one that is perhaps most different from the normal
psychosis of dreaming. Two differences are worth noting.

First, the waking hallucinations of schizophrenia, unlike those of
dreaming, are much more commonly auditory than visual. This observation suggests that while the I function in both states may be
similarly biased so that internal stimuli gain ascendance and produce
fictive perceptions, those false percepts arise in the auditory networks
of the temporal regions of the upper brain, not in the visual networks
of the occipital region.

Second, the delusions of schizophrenia are far more commonly
paranoid than are the delusions of dreams. Dreams have this paranoid aspect surprisingly rarely, given the high level of anxiety and
threat that is common to them. Why should this be? One possibility
is that the hallucinated voices that plague the schizophrenic occur
in the otherwise normal perceptual world of waking, and are thus
naturally projected onto that world. The cognitive system needs an

explanation for the heightened sense of threat and anxiety, and an obvious one is a malevolent external agency, which is assumed to exist even if it is invisible. We view this paranoia as a natural and inevitable response to the perception of threat and accusation in the hallucinatory voices. In dreams, it is paradoxically easier for us to explain anxiety and threat because we can visually hallucinate malevolent agents. Because our dream pursuers, attackers, and critics are visible, we are not stuck for an explanation of their malevolence, and our interpretations are not paranoid. This may be a surprising benefit of our being more completely psychotic in dreams than when schizophrenic in waking.

These two differences between dream and schizophrenic psychoses point up two important limitations of the AIM model. Note first that it makes no distinction among sensory modalities. A more complete model would display at least five I dimensions, one for each sensory modality. Note as well that the AIM model does not represent regional brain space, with its important geographical diversity, of which the sensory component is but one example. To deal with this deficiency we would need to visualize an AIM state space in each functionally distinct brain region. Our state space model, already far more complex than any other yet proposed, is thus grossly oversimplified.

We considered this latter limitation when we discussed temporal lobe epilepsy as a disorder of the I function. The brain locus of the internal stimulus is obviously an important determinant of its modality as well as of its emotional and cognitive effect. Interestingly, mounting evidence suggests that in schizophrenia, the temporal lobe is dysfunctional in ways akin to temporal lobe epilepsy. Recall that epileptic patients, like schizophrenics, may become quite paranoid as they struggle to explain their strong internally generated perceptions in terms of the motives of people in their surroundings.

What about the modulatory mediation of schizophrenia symptoms? The leading culprit in the disordered M function is dopamine, an aminergic neuromodulator that does not seem to play a major role in triggering the normal psychosis of dreaming. Dopamine is produced by neurons in the midbrain, the brain structure just anterior to the pons and medulla. But dopamine does share with norepinephrine and serotonin a functional interaction with acetylcholine. Because it is also interactive with serotonin, dopamine may indirectly mediate sleep-related changes in consciousness. Its interaction with acetylcholine subserves sensorimotor integration in the basal ganglia and related deep motor structures of the anterior brain.

Neuromodulatory interaction might thus account for the curious motor signs of schizophrenia, such as catatonia and waxy flexibility,

Schizophrenia *Some hint as to the consciousness of psychotic patients can be derived from our own dreams, but the distinctive bizarreness of schizophrenic hallucinations is perhaps best appreciated through their artworks. I myself have never dreamed of an eye in a fingertip, but one of my patients sees eyes everywhere, looking at her, menacing her, devouring her.*

that were seen before the advent of anti-dopaminergic narcoleptic drugs, and for the motoric side effects of those drugs, such as dystonia and rigidity. The enormous benefit to consciousness of reducing the parasitic perceptions and paranoid cognition of schizophrenia is often well worth these unfortunate side effects. Following the introduction of the phenothiazines in 1955, American mental hospitals were largely emptied, and many were closed.

The neuromodulatory concept was slow to emerge from the exciting turmoil of the psychopharmacology revolution. One reason is that antipsychotic drugs were introduced primarily for clinical reasons, without regard to how they affected the detailed workings of the brain. In fact, the breakthrough drug, Thorazine, was first tested as an antihistamine cold remedy and was given to psychiatric patients only because research subjects noticed its strong antianxiety effects. Second, next to nothing was then known about the function, or even the presence in the brain, of neurotransmitters such as acetylcholine, norepinephrine, and serotonin. I was a first-year medical student in 1955 and remember being taught that there was no rigorous evidence for accepting a central brain role for these chemicals, even though they were known to be powerfully active in the peripheral nervous system. Finally, dreaming, the normal behavior that best demonstrates clinically relevant changes in consciousness, had no known brain basis until 1953, and no specific brain basis until 1975.

Catatonia *Sure evidence that sensory and motor gating functions are deranged in schizophrenia is found in the bizarre postures of catatonia. But similar dystonias may also be produced in normal people by the same drugs that are used to control psychosis in schizophrenia patients.*

Thus it was only gradually that the concept of an M function controlling the balance of internal and external stimuli took hold. It became apparent that, in normal consciousness, the modulatory neurons balance the neural nets so that they can catch real informational fish and let the fictive fish go free.

The neuromodulatory chemistry of schizophrenia could also help explain the different conscious experience of its victims. In particular, a sense of isolation and social distance is a disabling symptom that distinguishes schizophrenia from dreaming. Schizophrenics are neither integrated as selves nor fit comfortably into the social world. This split is still another variation on the theme of binding that recurs in any discussion of consciousness. Getting consciousness together and holding it together is not an easy task for everyone.

M function theories of schizophrenia have broadened recently with the introduction of new and sometimes dramatically effective anti-schizophrenia drugs that not only counteract excess dopamine but also bolster norepinephrine and serotonin. Their success suggests that schizophrenic consciousness, like normal dreaming, is a state of the brain-mind caused by generalized and widespread neuromodulatory reorganization. Only when the unbalanced and deficient neuromodulatory systems of schizophrenia are tuned by external chemicals with versatile and widespread effects are the core disintegrative symptoms resolved. These deep effects allow more unified and saner selves to emerge even after lifetimes of disintegration and disarray.

The Affective Disorders: M is for Mood

We have used the M function of the AIM model to define the effect of modulatory chemistry upon the mode of information processing and especially upon the brain-mind's memory capacity. Thus we have seen that when aminergic modulation fails during REM sleep, we cannot remember our conscious experience, even though the brain is highly activated. These effects are short-lived, lasting no more than an hour at a time before NREM sleep rescues and restores half of the lost M function. After six to eight hours or so, waking restores it a hundred percent.

What happens if aminergic modulation is impaired in waking? And over the long term? In this case it is primarily mood and only later memory that is the victim, as the affective disorders, especially major depression and bipolar psychosis, make clear. The affective disorders provide perhaps the most emphatic support for the both/and approach to the organic-functional issue. Family histories provide strong evidence of a genetic predisposition to react to life's vicissitudes with marked changes in conscious state functions.

Bipolar mood disorders with alternating peaks of wild manic energy and troughs of despairing depression are not uncommon in affluent families. In Boston, they say, a typical Brahmin family has a house on Beacon Hill, a son at Harvard and an uncle at McLean Psychiatric Hospital. Among the many distinguished sufferers of manic depressive illness are the poet Robert Lowell, the novelist William Styron, and the painter Vincent van Gogh. Winston Churchill fluctuated between bouts of major depression (which he called his "Black Dog") and waves of exuberant self-confidence and indefatigability which he rode to success as England's wartime prime minister and historical chronicler. "Choose your parents carefully" is clearly good advice.

The story of the affective disorders and their relation to sleep and cognition also offers the most persuasive argument for the AIM state space concept available in the casebook of abnormal conscious states. The key to understanding this story is the recognition that the M function profoundly affects the fundamental energy supply of the brain-mind as well as its mode of information processing. In short, mode and mood go hand in hand. As this concept may seem paradoxical, counterintuitive, and even contradictory to the concept of the

Mood Disorder Pedigrees *The tendency of bipolar mood disorders to run in families of distinction is illustrated by the Churchills of England whose afflicted members include: John Churchill, the first Duke of Marlborough; Lord Randolph Churchill; and his son, Sir Winston Churchill, shown here with his mother Lady Randolph and his brother, John Churchill.*

activation (A) function, we need to distinguish between the metabolic (M) levels of energy controlled by the aminergic modulators and the electrical activation levels (A) controlled (mostly) by other neurotransmitters (like glutamate and GABA).

To grasp this difference, imagine a remote cabin in the woods whose electrical power is generated by a gas engine. As long as there is an adequate fuel supply, the generator can be used to power a wide variety of devices, including lights, heaters, and even—in the case of modern-day Henry David Thoreaus—word processors. But as the fuel supply dwindles, the lights dim, the house cools, and the computer disk crashes. In our brains, the same thing happens if we run out of cerebral gas. Our brightness, our warmth, and our ability to remember all ultimately fail if we become depressed. Depression occurs when the aminergic modulatory system is not topped off on a regular basis, as it is during sleep—especially during REM episodes. As this too is a paradoxical concept, we will return to it when we discuss the surprisingly beneficial effects of REM sleep deprivation on depressed mood later in this section.

Early on in our modular dissection of the components of consciousness, we reserved only one category for emotion, and we considered emotion in only reflexive terms. And certainly an emotion like anxiety may be triggered by stimuli and so heighten or disrupt conscious experience. But mood is pervasive emotion, and as such, is relatively independent of stimuli, seeming to arise spontaneously from our nonconscious depths and to determine our responses to stimuli rather than being swayed by them. When we are high, the world is our oyster: everything looks and feels good, even if it is actually harmful or dangerous to us. When we are down, we see and feel the world with foreboding: gloom and doom drain the color from even the most vivid inputs.

Sometimes our mood may change overnight, but usually the highs (as in mania) and lows (as in depression) take days, weeks, or months to develop and to clear. The difference between emotion as an acute reflex response and mood as a chronic, anticipatory emotional filter reflects the fact that each evolved in a unique way; thus, each has a dramatically distinct effect on consciousness.

To account for these differences, it is helpful to recognize that modulatory chemicals like norepinephrine, serotonin, dopamine, and acetylcholine all have one—acute—effect at the level of the nerve cell membrane onto which they are secreted and another—chronic—effect on the metabolic machinery in the nucleus of that cell. The translation of the membrane signal into the metabolic message is effected by second messenger molecules, which are knocked off the inside of the membrane by modulators, and which tell the nuclear DNA of the cell to make more protein and hence crank up one or another metabolic process within that cell. These second messenger molecules are cyclic nucleotides. The aminergic modulators norepinephrine, serotonin, and dopamine release cyclic AMP, which has energy-mobilizing effects on neurons. The cholinergic modulator acetylcholine releases cyclic GMP, which has energy-conserving effects. Too much cyclic AMP gives rise to hypomania, in which consciousness runs the risk of undue optimism. Too much cyclic GMP gives rise to depression, in which consciousness runs the risk of undue pessimism.

Each of us is born with a constitutionally embedded temperament, a propensity to optimism or pessimism that determines where we sit on the M axis of the AIM model. This propensity contributes to what we call personality. When colored by our moral sensibility and education, it constitutes what we call character. High M people tend both to be optimistic and to sleep little, while low M people tend to be pessimistic and to feel rested only when they have lots of sleep.

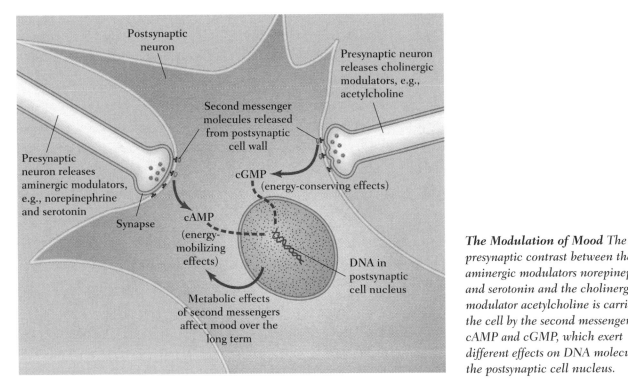

The Modulation of Mood The presynaptic contrast between the aminergic modulators norepinephrine and serotonin and the cholinergic modulator acetylcholine is carried into the cell by the second messengers cAMP and cGMP, which exert different effects on DNA molecules in the postsynaptic cell nucleus.

Each extreme has both enviable and problematic aspects. Short sleepers may get a lot done because they spend so much more time in a state of energized, acquisitive, and inventive consciousness, but in their bent toward overachievement they may fall prey to anxiety and stress and collapse in states of nervous exhaustion. Long sleepers may be more sensitively introspective, and hence more poetic in their response to the world, because they spend more time in inward absorption and reflective consciousness, but they are prone to disillusionment, withdrawal, lugubrious rumination, and collapse in states of despair.

High M people can't easily fall asleep and low M people can't easily wake up. Each may need the help offered by cognitive, behavioral, and pharmacological interventions designed to move them into that region of normal state space that chance and habit have conspired to avoid. It is in consideration of such treatment for disorders of consciousness that we can both appreciate the power of the AIM

"Malinconia," Edvard Munch
Edvard Munch conveys the doom and gloom of depression by depicting a man's dejection and by placing his subject in a lightless Nordic winter landscape. The dark black ink of his powerful woodcut completes the picture of melancholia. (Scala/Art Resource, NY. © 1998 The Munch Museum/The Munch-Ellingsen Group/Artists Rights Society (ARS), New York.)

model and foreshadow our discussion, in the next and final chapter, of the functions of consciousness. These functions include our ability to create a model like AIM, to apply it to the analysis of the risks of living within the constraints of such a system, and to maximize the benefits of altering consciousness by manipulations that honor—and profit from—its rules.

Consider major depression. Of the three main classes of psychosis, it is arguably the least severe from a cognitive point of view because its delusions (there is something wrong with my body) and hallucinations (I smell bad) are not so very far from the mark, reality-wise. But the energetic retardation, with its accompanying impairment of memory, can lead to states of cognitive imprisonment akin to dementia. And, worst of all, everything is black: shame, guilt, low self-esteem, and preoccupation with disease, death, dying, and loss cloud consciousness in a life-threatening way. Under these circumstances, consciousness is likely to be so pained by its own state as to prompt the one definitive act of redemption: self-annihilation.

In such emergencies it is helpful to pump up the aminergic modulators, tone down the cholinergic system, and thus jack up the M function so that consciousness can emerge from the slough of despond. And this is exactly what the antidepressant drugs do. They enhance the efficacy of noradrenergic and serotonergic modulatory molecules either by imitating them or by giving them a longer time to act in the synaptic cleft. At the same time they diminish the power of the cholinergic system by blocking the action of acetylcholine. And, true to the rule of acute synaptic versus chronic metabolic action, they have effects that are immediate and effects that are delayed.

One immediate effect is to correct the sleep disorder. Since dreaming is triggered by acetylcholine and restrained by norepinephrine and serotonin, chronically depressed subjects tend to enter REM sleep more quickly, to experience more intense REM episodes, and to stay in that state longer than do normals. As a consequence, they have less deep NREM sleep and tend to wake up earlier, feeling unrefreshed. This further contributes to their depressed state of consciousness. Antidepressant drugs fix the sleep problem right away. And when they do, the outlook for a delayed but positive effect on mood itself is brighter.

This two-step sequence implies that while the drug-induced synaptic effects benefiting sleep are immediate, the metabolic effects, benefiting mood, are the delayed consequence of those effects. In other words, we must sleep every night so that consciousness can be cognitively efficient the next day. But we must sleep night after night so that consciousness can be affectively balanced over the long term. Our nocturnal journey through AIM state space thus has at least two linked but distinct goals: short-term cognition (and emotion) and long-term energy regulation (and cognition-mood).

One of the paradoxes of chronic depression is the apparent negative effect of REM sleep on mood. Once the aminergic system has failed, running the cholinergic system during REM sleep makes depression worse—in the short term—while reducing REM sleep makes depression better—again, only in the short term.

Controlling Consciousness

For the student of consciousness who wishes to obtain insights that matter on a day-to-day basis, it should be clear that the proper care and maintenance of the brain-mind begins with the simple principles of cognitive and behavioral psychology. To give the AIM system maximal opportunities to enter the beneficial states of deep NREM and REM sleep, it is important to schedule—even to program—one's life so that somatic, cerebral, and conscious state mechanisms can interact positively and harmoniously. In this great balancing act, the tim-

Contre Danse *This handwritten score of one of Mozart's dance pieces records the mercurial flow of creative genius. We can easily visualize the composer's pen flying unhesitatingly over the paper as his hand raced to keep up with the torrent of gleeful notes that he heard—in his brain—as he wrote.*

ing, amount, and quality of physical exercise and diet, intellectual exercise and content, introspective self-reflection and extroverted sociability all play their part. With the luck of the genetic draw and with the skillful management of whatever constitutional hand we are dealt, we may emerge from the casino of conscious life a winner, or at least with our losses cut to tolerable levels.

What Is Consciousness For?

My apprehension of the vastness of the cosmos as I beheld the starry heavens that night in Maine was a vivid conscious experience that served to crystallize my nascent adolescent awareness of that universe within my head that I have come to call my brain-mind. But short of such transports—which make art and science seem to me to be a shared effort to understand ourselves—I experience a more mundane sense of awe as I use my now declining cerebral powers to order my life. I use my consciousness to plan, so that the needs of my family, my friends, and my colleagues may be met. I use my consciousness to observe, so that I may be truly present and open to the quotidian panoply of truths that my house, my garden, and my young children put before me. My awareness of my awareness now includes its impending extinction. In time, only these pages may remain. I therefore use my consciousness to reflect so that I may refresh my sense of priority. I want to be sure that I invest my consciousness in projects that will be as socially useful as they are personally satisfying. My wish to leave something of value behind grows stronger as the time remaining for its accomplishment inexorably dwindles.

Dream, Odilon Redon, 1904 *The autocreative capacity of consciousness is represented in this painting. From a hot spot deep in the darkness of the brain-mind arises an embryonic, protohuman vapor trail which writhes upward toward the light. Our aspirations, our ideas, and our models are all similar, emergent from germinal sources in our depths. (Giraudon/Art Resource, N.Y.)*

By enabling us to hold ideas, images, and impressions in mind, consciousness frees us from complete reliance upon our reflexes. The enormous evolutionary advantage of consciousness thus boils down to freedom. Freedom from automatism. Freedom from pure impulse. Freedom from ignorance. But the price of such freedom is high. Conscious awareness commits us to morality, to concern for others, to fair play, to guilt, and to indecisiveness because the choices that consciousness offers us are not always easy ones to make.

In a sense, then, the gift of consciousness contains within it the curse of obsessive doubt, of conflict, and even of neurosis. We do not need to postulate, as did Freud, a dynamically repressed unconscious to appreciate the inevitability of conflict. Conflict can—and does—arise within the domain of consciousness itself. But consciousness also enables us to recognize the unconscious, to confront the conflictual demands that it too presents, and to resolve them via reflection, decision, and compromise.

Skeptics and many theorists will object that freedom of conscious choice can never be scientifically proved. They say that freedom of choice is an illusion, a fiction of consciousness's own invention that fails to recognize the inevitability of the myriad deterministic, atomic, molecular, neuronal, and network-level events that render us all mere automata no matter what we may think or feel.

A Creative Automaton

It is certainly not my purpose to argue against the powerful automatic forces that shape and guide us. On the contrary, we must all be grateful that so much is done for us without our having to think about it.

Our brain and body create a history together. FLOYD BLOOM AND ARLYNE LAZARSON, 1985

Take the beating of my heart, for example. Even when I sleep, my heart goes on beating entirely automatically. But I know—because I am conscious—that my heart won't go on beating indefinitely. I know that one day, no matter what steps I take to safeguard it, my heart will stop beating. Consciousness thus helps me to appreciate and to accept the inevitability of my death. In the meantime it enables me to weigh the risks to my heart of, say, eating butter and steak (which I love), and the benefits of drinking red wine (which I also love) and of vigorous physical exercise (which I cannot live without).

You may say that the entire contents of my heart consciousness are in fact determined by essentially automatic processes outside my control. I will concede my consciousness's susceptibility to the claims of medical science, the media, and advertising messages, but this in no way impugns my freedom of choice. At every moment there exists an interplay of chance and determination over which—or in which—my consciousness decides. I have no doubt of it. In taking this stance, I am echoing William James in his pragmatist mode. Of free will, James would say, whether or not it can be proved to exist doesn't matter. What matters is that individuals and societies work well only if it is assumed to exist.

The complex reality of the organ of consciousness, the brain, is another reason for viewing freedom as the essential functional advantage of self-awareness. The behavior of the brain, like that of any complex system, presents a paradoxical dynamic in which predictability and unpredictability both play their parts. Unpredictability is not usually considered to be the guarantor of freedom. Quite the contrary. Obligatory randomness—or chaos—would seem to commit us to an unwanted lack of control. The almost wholly involuntary nature of conscious states like dreaming is a good case in point. Who could want to be in the grip of an essentially psychotic process? And yet dreams, with all their horror, also promise transcendence by revealing that creativity is the flip side of madness. This does not mean that artists are mad or that mad folk are artists. What it does mean is that madness and art are cousins in consciousness and that this familial relationship arises from the inextricable link between unpredictability and novelty.

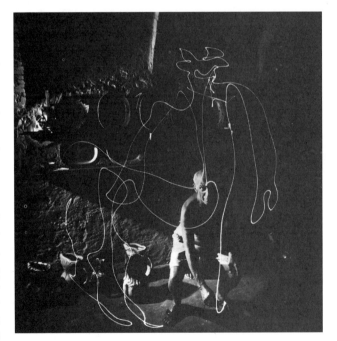

As we now look at the function of consciousness in four of its aspects—planning, critical evaluation, unexpected invention, and health maintenance—we will see that this interplay between chance and determination manifests itself in each aspect. It may seem unflattering to view humanity's highest cultural achievements as dependent upon randomness and chaos, but I believe that they are. In this chapter I attempt to flesh out my vision of the brain-mind as a creative automaton. The paradoxical nature of the phrase *creative automaton* conveys the very essence of this vision. Without automatism we could not survive. Without creativity we could not embellish and refine our survival. These apparent opposites, chaos and creativity, are the antipodes of our cerebral universe. Because we have brains that are conscious, we are both free to be determined and determined to be free.

Picasso's Passionate Line *One of the most prolific artists of all time, Pablo Picasso personifies the plastic potential of human consciousness. Hopped up on wild creative and sexual energy, Picasso turned himself loose on his canvas to create records of dynamic passion. Here he is photographed drawing on thin air in the dark, with a light instead of a pencil.*

Planning and Organized Behavior

Among those diehard skeptics who doubt that consciousness—or any other subjective aspect of mental life—can be scientifically studied, none are more obdurate than those behaviorists who follow the tradition of B. F. Skinner. It is a little-known fact that Skinner participated in some of the very earliest experiments on the brain basis of consciousness ever to be conducted in the United States. And those experiments proved that Skinner's own head was not a black box after all! Instead, it contained a brain whose electrical activity changed with his state of consciousness, and changed as well when he made deliberate, conscious decisions about his behavior.

The events of inner experience, as emergent properties of brain processes, become themselves explanatory causal constructs in their own right, interacting at their own level with their own laws and dynamics. The whole world of inner experience (the world of the humanities), long rejected by 20th-century scientific materialism, thus become recognized and included within the domain of science. ROGER SPERRY, 1982

I am poking fun at Skinner not to mock his memory, which I revere, but to make a point about the scientific study of consciousness, which can in fact be pursued using the conscious state paradigm. This is exactly what Skinner's friend and colleague Hallowell Davis had in mind when he hooked Skinner up to his EEG machine in the physiology department at Harvard Medical School one day in 1937. To demonstrate the dependence of conscious state upon brain (and vice versa), Davis asked Skinner to close and open his eyes, whereupon the alpha rhythm in Skinner's EEG waxed and waned. Then, to show the effect of intense mental effort on the EEG, Davis asked Skinner to solve some difficult math problems in his head. Amusingly, the most impressive EEG activation occurred when Skinner was told that one of his calculations was incorrect. Davis and Skinner were studying not only activation and alertness but the contribution of emotion to conscious state as well.

To Skinner's great credit, he carefully kept these precious historical artifacts and generously shared them with me. But I don't think he ever imagined that these very records would provide a link between his behaviorism and today's cognitive neuroscience, a field whose validity and promise he so steadfastly denied.

No human being, including B. F. Skinner, could possibly plan a day, a week, a year, or plot an overall career path without consciousness. The functional advantage of organizing behavior in advance of its occurrence is enormous and obvious. By setting goals and making lists, we escape the helter-skelter, stimulus-and-reward-driven realities of reflex behavior. This doesn't mean that conditioned reflexes of both the classical Pavlovian and operant Skinnerian types do not exist. They do. And yes, Professor Skinner, behavior is determined, in part, by its consequences. But consciousness helps us anticipate those very consequences and so favors desirable outcomes by shaping our behavior from the inside out.

If consciousness is to perform this important organizing function for behavior, the brain-mind must be properly maintained. In particular, it must be exercised regularly, kept free of toxic substances and toxic ideas, and allowed to wander through the regenerative regions of its conscious state space at least once a day. Sleep was essential even in Skinner's notorious box, in which he also carefully controlled the dietary and information inputs to his subject. To appreciate this point, consider the disorganizing effects on your own consciousness and your own behavior when you deprive yourself of sleep.

One critical consciousness function for the organization of behavior appears to be attention. Without attention, behavior descends to the Skinnerian level. It becomes stimulus-driven rather than consciousness-driven. It becomes directed from the outside in rather than the inside out. You know what I mean: after one or more nights of poor sleep, your desk becomes cluttered with papers, each one of which has an equally exigent claim upon the weakened attention of your sleep-deprived conscious state. Rather than organizing the papers by classifying and prioritizing them, as you would after a good night's sleep, you fiddle and fumble, sometimes handling an item three or four times without properly analyzing it or reaching a dispositional decision about it. You have a moderate case of attention deficit disorder. Fortunately, it is an acute case, and easily cured. Just get a good night's sleep.

Another way to appreciate the organizing power of consciousness is to imagine holiday shopping with and without a list of possible presents for your family members, some of whom are easy to please, others more difficult. The easy way out is simply to hit the stores and let the merchandisers suggest gifts to you. Sometimes this works, but more often, your trip is an endless series of distractions and you still can't find those two presents for the hard-to-please folk at the end of your list. A half hour spent thinking—and specifying at least the category of gift your beneficiary might want—can change the shopping experience from a data-driven chain of reflexes to a program-driven conscious search.

A trick related to anticipatory list-making is visualization. When I am preparing for an important lecture, I first formulate its emphasis, then outline its logic and arguments, usually in three segments. With this literary structure in mind I can begin to see, in my mind, those

Virtual Reality Now that an observer's behavior can be tied to artificial image generation by a computer, we can experience the disconcerting but instructive world of virtual reality. In this photograph, a student subject demonstrates the visor and pointer of a program called "Phobias" that was designed as an experimental treatment of the fear of heights. Of course, all conscious experience is a virtual reality that also ties our motor behavior to the abstract visual imagery in our brain-minds.

visual images from my extensive and exotic slide collection that will best convey my points and most convincingly document the scientific evidence for them. Once I have assembled the slides, I have a scenario sequence in mind that I need only review, visually, to rehearse the talk once or twice just before beginning to speak. Then I remind myself to sum up my story, if possible, with a provocative quotation from some inspiring wit—John Dryden, for example:

> *Dreams are but interludes, which fancy makes,*
> *When monarch reason sleeps, this mimic wakes:*
> *Compounds a medley of disjointed things,*
> *A mob of cobblers, and a court of Kings:*

Dryden's rationalism would have delighted in today's recognition that dreaming is virtual behavior because of the vivid conviction that we are actually doing things that are only imaginary. Whatever the specific function of dreaming may be, its convincingly fictive aspect speaks volumes about the brain-mind's capacity to simulate the world. It is this model of the world that helps each of us as conscious human beings to deal with the infinite set of behavioral options that each day presents to us. Without conscious planning we are slaves of the world and doomed to inefficiency and inefficacy. With a conscious plan we have at least a chance of accomplishing something.

Critical Evaluation of Past Behavior

When we launched our first study of waking fantasy at Harvard, we were not surprised at the reluctance of our subjects to participate. Who, after all, wants their hidden thoughts and desires known to the world? What did surprise us, when we overcame the understandable resistance of our subjects, was how banal was the content of most of their normal daily ruminations. Banal compared with the vivid fictional exploits of James Thurber's Walter Mitty or Henry Miller's Henry Miller, who always seemed to live on the edge of aggressive or sexual mastery. But not banal when considered from a more functional, adaptive point of view. In today's urban world, successful breeding and the provision of nest and territory for one's self and offspring have more to do with bosses, bureaucracies, co-workers, colleagues, and companions than with tigers, tropical storms, or teams of tempestuous lovers.

What most people think about, most of the time, is their own behavior. They review and rehearse it as if life were at once a theatrical play and a courtroom trial. They audition and they testify in their minds. They want to anticipate—as an extension of the planning function of consciousness—different possible scenarios and how to react to them. And once the anticipated encounter has been concluded, they want to know how well they did and how they might have done better. Consciousness is thus, first and foremost, eminently practical.

When I refer to this kind of consciousness as fantasy, you may object and say that I should call such reality-based rehearsal and review just plain old thinking and reserve the term "fantasy" for more exotic imaginings—the impossible or highly improbable flights of fancy we sometimes take. I won't quarrel over classification, but one other surprise our study held was the recognition that even very practical imaginings are just barely conscious. They float just below the surface of consciousness in what the psychoanalysts call the preconscious.

Indeed, it is only the enforced discipline of introspection—as in our first study—or the intrusion of a beeper—as in the experience sampling we are doing now—that makes people at all mindful of their ongoing mental activity. This means that consciousness is not only graded across life spans, species, and days, but that it is also continuously graded, at every instant, from the fully automatic nonconscious processing of reflex adjustment (B. F. Skinner) to the equally automatic but exigent and intrusive forces of instinct (James Thurber and Henry Miller) to the semiconscious ruminations about success and failure (our subjects) to the fully conscious, deliberate plan (a holiday shopping list). We can separate these aspects of consciousness for analysis and experimentation, but in reality, they are as seamlessly bound together as the plants, grass, and trees of my garden that I perceive, in the corner of my mind's eye, as I write.

So fantasy can go either way, toward the exotic or toward the commonplace. But wherever it goes, it is always with the purpose of mastery, be it fictive or actual. In this sense, creativity, which becomes codified, packaged, and even sold by some as art and science, is a universal aspect of consciousness that anyone can tap, free of charge.

Controlling the Dictates of Consciousness

Having extolled semiconscious review and rehearsal as the mental handmaiden of behavioral success, I need to point out that she can be overworked. Picking up on the themes of the last chapter, the mix

Merchandising Consciousness This woman is not drying her hair. She is instead undergoing a personality analysis by the psychograph, a device evolved from the practice of phrenology. Psychograph proponents claimed that it mechanically translated the user's skull bumps into an accurate analysis of character traits. In reality, the psychograph produced results not unlike those offered by a fortune cookie or daily horoscope, printing up its output such epigrammatic statements as, "You are fairly secretive but can improve."

between planning and spontaneity can be tilted too sharply in either direction. The unexamined life, as Emerson said, is not worth living. But the excessively planned life is no life at all, as our overly compulsive fellow humans make clear. The phrase "moderation in all things" means that in the state space of consciousness, automaticity, instinct, and emotion must be given free reign by conscious choice. Otherwise, life is choked off at its root.

Consider a patient I'll call Myles Suitor, who had consciously decided he must wed. In today's world that means, first, bed! Both thoughts, however enticing, also filled poor Myles with dread. He didn't have a how-to manual for either task. So he wrote one. His consciousness-as-planner tried to imagine all the possible scenarios that might ensue when he rang every prospective Ms. Suitor's doorbell on the first date. But no matter how actively he imagined the sequence of communications, by the second or third exchange he found himself in uncharted waters. This caused him to panic and mentally block. For Mr. Suitor, the infinite freedom of the world, of biology, and of psychosexual discourse was a terror.

The clinical help he sought did not include the ability to recognize and accept the unknown. He wanted only to be made into a more effective planner. So, there was an imbalance not only between the volition module of his consciousness and the chaotic aspects of his life experience but also between his anticipatory consciousness and his critical review consciousness. He knew he was failing all right, but he couldn't see that he needed to plan *less*, not more. His critical review function was stuck in the analytic mode. Obstinate progression is one name for it. Obsessive compulsive disorder is another.

Whatever the label, these behaviors all boil down to an overactive cerebral cortex. Too much top-down direction from the frontal lobes, not enough brainstem-limbic play. Not enough dreaming. Time to shift position in the conscious state space. But how? Decrease the activation level via meditation or the relaxation response. Increase positive emotion via the conscious cultivation of free play and humor. Try finger painting and rent Woody Allen movies. Change the input-output dimension by dropping the scenario writing and increasing the internal signal strength. Listen to your dreams. They are telling us something important about how our brain-minds work.

Last but not least, perhaps reach for the Prozac. Move yourself up—or better—down on the modulatory axis. Give the cholinergic system a chance. Why Prozac, which enhances serotonin, which increases behavioral inhibition, should help patients like Mr. Suitor, I don't know. On paper, at this writing, it shouldn't. But it does. So we have to keep experimenting and find out why. Like Mr. Suitor, we have to admit that we can't control everything. At times, it's best to go with the flow.

We are still, despite all the current hype, in the Dark Ages when it comes to understanding consciousness. To realize just how dark our age really is, consider that only 50 years ago Egaz Moniz won the Nobel Prize for his pioneering prefrontal lobotomy. And recognize that such so-called psychosurgery was prescribed for many of the Myles Suitors of that day! But however barbaric it may seem to us now, it did—often enough—work. How?

Lobotomy works by severing the connections of the frontal lobes with the rest of the brain. This takes worry out of the loop. Without an executive cortex to weigh every decision with agonizing care, some previously obsessive and ornery characters became docile, even pleasant. Others, like Phineas Gage, whose frontal lobes were disconnected when the dynamite he was tamping blew the rod up through his head, turn rude and crude as their limbic lobes escape frontal cortical governance. Lobotomy causes a personality change, which

The Power of Positive Emotion
Laughter has been claimed to heal as well as to amuse. Norman Cousins fired his doctor and hired the Marx Brothers, whose antics seemed more curative than pills. A good belly laugh will certainly tickle your brainstem and thereby, perhaps, open the door to the drugstore between your ears.

proves that consciousness is intimately involved in shaping character, a practical behavioral matter if ever there was one.

By taking the frontal lobes out of the consciousness game, lobotomy acts like sleep, only in waking. Recall that in both NREM and REM sleep the frontal cortex is deactivated, and in our dreams we certainly do not overplan our behavior. In fact, we don't plan at all! From this observation a prediction follows: Obsessives, like Mr. Suitor, should be freer, more spontaneous, and more tuned to their feelings in their dreams. This suggests a way to teach them about alternative states of mind. Instead of interpreting their dreams, perhaps we should train obsessives to live them out.

Come to think of it, one of the worst things to do to an obsessive is to offer interpretations of a symbolic variety. Obsessives, being concrete, take symbolic interpretations literally. These interpretations can thus become a more elaborate embellishment of the thought trap that the obsessives' consciousness is caught in, rather than the key to escape that the unwitting psychoanalyst hoped to cut for them. My patient Daisy Counter was one such unfortunate. So obsessed was she with food that normal dining was impossible. She therefore resorted to consuming garbage. When her well-meaning analyst suggested that each of the dreaded foodstuffs represented to Daisy a family member (or his or her body parts), Daisy became convinced that she was not only unworthy of a normal meal but also guilty of

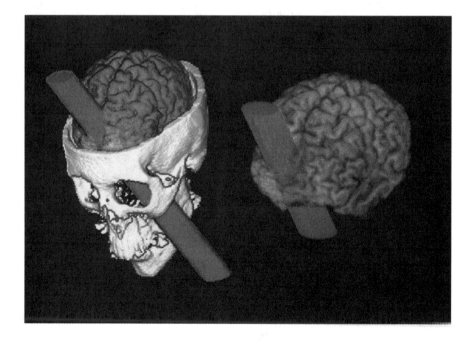

The Strange Case of Phineas Gage
The actual tamping rod and Gage's perforated skull can be seen in the Warren Anatomical Museum at Harvard. Using these display objects, Antonio and Hanna Damasio have reconstructed the damage that must have occurred in this simulated scan of Gage's brain.

cannibalism. As a good Catholic, she thereby became addicted to the confessional box instead of the garbage pail. You have to have a very generous nature to consider this progress. And still, Daisy couldn't eat. To this day—30 years later—Daisy still thinks that soft white food is her mother.

One joke about psychosurgery goes like this:

I'd rather have a bottle in front o' me,
Than to have a prefrontal lobotomy!

Alcohol dissolves obsessive concern and turns down the worry machine, possibly by depressing the frontal cortex after the fashion of sleep. It is this capacity to dissolve paralytic self-consciousness that makes alcohol such a popular social lubricant and so welcome an anodyne to the conscious concerns that continue to reverberate in our heads when we come home from work. Our muscles relax, our tongues loosen, and our affiliative emotions run free as our ever so lightly pickled frontal lobes release their braking action on the subcortical engines of desire. But by weakening judgment, alcohol may make us go too far. It may turn us rude and crude like Phineas Gage. Or, as Shakespeare said through the mouth of Macbeth's porter, "It provoketh desire but it taketh away the ability."

Some discover that falling asleep is enhanced by alcohol. But, as every drinker soon learns, alcohol is not a good sedative because its metabolic breakdown products cause arousal later in the night. And while alcohol may induce dreamy states in waking, it powerfully suppresses REM—and with it dream consciousness—in sleep. For the chronic alcoholic, this REM sleep deprivation becomes a driving force in the ultimate ruination of waking consciousness. It is, in part, the release of massive pent-up REM pressure that triggers the breakthrough of the visual hallucinations, the disorientation, the confabulation, and the memory loss of dreaming in the delirium that often follows alcohol withdrawal.

Electric shock therapy is no less heavy a hammer with which to bludgeon the brain and push consciousness around the state space. By virtue of its hyperactivation and its preemption of input-output operations, it must have immediate and extreme effects on factors A and I. But by causing a generalized seizure, EST quickly drives the brain-mind in the direction of NREM sleep and coma, where it remains for several hours. The fact that memory is poor even when conscious awareness is regained indicates that EST also affects the M system.

Today, EST is not so much used to treat obsessive compulsive consciousness as it is to improve the negative mood states of depression. And since mood, like memory, is an M dimension function, it is almost certainly the M dimension of conscious state space that is altered in the treatment of depression with EST. How might this work? To answer this question, we can again take a leaf from the sleep book. When electric current is passed through the brain, it causes convulsive discharge of neural cells. The net effect is to overdrive them in the waking direction, but because of the chaos of convulsion, consciousness is lost.

Among the neurons overdriven by EST are the noradrenergic locus coeruleus and serotonergic raphe nuclei, whose aminergic modulators are depleted—or less efficacious—in depression. Turning them on by the strong stimulation of EST could thus be beneficial—in the same sense that keeping them on is beneficial when REM sleep deprivation is used to raise mood (M). But in the case of EST, the initial convulsion is followed by a prolonged recovery period, which is sleeplike in that it allows the net increase in aminergic

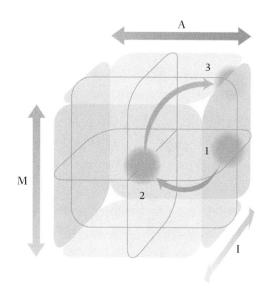

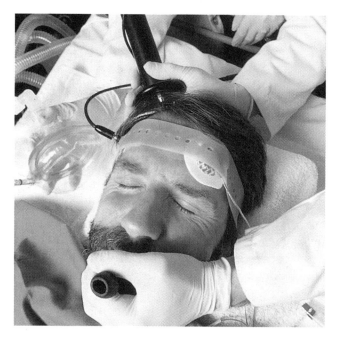

Treatment using Electric Shock Therapy *Similar to the conscious state space rendering of spontaneous epilepsy shown on the left, an electrically induced seizure, shown at right, moves the patient from a starting point in M-depressed waking (1) rapidly down the I axis. As the seizure develops, the brain is deactivated and slow waves are generated much as occurs in NREM sleep (2). After recovery (3) the patient is, hopefully, at a higher M level in the AIM state space.*

metabolism to be conserved. It is interesting that mood improves only after 4–8 shocks given on successive days or alternate days. As with antidepressant drugs, the M pump must be primed for some time before the positive effects on mood are observed.

The review and rehearsal functions of consciousness are impaired not only by the hypercriticism of obsessive thinking but also by the blue coloration of depressed mood. Consciousness cannot be objective, optimistic, or creative if it is clouded by dark emotion. As we noted in Chapter 8, everything seen through the lens of depressed consciousness is gloom and doom—so dour, in fact, that suicide may seem attractive, and may be tried. In this dark sector of the state space, consciousness becomes the enemy of life itself. To once again serve as the benevolent director of behavior, consciousness needs to be shifted to a more favorable position by changing the value of the M dimension.

Consciousness and Creativity

The ability to anticipate the world and therefore to plan behavior and the ability to evaluate behavior and therefore to better adapt to the world are both based upon the capacity of consciousness to create abstract models. This capacity reaches its apex in human creativity. In creativity, consciousness transcends the world by making worlds of its own: the world of art and the world of science, worlds that would not exist at all without the supervention of consciousness. Creativity goes beyond the day-to-day management of behavior to the discernment of the underlying rules of the world (science), to the elaboration of complex aesthetic responses to it (art), and collectively, to the evolution of consciousness itself.

Poetry is made in bed like love.

ANDRÉ BRETON, 1948

But, make no mistake, the path to creativity is a straight and direct one from the brain's intrinsic talent for representing stimuli in its neural discharge patterns and chemical codes. As we have seen, even sensation, that most primitive and primary component of consciousness, involves abstraction. Light does not enter the brain. Electrical energy transduced from light energy by the retina represents light. This is already a symbolic transformation, a first level of abstraction. At a second level, a visual image, once perceived and stored as neural code, can be summoned voluntarily into consciousness so that we can behold the world in the absence of external stimuli. Armed with such symbol-manipulating power, we can rotate images, analyze their structure, and describe their geometry (in numbers) or their form (in painting or sculpture), all via the neural codes that are the fundamental property of even the simplest neurons.

It is in this sense that I say that the brain-mind question and the problem of consciousness are already solved. Creativity is inherent in the basic operation of the nervous system. Of course we need to know more about how the world comes to be re-represented in primary conscious awareness, and how these re-representations come to be re-re-represented in the awareness of awareness in secondary consciousness. But, qualitatively speaking, we have already made the biggest leap by entering the brain and seeing one form of informational energy (light) translated into the lingua franca of the neuronal code (action potentials).

What we call "subjectivity" is thus an emergent property that inevitably arises in any sufficiently complex sensory system composed of sensory neurons. The brain that is subjective is just a brain with enough neurons organized in a fashion such that its codes can be carried up a bucket brigade of hierarchically ordered representations to selfhood.

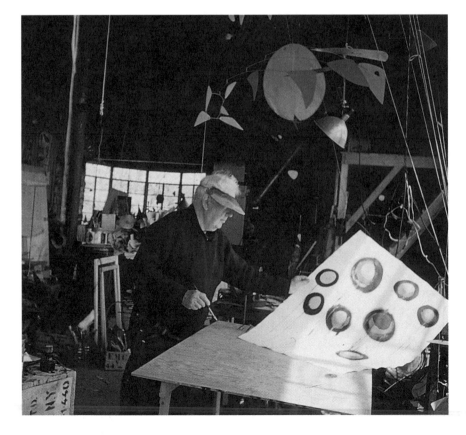

The Art of Movement Sculpture dances, even as it flies, in the mobiles of Alexander Calder, who created this endearing art form. His abstract space models display an infinitude of states and constantly shifting configurations, thus mirroring the endless variety of consciousness. Playfulness was Calder's lifelong passion, and his output was prolific. In 1931, he was married to Louisa James, whose great uncles were William and Henry.

We are ourselves, nothing more, nothing less, and nothing but the integrated neuronal activity representing our sensations of the world and our bodies—including our emotions, and all the other modalities that make up our conscious and unconscious minds, especially memory. It is the most remarkable situation—so paradoxical as to be mind-numbing. But how can we any longer doubt that our brains—and all the information represented in them—are ourselves?

Guided by consciousness, and followed by consciousness, the imaginative acts of which our brain-minds are capable make us far more than King of the Beasts. Mind power confers upon us the heaviest of responsibilities and the loftiest of privileges. Although we are not birds, we can, in our dreams, fly. And in waking, we can use mind power to construct flying machines that escape earth's gravity and become literally weightless. We can even quite seriously contemplate exploring cosmic space with automatic probes of our own devising. At this time we can only imagine sending our brains to other planets, but inner space has already met outer space with Neil Armstrong's lunar giant step.

In my view, the much vaunted qualia of the philosophers are nothing more—and nothing less—than sensations and sensations of sensations. Subjectivity begins at the sensory transducer. It builds with each level of symbolic transformation until an image—a dynamic symbolic representation—emerges in the iterative activity of neural networks encoding the symbols in their firing patterns. With images coming and going, often without the stimuli that originally shaped them, consciousness is now offline, sufficient unto itself. It can play with, recombine, manipulate, and transform images into any of several symbolic domains. And so consciousness can make "discoveries" that are entirely abstract but which have some relationship to the real world that gave birth to them in the first place, and to which they must ultimately return.

I was in Vermont that night in 1969 when Neil Armstrong walked on the moon. To keep my mind free to communicate with Nature, I had consciously and volitionally excluded from my country retreat two of the most fabulous mental models of our time, the telephone and the television. But I wanted to see that flag unfurled and to hear that voice declare its proud message—in real time. So I walked in the moonlight to the house of my Vermont farmer neighbor, who had bought a TV shortly after installing indoor plumbing. And there I witnessed that most remarkable triumph of human consciousness, the integrative culmination of physics, centuries of mathematics, and engineering.

Cosmic Consciousness *New knowledge and new technologies—themselves the creative products of consciousness—allow us to map and to explore outer space as well as the cosmos that is our brain-mind.*

Like many of his fellow Americans, my farmer neighbor was unimpressed. Indeed, he was snoring loudly in his Barcalounger, the only other piece of furniture in his living room besides the TV. As my consciousness buzzed with excitement at these improbable doings in outer space, his was transported into the center of his AIM state space, where it recovered from a very long day of haying and prepared for another.

On my way home I gazed at the moon with new eyes. The fact that at that very moment Neil Armstrong was up there meant that all those abstractions that had made the rocket, the Apollo spacecraft, and the lunar rover possible were really true. The crunch of my feet on the gravel road and Armstrong's playful scattering of lunar dust were proof that the theory of gravity still held. Now my consciousness returned to earth and to the brain that had just beheld these wonders. What are its laws of gravity? How is it held in orbit? Can it gives some preliminary answers to these youthful questions.

The Physics of Qualia

Saying that qualia are not mysterious, that they are nothing more than dynamic forms of matter, does not rob them of their wonder. Denying them other-worldliness is simply insisting on their this-worldliness. Why, after all, should subjectivity be regarded as immaterial? One reason is the difficulty of imagining it as material. And there is another, deeper, nonscientific reason for resisting even the effort to understand the materiality of consciousness.

And that, of course, is the notion of soul or spirit with its putative immortality. The monistic view of consciousness is obviously incompatible with this fondest of all of humankind's hopes. Just as we are at pains to conceive of the universe—and human life—as emerging by chance from cosmic chaos, so we balk at realizing that when our brain dies, our consciousness, including our spirit and soul, dies with it. Except, of course, in the consciousness of other living brains! And here we see that creativity confers transcendence in just the way that the religious impulse in all of us would like.

How to achieve immortality? One way is to follow Blaise Pascal's gamble and simply believe in it. Pascal the mathematician reasoned that while matters of faith couldn't be proved, it was unwise to reject them because they couldn't be disproved either. Faith, after all, is one aspect of consciousness. None of us hard-headed scientists could possibly function in the world without faith. We go around accepting all sorts of assumptions that cannot now be proved, and may never be proved. But there is another way to achieve immortality. And that is to exercise the creative function of our consciousness to the full.

We use our brain-minds to image, to imagine, to draw, to paint, and to write. Please don't say you can't do any of that because you have no talent. Everyone has the talent of abstract representation. It is inherent in sensation. Consciousness must be used to foster its own intrinsic creativity. Even the humblest human being can keep a record of his or her experience. Whether it be photographic or autobiographical, creativity begins with imaging the world, our feelings, and our deep selves.

For the past 25 years—ever since I turned 40—I have been keeping a journalistic record of my experience. It now runs to 99 volumes, which may seem prodigious or pathological depending on your point of view. This creation contains my thoughts, my dreams, my

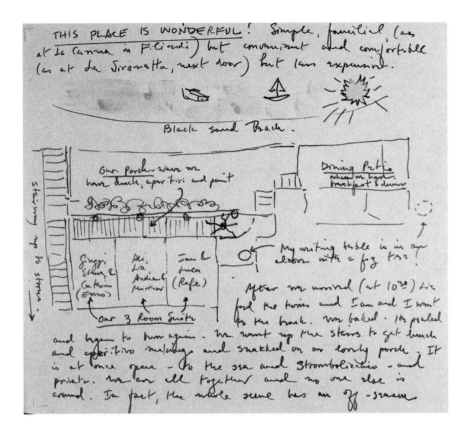

Extensions of Consciousness Volume 98 of my journal was composed in the summer of 1996 in parallel with the writing of the first draft of this book. This page shows where I sat—and what I saw—as I looked up from writing.

sketches, my photographs, my notes on science, and my thoughts about art. It even contains the first drafts of some of my papers written while traveling in the world. I make no claim that any of this is either science or art that is of any value to anyone but me.

Whatever their value, I know that these journals will outlive me by at least a day, and maybe more, if my family doesn't immediately put them all out in the trash. Of course, my published works, including this book, have a better chance of surviving in the archives of the world's collective memory than do my journals. But the journals are a closer record of my day-to-day conscious experience. And the personal journal is a form of creative self-expression available to anyone who is conscious.

Consciousness and Health

Humans are the only animals who understand that their minds, spirits, or souls are functions of their material bodies. And whether or not one believes in the unity or the separability of mind and body, the evidence is overwhelmingly strong that mental states can be voluntarily changed in order to affect bodily states. This means (as I have insisted from the outset) that consciousness is causal, and in a very material way. Simply by inducing a state of relaxation, it is easy to reduce muscle tension, to lower heart rate, to slow respiration, and to decrease the output of neuromodulators within the brain and in the body. The easiest way to explain this mind-body effect is to assume that since subjectivity is itself a brain function, it very naturally can redirect its own energy from one neural region to another.

Meditation and other techniques associated with Eastern traditions such as Buddhism thus offer the power to channel consciousness without in any way entailing mystical belief or ascetic practice. As for the Buddhist idea that consciousness is an independent, universal force, preceding and surviving earthly life, science is as free to doubt it as the faithful are free to believe it. One severe problem faced by proponents of the religious idea of the transmigration of souls is how the constantly expanding populations of the world could possibly be equipped with consciousness if consciousness were a finite commodity, limited to some preordained number of souls.

By utilizing consciousness to control itself (that is, change its focus and its content) and to control the body (that is, shift it to a less energy-consuming mode), relaxation techniques demonstrate the advantages that conscious animals have over those with purely reflexive behaviors. One of the effects of relaxation is to reduce the level of certain reflexes and thus render behavior less automatic and more "mindful," in the language of meditation adherents and adepts. For everyone, this approach offers at least momentary escape from the stress and strain of a life that has become all too reflexive.

Another mind-body phenomenon related to meditation-relaxation, but distinctly different from it, is hypnosis. Hypnosis has enjoyed wider acceptance in the West than has meditation, perhaps because it is an active, instrumental technique that depends upon the interaction of an agent, the hypnotist, and a subject. Hypnosis takes advantage of the modular character of consciousness, which allows its component parts to dissociate from each other. This is not a prerequisite of relaxation. Only some people are capable of achieving trance in hypnosis; everyone is capable of doing so via relaxation. But hypnosis shares with relaxation the induction of an altered conscious state. Both move the brain-mind from one part of conscious state space to another. In the desired locus of the state space, the hypnosis subject abandons volitional control of behavior and accepts, seemingly unconsciously, the will of the hypnotist.

The involuntary aspect and the trance aspect of hypnosis have combined to suggest a kinship with sleep and with dreaming. The

French term for trance, *somnambulism,* means, literally, sleepwalking. And indeed, real sleepwalkers are both dissociated and highly suggestible. But, so far, it has been impossible to find physiological similarities between the states of sleep and hypnosis using the techniques of surface electrical recording. In fact, the failure to establish a physiological substrate of hypnosis has hindered its scientific investigation severely.

All that may be about to change with the availability of brain imaging techniques. Now, instead of being limited to amplifying weak electrical signals from the scalp and skin, it is possible to assess the regional activation of the brain in subjects who are hypnotized. When these subjects are told to increase—or decrease—functions like vision (trance-susceptible subjects can hallucinate or become blind), their visual systems should increase or decrease their activation.

Control of pain—psychic and somatic—is one of the desirable goals of hybridizing relaxation and hypnotic techniques. I am not highly hypnotizable, nor am I anywhere near as mindful as a Buddhist, but I have learned to reduce dental pain to a tolerable minimum by a combination of relaxation and self-hypnosis. My decision to attempt this analgesic redirection of consciousness was encouraged by my success in the autosuggestion of lucid dreaming, following the eminently sensible and down-to-earth lead of Mary Arnold-Foster, an English intellectual who taught herself to fly in her dreams.

The Point of It All

We have considered only the most immediate uses of consciousness to positively affect health. What about longer-term health issues— risk management, diet control, weight and cholesterol reduction? And how might we increase our longevity and our vigor? Consciousness is the answer because all of science depends upon it. And consciousness is the answer because scientific knowledge can be translated into health-promoting behavior only by conscious individuals. Come to think of it, it would almost appear that consciousness had evolved in order to permit us to understand ourselves and to manage ourselves in a more adaptive fashion.

Whether cognitive neuroscience is viewed as a spectacular leap or only as a small but significant step, the renewed scientific focus of attention upon consciousness must be warmly welcomed. Consciousness is, after all, our most impressive attribute and our most potent tool in our quest for happy, healthy, morally responsible, and creative lives. The proper appreciation and use of consciousness may be helped by the scientific study of its material basis, but it remains the responsibility of each individual to accept, understand, and apply it by living, loving, and learning to the full.

The Unthinkable, 1957, Roberto Matta The Chilean surrealist artist, Roberto Matta seems to be reaching beyond narrative and beneath visible surfaces in his attempt to convey the mechanisms of conscious and unconscious mental processes. This science-fiction phantasmagoria suggests the brain in action to me. (Galerie Thomas R. Monahan, Chicago.)

Acknowledgments

While the ideas in this book are my own responsibility, they have been inspired by many people who have star-gazed with me over the past fifty years. I can acknowledge only a few of them here. I doubt that my first mentor, Page Sharp, went to any real neuropsychologists' heaven after he died in 1958. But his guiding star still shines bright in the constellation of my scientific imagination. And his personal passion still powers my lifelong search for transparent authenticity. That search has recently been realized with my luminous companion, Lia Silvestri. It is embodied in her sweet children, Luca and Caterina. And it's especially radiant in Andrew and Matthew, our two-year-old twins whose rapidly budding brain-minds excite our wonder under the starry skies of Stromboli and Vermont. My scientific colleagues now include Bob Stickgold and Edward Schott, whose work is as inextricably linked to this book as our minds are linked to our brains.

Robert McCarley helped me get going when I moved the lab from the Physiology Department at Harvard Medical School to the Massachusetts Mental Health Center. There we did the first single-cell recordings, developed our physiological model of REM sleep, and used it to create the activation-synthesis hypothesis of dreaming. Ralph Lydic and Helen Baghdoysian contributed signficantly to the development and testing of our model using neuropharmacology and very long-term monitoring techniques.

During the past decade, the flowering of the ideas that grew in my scientific garden has been greatly enhanced by my membership in the most ideal collegial group imaginable, the Mind-Body Network of the John D. and Catherine T. MacArthur Foundation. Words cannot adequately convey my gratitude for this golden intellectual opportunity. And, from start to finish, I have been fortunate to have the continual support of the Neurobiology of Behavior Branch of the National Institute of Mental Health.

Many of the visitors to my dilapidated laboratory at state-subsidized Massachusetts Mental Health Center asked in wonder "Is this supposed to be Harvard?" In reply I smile ironically saying, "Well, yes and no!" Like so many arranged marriages, its convenience has outlasted its commitment, but I remain convinced of its mutual benefit.

My editors at W.H. Freeman and Company have helped to keep me on track—and when they could not—have generously helped to make my message as clear as it was loud. I hope this book responds to the inspiring vision of Linda Chaput, founding editor of the Scientific American Library. It is a pleasure to thank her, in this way, for her enthusiasm and encouragement.

When *Consciousness* was in the proposal stage of its conception, Jonathan Cobb helped me move from chaos to order. The manuscript was prepared from my longhand draft by Dolly Abbott who also typed the revisions. Barbara Brooks proved an enthusiastic ally of my impulse to embrace subjectivity and to reach out to literature and the arts in search of verbal and visual echo-reflections of my thoughts and my theories. George Adelman, Ralph Lydic, and David Spiegel provided useful comments on the first draft of my manuscript. I appreciate their candor as well as their tolerance. Producing the finished book was a wild adventure to which June Lundborg Whitworth, Diane Cimino Maass, and Philip McCaffrey contributed calm and wise direction.

Selected Readings

Ned Block, Owen Flanagan, and Güven Güzelderz. *The Nature of Consciousness.* Cambridge, MA: M.I.T. Press, 1997. 843 pp.

Jonathan Cohen and Jonathan Schooler, eds. *Scientific Approaches to Consciousness.* Mahwah, NJ: Lawrence Erlbaum, 1997. 538 pp.

Francis Crick. *The Astonishing Hypothesis.* New York: Scribner's, 1994. 317 pp.

Antonio Damasio. *Descartes' Error.* New York: Grosset Putnam, 1994. 312 pp.

Daniel Dennett. *Consciousness Explained.* Boston: Little Brown, 1991.

Gerald Edelman. *Bright Air Brilliant Fin.* New York: Basic Books, 1992. 280 pp.

Stuart R. Hameroff, Alfred W. Kasniak, and Alwyn C. Scott. *Toward a Science of Consciousness.* Cambridge, MA: M.I.T. Press, 1996. 790 pp.

William James. *Principles of Psychology.* Henry Holt © 1890. Dover Edition, 1950.

William James. *Varieties of Religious Experience.* Random House, 1994.

Roger Penrose. *The Emperor's New Mind.* New York: Penguin, 1991. 466 pp.

References and Sources of Illustrations

Diagrams by Fine Line Illustrations

Front cover: Odilon Redon, Dream, 1904, Giraudon/ Art Resource, NY.

Back cover: Courtesy Paul Coupille.

Prologue

Page vi: Courtesy Paul Coupille.

Page viii: Quotation from William James: *The Varieties of Religious Experience* (New York: Random House), 1994.

Chapter 1

Page 0: Pablo Picasso, *Girl Before a Mirror*, Boisgeloup, March 1932. Oil on canvas, 64 × 51 1/4 inches. The Museum of Modern Art, New York. Gift of Mrs. Simon Guggenheim. Photograph © 1998 The Museum of Modern Art, New York. © 1998 Estate of Pablo Picasso/ Artists Rights Society (ARS), New York.

Page 3: From P. E. Roland and L. Friberg, 1985. Localization of cortical areas activated by thinking. *Journal of Neurophysiology* 53: 1219–1243.

Page 5: Greek Attic red-figure vase depicting Odysseus with the Sirens, Stamnos, c. 490 BC, PHD982. British Museum, London/ The Bridgeman Art Library International Ltd.

Page 7: (*Both*) Sigmund Freud Copyrights/ Mary Evans/ Picture Library, London. (*Right*) Drawing from Freud, *Standard Edition* 1:324.

Page 10: Quotation from Thomas Huxley, *Nature*, vol. 1, no. 1 (Nov. 4, 1869): 10.

Page 11: The Granger Collection.

Page 12: Quoted in *Newsweek*, Nov. 30, 1959.

Page 13: Corbis- Bettmann.

Page 19: The Natural History Museum, London.

Page 20: Courtesy Donna Bierschwale, USL, New Iberia Research Center.

Page 22: Courtesy Timothy Murphy and Gil Wier, The University of British Columbia.

Chapter 2

Page 24: Salvador Dali, *Illumined Pleasures*, 1929. Oil and collage on composition board, 9 3/8 × 13 3/4 inches. The Museum of Modern Art, New York. The Sidney and Harriet Janis Collection. Photograph © 1998 The Museum of Modern Art, New York. © 1998 Fundacion Gala—Salvador Dali/ Artists Rights Society (ARS), New York.

Page 26: Quotation from *The Notebooks of Leonardo da Vinci*.

Page 96: Quoted in Ingo F. Walther: *Pablo Picasso: Genius of the Century* (Cologne, Germany: Benedikt Taschen, 1986), 43.

Page 98: (*All*) J. A. Hobson.

Chapter 5

Page 102: Paul Delvaux, *L'Ecole des Savants*, 1958, Museum of Modern Art, Ludwig Foundation, Vienna © P. Delvaux Foundation, St. Idesbald, Belgium/Licensed by VAGA, New York, NY.

Page 104: Leonardo da Vinci, *The brain injected to demonstrate the shape of the cerebral ventricles*, RL 19127r, The Royal Collection © Her Majesty Queen Elizabeth II, Royal Collection Enterprises, Windsor Castle.

Page 107: Quotation Copyright © 1982 by the Nobel Foundation. Reprinted in *Science*, vol. 217, Sept. 24, 1982, 1224. Copyright © 1982 AAAS.

Page 108: Mark Rothko, *Light Red over Black*, 1957. Oil on canvas. Tate Gallery, London/Art Resource, NY. © 1998 Kate Rothko Prizel & Christopher Rothko/ Artists Rights Society (ARS), New York.

Page 110: Ken Heyman/ Woodfin Camp & Associates.

Page 112: Quotation from Marcel Proust, *Swan's Way*. (New York: The Modern Library, 1956), 61.

Page 113: J. A. Hobson.

Page 116: Courtesy Stephen M. Kosslyn, Harvard University and Massachusetts General Hospital.

Page 117: Courtesy Richard Davidson, University of Wisconsin Laboratory for Affective Neuroscience.

Page 118: Courtesy David Spiegel, Stanford University School of Medicine.

Page 120: Courtesy Kenneth Hugdahl, University of Bergen.

Page 121: J. A. Hobson.

Page 123: From C. P. Stevens, The Neuron, in *The Brain*, a Scientific American book, W. H. Freeman and Company, 1979.

Page 126: From Nobutaka Hirokawa (1991) in the *Neuronal Cytoskeleton* (ed. R.D. Burgoyne) pp.5–74. Wiley-Liss, N.Y. Reprinted by permission of Wiley-Liss, Inc., a subsidiary of John Wiley & Sons, Inc.

Page 126: Based on Figure 2.3 in Richard F. Thompson: *The Brain: A Neuroscience Primer* 2d ed. (New York: W. H. Freeman and Company, 1993).

Page 127: J. A. Hobson.

Chapter 6

Page 128: Rene Magritte, *The Mysteries of the Horizon*, 1955. Giraudon/ Art Resource, NY. © 1998 C. Herscovici, Brussels /Artists Rights Society (ARS), New York.

Page 130: Quotation from John Keats, "Ode to a Nightingale."

Page 133: J. A. Hobson.

Page 136: Salvador Dali, *Dreams Caused by the Flight of a Bumblebee Around a Pomenegrate a Second before Awakening*, 1944. Nimatallah/ Art Resource, NY. © 1998 Fundacion Gala—Salvador Dali/ Artists Rights Society (ARS), New York.

Page 139: (*Above*) Reuters/Claudia Daut/ Archive Photos; (*below*) Shizuo Kambayashi/ AP/ Wide World Photos.

Page 140: Quotation from Charles Sherrington: *Man on His Nature* (New York: Doubleday, 1955), 184.

Page 143: Courtesy Allen R. Braun, National Institute on Deafness and Other Communication Disorders, NIH.

Page 148: Based on Figure 5.5 in Richard F. Thompson: *The Brain: A Neuroscience Primer* 2d ed. (New York: W. H. Freeman and Company, 1993).

Page 229:   Quotation from Andre Breton, "On the Road to San Remo" in *What is Surrealism?* (Franklin Rosemont, 1978).

Page 230:   Inge Morath/ Magnum Photos.

Page 232:   *(Left and right)* NASA.

Page 234:   J. A. Hobson.

Acknowledgements

Page 238:   Roberto Matta, *The Unthinkable*, 1957. Oil on canvas, 78 × 118 inches. Galerie Thomas R. Monahan, Chicago.

Index

If you would like to purchase additional volumes in
the Scientific American Library, please send your
order to:

Scientific American Library
41 Madison Avenue
New York, NY 10010